Black Fire

Black Fire

African American Quakers on Spirituality and Human Rights

edited by
Harold D. Weaver, Jr., Paul Kriese,
and Stephen W. Angell

with Anne Steere Nash

foreword by
Emma Lapsansky-Werner

PHILADELPHIA, PA

Copyright © 2011 QuakerPress of Friends General Conference
All rights reserved
1216 Arch Street 2B
Philadelphia, PA 19107

Printed in the United States of America.

Composition and design by David Botwinik.

ISBN 978-1-888305-88-3 (paperback)
    978-1-888305-90-6 (electronic version)

Library of Congress Cataloging-in-Publication Data
Black fire : African American Quakers on spirituality and human rights / edited by Harold D. Weaver, Jr. ... [et al.] ; foreword by Emma Lapsansky-Werner.
  p. cm.
 Includes bibliographical references.
 ISBN 978-1-888305-88-3
 1. Quakers--United States--Biography. 2. African Americans--Biography. 3. Society of Friends--Doctrines. 4. African Americans--Religion. I. Weaver, Harold D.
 BX7791.B53 2011
 289.6092'396073--dc22
 [B]
            2010054554

To order more copies of this publication or other Quaker titles call
1-800-966-4556 or see the online catalogue at www.quakerbooks.org

Contents

Illustrations   vii

Permissions   ix

Foreword   xi
by Emma Lapsansky-Werner

Preface I   xvi
by Harold D. Weaver, Jr.

Preface II   xxvi
by Paul Kriese

Preface III   xxviv
by Stephen W. Angell

Introduction   xxxii

I
The Early Period   1
edited by Stephen W. Angell

Benjamin Banneker (1731–1806)   1

William Boen (1735–1824)   6

Paul Cuffe (1759–1817)   15

Elizabeth (1766–1866)   20

Sojourner Truth (1799–1883)   21

Sarah Mapps Douglass (1806–1882)   27

Robert Purvis (1810–1898)   30

II
N. Jean Toomer (1894–1967)   45
edited by Paul Kriese

III
Howard Thurman (1899–1981)   63
edited by Stephen W. Angell

Contents

IV
Ira de Augustine Reid (1901–1968)   97
edited by Harold D. Weaver, Jr.

V
Barrington Dunbar (1901–1978)   125
edited by Paul Kriese

VI
Helen Morgan Brooks (1904–1989)   139
edited by Anne Steere Nash

VII
Bayard Rustin (1912–1987)   151
edited by Harold D. Weaver, Jr.

VIII
Mahala Ashley Dickerson (1912–2007)   179
edited by Harold D. Weaver, Jr.

IX
Bill Sutherland (1918–2010)   195
edited by Harold D. Weaver, Jr.

X
Charles H. Nichols (1919–2007)   203
edited by Harold D. Weaver, Jr.

XI
George E. Sawyer (1925–2002)   219
edited by Paul Kriese

XII
Vera Green (1928–1982)   233
edited by Paul Kriese

Bibliography   241

Acknowledgments   245

About the Editors   250

Illustrations

Bayard Rustin, 1965 photo by Stanley Wolfson, *New York World-Telegram* and the *Sun Newspaper* Photograph Collection, Library of Congress.	*cover*
Benjamin Banneker's Almanac for 1795, courtesy of the Maryland Historical Society, Baltimore.	*page* 1
Cover of William Boen's *Anecdotes and Memoirs*, courtesy of Friends Historical Library, Swarthmore College.	*page* 6
Paul Cuffe sillhouette, courtesy of Friends Historical Library, Swarthmore College.	*page* 16
Abolition stamp, courtesy of Friends Historical Library, Swarthmore College.	*page* 20
Sojourner Truth photo, courtesy of Friends Historical Library, Swarthmore College.	*page* 21
Watercolor by Sarah Mapps Douglas, courtesy of the Library Company of Philadelphia.	*page* 27
Robert Purvis photo, courtesy of Friends Historical Library, Swarthmore College.	*page* 30
Jean Toomer photo, source unknown.	*facing page* 45
Howard Thurman photo from U.S. Department of Health and Human Services.	*facing page* 63
Ira de A. Reid photo of portrait taken by Dick Jones, courtesy of Lower Merion Historical Society.	*facing page* 97
Barrington Dunbar photo, courtesy of Friends Historical Library, Swarthmore College.	*facing page* 125

Illustrations

Helen Morgan Brooks photo, courtesy of Friends Historical Library, Swarthmore College. — *facing page* 139

Bayard Rustin (center) speaking with (left to right) Carolyn Carter, Cecil Carter, Kurt Levister, and Kathy Ross, 1964. Photo by Ed Ford, *New York World-Telegram* and the *Sun Newspaper* Photograph Collection, Library of Congress. — *facing page* 151

Mahala Ashley Dickerson photo by Michael Avedon, courtesy of Mahala Ashley Dickerson estate. — *facing page* 179

Bill Sutherland photo, courtesy of American Friends Service Committee. — *facing page* 195

Charles Nichols photo courtesy of Brown University. — *facing page* 203

George Sawyer photo circa 1970, Earlham College. Used by permission. — *facing page* 219

Vera Green photo courtesy of Haverford College Library. — *facing page* 233

Harold D. Weaver, Jr., photo provided by Anne Steere Nash. — *page* 250

Paul Kriese photo provided by Indiana University East. — *page* 251

Stephen Angell photo by Joanne Clapp Fullager for Friends General Conference. — *page* 251

Permissions

Source notations may be found at the end of each selection.

"Keep the Inward Watch" by N. Jean Toomer on page 57 is used with permission of Friends Publishing Corporation (www.friendsjournal.org).

All selections by Howard Thurman, pages 64–93 are used with permission of the Howard Thurman Estate.

"Peace and Tranquility: The Quaker Witness" by Ira de A. Reid on page 98 is used with permission of Philadelphia Yearly Meeting of the Religious Society of Friends.

"Negro Immigration to the United States" on page 105 and "Methodological Notes for Studying the Southern City" on page 114, both by Ira de A. Reid, are used with permission of the University of North Carolina Press (www.uncpress.unc.edu).

"The Society of Friends and the Negro Revolution" by Barrington Dunbar on page 125 is used with permission of the American Friends Service Committee.

"Black Power's Challenge to Quaker Power" by Barrington Dunbar on page 127 is used with permission of Friends Publishing Corporation (www.friendsjournal.org).

"The Revolutionary Jesus" on page 129 and "Sharing My Experience in Friends Schools" on page 137, both by Barrington Dunbar, are used with permission of *Quaker Life* magazine of Friends United Meeting.

"Friends and the White Backlash" by Barrington Dunbar on page 131 is used with permission of Earlham School of Religion.

The following selections by Bayard Rustin, "Letter to His Draft Board" on, "Non-Violence in Action" on page 155, "You Don't Have to Ride Jim Crow" on page 157, "In Apprehension How Like a God!" on page 158, and "From Protest to Politics" on page 164, are all used with permission of the Bayard Rustin Estate.

The selection from *Speak Truth to Power* on page 161 is used with permission of the American Friends Service Committee.

"Negro Lawyer in the South—Parts I and II" by Mahala Ashley Dickerson on pages 180 and 184 are used with permission of Friends Publishing Corporation (www.friendsjournal.org).

Permissions

The selections from *Guns and Gandhi in Africa* ("Why Examine Nonviolence in Africa" on page 196 and "The Future of Nonviolence, Armed Struggle, and Revolution in Africa" on page 198) by Bill Sutherland and Matt Meyer are used with permission of Africa World Press.

The selections from *Many Thousand Gone: The Ex-Slaves' Account of their Bondage and Freedom* (from the "Introduction" page 204, "Prologue" page 208, chapter 1 page 210, and chapter 8, page 213) by Charles H. Nichols are used with permission of Koninklijke BRILL NV.

"National Conference of Friends on Race Relations" on page 222 and "The Stranger Among You" on page 224, both by George E. Sawyer, are used by permission of *Quaker Life* magazine of Friends United Meeting.

Every effort has been made to credit the sources of copyrighted material used in this book and to obtain permission for their use. If any such acknowledgment has been inadvertently omitted, miscredited, or if we failed to locate a rights holder, we offer our apologies. Receipt of such information would be appreciated and would be used to correct future printings of this work.

Foreword

by Emma Lapsansky-Werner

"No country can tell its history truthfully until all its scrolls are unrolled." Thus Philadelphia's Negro Historical Society proclaimed its agenda at the end of the nineteenth century. In this same era, the Friends Historical Association was founded, which defines its mission as promoting "the study, preservation and publication of material relating to the history of the Religious Society of Friends."

Gracefully, *Black Fire* takes a big step toward addressing both concerns—unfurling long rolled-up scrolls, and stimulating the study of the history of the Religious Society of Friends. African American history, and Quaker history—and especially the intersection of the two—have been my interests for many decades, and I have often been disappointed by the array of misinformation and garbled information that have surrounded these topics.

I am honored to have been invited to write a foreword to this wonderful anthology that mirrors the hard work and dedication of religious believers and practitioners, philosophers, and scholars across several centuries. Hal Weaver, Paul Kriese, and Steve Angell have made a major contribution by unrolling some of the many scrolls of both the Religious Society of Friends and Americans of African descent.

The question of race and race relations has bedeviled Quaker individuals and communities since the days of Quaker founder George Fox, who, upon visiting the Caribbean and the American mainland in the 1670s, cautioned slaveholders to make sure that their black chattel received religious instruction. By the end of the seventeenth century, a group of Philadelphia Friends cautioned their community to consider the many dangers—moral and physical—of holding humans in bondage. Slavery violated the Golden Rule, and it could not be sustained without violence, or the threat thereof, these Friends reminded their community. Their petition was tabled for many generations, but the problem would not go away. William Penn grappled with it—releasing his slave Yaff, but only on the condition that Yaff remain in England. Eighteenth century Quaker philosophers and activists—including those in North America, Britain, France, and the Caribbean—remonstrated with their friends and created enemies over the issue. And despite the common belief that "the Quakers" were early and devoted participants in the pre-Civil War Underground Railroad slave escape network, much controversy, strife, and wringing-of-hands accompanied the desegregation of Quaker schools in the mid-twentieth century.

The problem is that the scrolls to be unrolled have a great deal of smudged ink and many cracks and creases where information is distorted. Consider, for example, the great number of moving parts, resulting in myriad permutations and possibilities for smudges. To get the stories straight we need to look at African Americans as a group(s), while simultaneously exploring African American individuals (for example, Barrington Dunbar, Howard Thurman, and Robert Purvis, whose stories are explored here in *Black Fire*). Gender, region, and era add to the mix: the mid-twentieth century reality experienced by Helen Morgan Brooks is as different from the nineteenth century life of Sarah Mapps Douglass as it is from the mid-twentieth century story of her neighbor Bayard Rustin, and from the story of Elizabeth, born a Maryland Methodist, whose life encompassed both of the wars that defined the meaning of "American." In *Black Fire*, as these narratives unfurl, the reader gets a close look at the broad diversity within the black Quaker experience.

Yet, even as *Black Fire* helps us get a glimpse of African American Quaker diversity, the creases of the scrolls hide other stories waiting to be brought into the light. For example, of the eighteen African American voices included here, only three lived their stories west of the Appalachians. And there is a gap in time between Robert Purvis (born in 1810) and Jean Toomer (born in 1894). Scholar Linda Selleck tells us that the Civil War and Reconstruction eras were a time of great ferment as activist Quaker women sought to bring Friends ideas to Southern and Midwestern black people, and to bring black people to Friends. Can the faces and voices of late nineteenth century black Friends be found among the creases of the scrolls?

And there are other moving colors in the kaleidoscope: "white" Quakers, as a group, have a somewhat deserved reputation of racial liberalism. But "white" Quakers as individuals have interacted with the phenomenon of "race" in varying and sometimes contradictory ways. And "white" Quakers come in many shades of white—North and South, liberal and conservative, prejudiced and not so—for they live in and are shaped by prevailing notions of the social and political meanings of "race."

Then there is the issue of "race" itself as a phenomenon. To what degree is race about skin color? To what degree about culture? To what degree about the intersection of the two? How many different ways shall we dissect "whiteness" and "coloredness"—especially if we add region and class to the array of variables by which we categorize "white" Quakers and "Quakers of color." Similarly vexing is the phenomenon of "religion" or "spirituality" versus belief systems and styles of worship and prayer. An example of this confusion is the persistent myth that "black people are not drawn in great numbers to the Religious Society of Friends because they prefer a more active style of worship—with music, more demonstrativeness, and not so much silence." Where does such a generalization fit with the number of "white" worshipers who visit Friends meetings only to return to the chants and structure of other denominations?

How do we delineate what people believe from how that belief plays out in worship and in daily life? What can the lives and writings of such individuals as Howard Thurman, Charles Nichols, Jean Toomer, and Ira Reid—all of whom *lived* parts of their lives in Quaker circles—tell us about the intellectual, academic, and spiritual lives of some modern black intellectual Quakers? Toomer moved through Quakerism to end his life as a Catholic, yet one could not ask for a better description of Friends belief and worship than his writing excerpted here. Toomer is among a long list of Friends—black and white—for whom Quakers and Quakerism served as a "vestibule" or transitional experience into another denomination. And what of the black Quakers who are missing from this volume? The editors made some hard choices in order to give the volume coherence, but in deciding whom to *include*, decisions were made about whom to *exclude*.

Part of the problem is that often "Quakerism" (a set of religious beliefs and practices) is conflated with what I call "Quakerliness" (a set of political, social, and economic postures that often flow from stereotypes created by or about Friends). And lacking a catechism or other definitional documents, it is sometimes hard to distinguish Quakerism from Quakerliness.

The three compilers of this wonderfully stimulating anthology have each wrestled—individually and with each other!—with these and many other thorny questions. How, they asked—and ask us readers—do we begin to unroll and flatten the scrolls without creating the sort of distortion that occurs when one unrolls a globe onto a flat surface? Which sectors get enlarged, which shrunk, which omitted?

With its far-reaching span of people, times, and places, *Black Fire* asks and hints at—and invites readers to probe—these questions. Modern scholars like Kenneth Ives, Linda Selleck, Rosalind Wiggins, Thomas Hamm, Margaret Hope Bacon, Vanessa Julye, and Donna McDaniel have built on the foundation set by Henry Cadbury many decades ago to give us a peek into the lives of African American Quakers and the meetings they encountered. However, as *Black Fire* shows, there are still many creases to iron out and cracks to fill in before the scrolls will not only lie flat, but also tell a full story. For example, we need to know more about William Boen and why his local meeting refused him membership. Maybe it was about "race," but maybe it was about something else. (Did he have a tendency to violence, or did he drink too much? Was his meeting concerned about his finances: worried they might have to support him?) In assuming that it was "race" that barred Boen from acceptance into membership, are we doing him or his meeting an injustice?

One thing becomes increasingly clear as the list of works by and about Quakers and race relations grows: this issue that has vexed Quakers since George Fox's time challenges us to think about it in present time. For nearly a century, historians and philosophers, such as Henry Cadbury, Rufus Jones, Douglas and Dorothy Steere, and others in the Quaker communities of Pendle Hill and Earlham School of Religion, and in the interfaith Fellowship of Reconciliation—to name just a few—have struggled to understand and interpret the many moving parts of race, race relations, religion, and social justice. *Black Fire* presents some of those moving parts of the "history relating to the Religious Society of

Foreword

Friends," unrolling some new scrolls and offering us new foundations from which to continue to explore African American stories, Quaker stories, and the intersections between the two.

Emma Lapsansky-Werner
Emeritus Professor of History and Curator of the Quaker Collection
Haverford College

Preface I

by Harold D. Weaver, Jr.

I. Identity Shapes the Framework

Ongoing discussions about this volume with my fellow Quaker scholar-editors Paul Kriese and Steve Angell have helped me to put into perspective how and why some of our interpretations and assessments and preferred selections are different, though all of us are active in the Society of Friends. Our struggles to agree on the content of this collection have been an occasion for me to think about identity. For example, as an African American, and a student of Africana studies for over five decades, I spiritually and intellectually link Africa with African America. This link is not vital to my co-editors. Such differences in perspective were part of a challenging process that required compromises not only at the practical, page-counting level, but also at a deeper and more uncomfortable level where the meaning and integrity of identity must be wrestled with. Thank you, Steve and Paul, for helping me understand both our subtle and profound differences in perspective, interpretation, and focus. Below I describe four aspects of my identity that have been integral to my work on this project.

My African ancestry is the dominant part of my membership in the human race—the sole race of people. Yes, as singer James Brown often proclaims in his music, "I am Black and proud." This dominant African ancestry means, in the context of my U.S. citizenship, that I have had to bear three major stigmas throughout my entire life: (1) dark skin color (permanent caste status of perceived inferiority), (2) the heritage of chattel enslavement in the Americas, and (3) the heritage of the "Dark Continent," with its continued images of savagery, cannibalism, violence, and other "uncivilized" associations. Apologists have long claimed, along with scholars and the media, that Africa is an uncivilized land mass, thus justifying dehumanizing slavery, colonialism, and neo-colonialism. Hence, this dominant African ancestry has become—consciously, subconsciously, or unconsciously—a motivating factor in both my professional and personal lives.

Yet, the reality is that my ancestors were of diverse origins. They were among the indigenous—pre-African, pre-European—inhabitants of the Americas, probably having immigrated to this continent from Asia, perhaps China or Siberia. They were also European American slave owners—including a great-grandfather who was a colonel in the Confederate Army and who took my grandfather, identified as "black" though white in appearance, shopping every Saturday when he was a child. This same colonel also enslaved human chattel. My ancestors were resisters to European conquest and occupation and also active implementers of European conquest and capture of indigenous North American and African peoples. Victims and perpetrators, both shared the same space but on different rungs of the ladder in the hierarchy of power. My ancestral oppressors and oppressed all lived under the same ideals and principles of our country's founding fathers: that "all men [people] are created equal" and that among their inalienable rights are "life, liberty, and the pursuit of happiness."

For over fifty years I have been a student and pioneer in Africana studies, the scholarly study of Africa and the African Diaspora. In 2009 I returned as a Fellow to Harvard University's W.E.B. Du Bois Institute for African and African American Research. I have spent a lifetime intellectually challenging the myths of white superiority and white supremacy perpetrated by media, scholars, politicians, and educators.[1] (As I mature in age, I have become increasingly impatient with untruths in the media and in academic scholarship, whether disseminated through misinformation or disinformation.) My activities have included participant-observation research beginning in 1959 in Soviet Russia. There I established close relations with African students who went on to play important roles in their respective countries' development. I have produced publications and lectures on the cultural relations of Soviet Russia and Africa as well as on Paul Robeson, Ousmane Sembene, and African and African-Diasporic cinema and culture. I have taught, consulted, and curated film in various countries in Asia, Africa, Europe, and the Americas. My pioneering Paul Robeson publications, lectures, television interviews, film festivals, courses, and advocacy in the United States and abroad have helped restore the Robeson name to its rightful place in history. This included initiating an honorary doctorate for Robeson at his alma mater, Rutgers University, in 1973 in honor of his 75th birthday. Through The BlackFilm Project and The ChinaFilm Project, I am currently involved in using film and moving images to facilitate cross-cultural respect and understanding of African, African Diasporic, and Chinese societies and cultures. Since 2006, at UNESCO's initiative, I have been fortunate to present lecture-film presentations around the world on black filmmakers' revolutionizing of the representation of chattel slavery in the Americas and the trans-Atlantic Middle Passage.

The tumultuous 1960s were an important decade of struggle and achievement for African Americans, and I was privileged to be a part of those advancements in the education of teachers and students in the United States and in France. Before establishing as chair in 1970 the new Africana Studies Department at Rutgers, I accepted an invitation in 1969 to teach at the new, radical University of Paris VIII (Vincennes/St. Denis). At that time our university in Paris was offering more courses in African American studies than any U.S. institution of higher learning. After finding that the course material included information that was incorrect or biased, my whole career has been spent in researching, teaching about, and informing students and the general public about these matters. In 1969, I helped conceive and served as director of a multi-disciplinary team of educators at Cornell University of an innovative summer institute that recruited teams of teachers, school administrators, and school board members from major urban areas to learn about and then teach, in innovative ways, the relationship between African studies and African American studies.

I have a long background in Quakerism. Sixty years ago, I was first exposed to Quaker thought and values, institutions, and religion as a sixteen-year-old, eleventh-grade student attending Westtown School, near Philadelphia. This experience was to change my life significantly and forever in ways that a teenager could not possibly have imagined at the time. Two years at Westtown, followed by four years at Haverford College, another Quaker institution, were to be filled with discovery, self-discovery, self-fulfillment, accomplishment, growing self-confidence, and growing empowerment, lovingly fostered in a welcoming Quaker environment. My success in multiple varsity sports was also a boost to my self-confidence. The affective and cognitive impact of a Quaker secondary school, boarding education, and a Quaker college is clear.

> [Westtown's] influence on me was through the exposure to Quakerism, despite the hypocrisy, the beliefs and practices. When I later became president of my class at Haverford I tried to apply the Quaker business process to class meetings.[2]

"That of God in every person" is a belief that certainly affected how I raised my kids and how I behave. These were two of the main reasons why I reconnected with Quakerism at Wellesley Monthly Meeting in 1992 and am an active member of that meeting.

The BlackQuaker Project is a Quaker ministry of Wellesley Monthly Meeting dedicated to examining, celebrating, preserving, and presenting the contributions and experiences of black Quakers around the world. It is divided into the following components: (1) research and publication of books and pamphlets, (2) developing plays and films, (3) oral history, (4) dialogue within the Society of Friends between Quakers of differing theologies and geographies, (5) providing outreach information and training to educational and cultural institutions and to Quaker meetings (including the 2008 Weed Lecture in "Facing Unbearable Truths"),[3] and (6) setting up a major project on Quakers and chattel slavery in the Americas.

Work in cross-cultural and international diplomacy constitutes my fourth identity influencing this anthology. Fifty years ago, I began my lifelong involvement as an international cultural ambassador in person-to-person diplomacy. Selected to participate in the second year of the youth exchange program between the major protagonists in the Cold War, I spent the summer of 1959 in the USSR. Even then, I was impressed by its comprehensive healthcare system (including witnessing natural childbirth in a free public hospital) and its system of free public education at all levels, where international students from Africa and other developing countries were coming for training related to their national needs, rather than to colonial or neo-colonial needs. I was also impressed by its attention to—some would say propaganda about—the significance of equality and cooperation between the races of mankind, yellow, white, brown, and black. My research culminated decades later in the completion of my doctoral dissertation on "Soviet Training and Research Programs for Africa." I have recently observed in a variety of African countries the positive impact of Soviet and other socialist training in creating national indigenous infrastructures to replace their dependency on foreign, colonial structures and personnel. This topic deserves research attention today. (To date my dissertation is the only one to tackle this subject. One potential dissertation adviser at another university where I was enrolled admitted to me that "they"—whoever that was—did not want me to research and write on that subject.)

Since 1959, I have been actively involved in international and cross-cultural diplomacy involving Asia, Africa, Europe, and the Americas. One result, I am convinced, is that I can feel at home almost anywhere in the world. This ability may even have started earlier when in 1944 my family moved from an all-African American community on the campus of Savannah State University (then called Georgia State College) to the almost all-white State College in Pennsylvania. There I was the only person of color in the entire public school system. Penn State, the local university, had few African American students that academic year, 1944-1945, the final year of World War II. This was the year of my introduction to organized athletics that were to be instrumental in developing my self-esteem and collaborative spirit in the immediate years to come.

In conclusion, these dominant identities all contribute to my interest in and commitment to this anthology. Additionally, a half century as a Quaker conscientious objector and social justice activist lead me to the hope that we can have a more accurate understanding of the roots of political, economic, and social phenomena as we attempt to solve and resolve social problems and to develop social, political, and economic policies and practices that are just. To do so, we need to begin with the Truth.

Hence, this initial volume of selected writings by African American Quakers.

II. Origin and Evolution of Black Fire

In January 2003 representatives from various Quaker yearly meetings were convened in Pittsburgh by Friends General Conference (FGC) to discuss issues of race and racism within the Society of Friends. We worked in teams consisting of two persons: one African American and one European American. We spent five days in interracial dialogue in a "Beyond Diversity 101" workshop led by Niyonu Spann.

For me, representing New England Yearly Meeting, the FGC workshop was both rewarding and (at times) frustrating. Although we produced few concrete results or pragmatic solutions and applications, we were able to develop some trust and to use the opportunity for networking. In the past, when I had offered training workshops and courses for teachers and school administrators, there had always been cognitive behavioral objectives for both knowledge and skills. At the Pittsburgh event, I felt that there was too much focus on the affective, the heart, and too little focus on the cognitive skills and knowledge needed to go forward to facilitate racial equality and justice in the Society of Friends. I came away determined to initiate something that would allow positive, pragmatic follow-up in the form of collaboration between African American and European American Quaker scholars.

Several factors seemed to converge in the conception of this anthology. The Pittsburgh experience provided the occasion for my interaction with a fellow scholar, Paul Kriese; for my reading of *The Many Lives of Jean Toomer: A Hunger for Wholeness* by Cynthia Earl Kerman and Richard Eldrich; and for my recognition of a void in knowledge about the writings of Quakers of African ancestry. This recognition led to my further desire for additional knowledge about some of the committed African American Quakers with whom I had previously interacted: Ira Reid, Bayard Rustin, and Bill Sutherland.

During the workshop and for months afterward, I repeatedly mulled over the question: "What might I do to advance this concept of black-white Quaker cooperation and collaboration aimed at improving racial equality and justice within the Society of Friends?" The result was that during my winter/spring semester 2003 as a visiting professor of African American Cinema Studies in far-off Taiwan, I hit upon the idea of an anthology of works by Quakers of African ancestry. I invited European American Paul Kriese, fellow participant in the FGC workshop, to join me in editing an anthology of writings of black Quakers from around the world. Paul Kriese is a political science professor at Indiana University

East in Richmond and has been active in civil rights and teaching about aspects of the black experience. Later, in March 2006, at a Friends World Committee for Consultation, Section of the Americas, meeting in Guatemala, I invited Earlham School of Religion historian Steve Angell to join our project. Steve, a European American, had earlier done work on the history of the black church. In May 2006, when Steve accepted the invitation to join the project, he contributed the idea of the two foci: spirituality and human rights. With his involvement we would have a trio that I hoped would move forward harmoniously.

During the FGC workshop I read the intriguing biography of Jean Toomer. The impact of this book was mind-boggling. I absorbed with fascination the lifelong searching, achievements, denials, and experiments of this incredible figure, whose ancestors had come from segregated Louisiana (an important place in my own life) to our segregated national capital, where he grew up. How could this restless, creative individual, who is often given credit for launching the Harlem Renaissance in the 1920s, function in such a racialized, divided, oppressive, totalitarian society as the United States of America?

The book raised many other questions for me as well: What did Toomer want from his life? Why did he never finish his undergraduate studies? Were undergraduate studies in the country too superficial at a time when Toomer, the persistent seeker, was probing deeply into life and its meaning? As a seeker, he was not satisfied by his formal education but found, for a period of time, his needs met in the Society of Friends.

I could not put the book down. Perhaps the first seed of the anthology was planted at this time only to emerge later. This reading produced in me an awareness of exciting material in African American and Quaker studies that was virtually unknown. As an example, the clerk of our meeting, who taught Toomer in his African American literature course, was surprised when I told him that Toomer was a Quaker.

My strong desire to know more about some of the people with whom I had been fortunate to interact—Bayard Rustin, Ira Reid, Bill Sutherland—were also important in my decision to pursue this anthology. In 1959 I worked with Bayard Rustin in Harlem as a volunteer planning the Youth March for Integrated Schools, which I also attended in Washington, DC. Ira Reid was my mentor and major advisor in sociology at Haverford College, 1952-1956. Bill Sutherland had been my guest for dinner and as a speaker, co-sponsored by the AFSC, in the early 1980s when I was teaching at Smith College.

Some of the questions that arose in my mind as I thought about these people and discussed their lives with F(f)riends were:

- What did black Quakers say and do that made them unique, pioneering, and innovative? What can we learn from them now in the twenty-first century? Were they ahead of their times in their ideas and contributions? How did they translate their thoughts and feelings into actions? What have African American Quaker writers contributed to Quakerism, to the nation, and to the world?

- How did early African American Quakers feel about some of the great pressing policy issues facing the Republic: retrospective justice ("reparations"), racial injustice and inequality, systemic discrimination/institutional racism, and individual racism? What special insights did they offer?

The anthology idea evolved during my time in Taiwan during 2003. I found myself teaching in a distant, international setting during the SARS pandemic and the Bush invasion of Iraq. The powerful impact of isolation, imposed both by the social culture and by the dynamics of a health pandemic, helped the creative juices to flow. During that time I was often away from the campus in a Seventh Day Adventist life center in the mountains, which provided a healthy and supportive environment for thinking, reading, and writing.

Active work on this project has continued from 2003 through 2010. The years 2003-2007 were spent on cultivation, including communication with a wide variety of Friends and non-Friends and collecting materials by and about prominent African American Quakers. Many of the individuals who assisted during this period are named in the Acknowledgements section. I have been fortunate to find encouragement for the anthology wherever I have traveled among a broad range of Quakers and Quaker organizations as well as non-Quakers and those involved in African American and African studies, religious studies, and Quaker studies.

In 2004 dialogues about publication of the anthology were initiated with Friends General Conference, beginning with members of its Ministry for Racial Justice and with its general secretary, Bruce Birchard, followed by discussions with publications personnel, the late Barbara Hirshkowitz, and, subsequently, with Barbara Mays. Original writings, biographies, and bibliographies were presented to make the case for the anthology. In 2007 our final proposal was submitted to the QuakerPress of FGC and to FGC's general secretary.

This project has taken many turns in the road, many hundreds of hours, and there were many challenges along the route, including my own dissatisfaction with some of the pieces that were selected by my colleagues. Our different identities—ethnicity/race, field of study, and differing life experiences, domestic and international—brought both richness of perspective and conflict of opinions.

Two crucial working sessions of the three editors led to critical decisions. For five days in July 2008 at the Nash/Weaver home in Newton, Massachusetts, we worked on finalizing the scope of the project and the role of each editor. In December 2009 at the Friends United Meeting center in Richmond, Indiana, the editors met with Barbara Mays to pull together bits and pieces needed to finalize the anthology. Barbara left FGC soon after, and Chel Avery has been implementing FGC's part in the plans we developed.

At our July 2008 working session, after contentious discussion, the editors agreed to include only writers from the United States, leaving out major African scholars. Our compromise included a 1930 cut-off point for the date of birth, eliminating all writers born after that date. Hopefully, in a future anthology, The BlackQuaker Project, dedicated to celebrating the lives and achievements of black Quakers worldwide, will be able to publish works of persons and themes omitted from this book, including: (1) books, pamphlets, and articles by African American Quakers born after 1930; (2) representations of the impact and centrality of Africa as a source of inspiration; (3) thoughts about retrospective justice (a comprehensive term more attuned to Quaker testimonies than the highly emotional "reparations"); and (4) discussions of some of the great policy issues related to racial equality and justice, past and present.

Preface I

Some of the late twentieth and early twenty-first century writers who might be anthologized in a future volume include historian Emma Lapsansky-Werner, Kenyan theologian Esther Mombo, sociologist Harriette McAdoo, restrospective justice advocates Jerry Leaphart and Helen Toppins, writer Vanessa Julye, university administrators Jim Fletcher and Tracye Peterson, political scientist Syl Whittaker, playwrite Amanda Kemp, spiritual leaders Ernestine Buscemi and Deborah Saunders, children's author Becky Birtha, photographer/artist Wendy Phillips, community activist James Varner, diversity trainer Niyonu Spann, the venerable husband-wife team of Daisy and Noel Palmer, educators Dwight Wilson and Hal Weaver, and other dedicated Friends of African descent. We also intend to add additional writings of some of the authors in this present volume for which there was not space in this first volume.

I am honored to have conceived and shepherded this anthology to the point that it was finally accepted for publication by the QuakerPress of FGC in the fall of 2007. I am grateful for the high quality work of my co-authors, Steve Angell and Paul Kriese.

Cambridge, Massachusetts, June 27, 2010

Endnotes

1 See James Loewen, *Lies My Teacher Told Me: Everything Your American History Textbook Got Wrong* (New York: The New Press, 2008).

2 The impact of my time at Westtown—and the experiences of other Aftrican American students at Germantown Friends School and Westtown—is documented in the Friends Council on Education publication *Schooled in Diversity Action Research: Student and African American Alumni Collaboration for School Change* (Philadelphia: Friends Council on Education, 2001).

3 Harold Weaver, *Facing Unbearable Truths* (Boston: Beacon Hill Friends House, 2008).

Preface II

by Paul Kriese

I LOVED SUMMERS MOST growing up in Buffalo, New York. It was during the summer when my father and I would spend quality time together. We would walk the neighborhood in the early evenings. We would go for rides in our car and stop for lunch along the way. We would sit in our living room and watch sunsets with a companionship that needs no words. In fact, words would have destroyed the mood. He was my model of Quaker simplicity and gentility. He was born Jewish and was converted at the age of five to Roman Catholicism by a terrified father who had snuck him and his wife out of a Jewish hell in northwest Germany. He converted to Quakerism when he married my mother who matched his gentility with a worldly unworldliness. She never raised her voice, but she was also never contradicted when she asked for compliance. It was this environment in which I grew up.

My father had been in a great many different and not always positive environments as he grew to adulthood. He knew the evils that people can foist upon each other. But he always reminded me that good and bad live together, and the definition of these terms is up to you. He believed that, if we but sit and wait upon God, we can see where we should travel. It is up to us then to discern if we wish to go in that direction. Silence has always been my friend. From the mystical tradition of Judaism and Catholicism, my father was already prepared to move into the realm of Conservative and General Conference Quakerism. It was in this universalistic religious context that I first came to know my place in the Religious Society of Friends. It was in this holistic sense of inclusion that I came to fashion my relationship with other people, within and outside of Friends.

I grew up in as mixed an ethnic and cultural reality in the outside world as I did in my inward genesis. I grew up in a working class neighborhood on the Buffalo waterfront. I grew up with African Americans,

Native Americans, and Hispanics. My neighborhood had fundamentalist and mainline Christians, Jews, store front churches, and, of course, our small Friends meeting, which met in the local downtown YMCA. I grew up in a world of diversity and pluralism in every sense of the word. This multiplicity was natural for me. I grew up theologically with Rufus Jones's "flowering of mysticism," Douglas Steere's sense of wonder at the world, Janet Scott's vibrant but silent waiting God. And, above all, I grew up with my favorite Quaker "continuing revelation" sense that God's world is always unfolding, if we but allow ourselves to see it unfold, and often from places where we least expect that unfolding or that flowering.

It is from this sense of wholeness, completeness, and relatedness with that which is around me, that I so unhappily came to learn that, in one sense, many Friends were all too like the world about them, at least in the United States. Hidden in plain sight, European American Friends relations with Friends of color historically have had and continue to exhibit negative behaviors. Friends have an admirable history in our relations to the human struggles of our African American cohorts, but an equally sad and discriminatory relationship with these Friends personally. It is a sad history, which we have often ignored, or even worse, have had no knowledge of at all. Yet Friends of color have for over three hundred years lived in a bifurcated world: as Quaker (or 'visitor') yet denied a place at the table because of their color. We can see this duality in the fact that this present volume is the first volume of the writings of Friends of color to be published. During our work on this collection, we encountered some well known Friends who have been quite ignorant of many negative experiences that Friends of color have experienced while holding membership in various monthly and yearly meetings. Some of these realities have matched the negativity of the outside world beyond the "hedge" of Quakerism.

We cannot expect non-Friends to repair the breach of human community, of spiritual collectiveness, of simple neighborliness unless we address this breach. Our valiant history needs to be told in its entirety if we are to be justly seen as a bearer of God's Truth in Meeting House and Counting House (to use Frederick Tolles's book title). To be true to that "still small voice of God," to the "Presence in the Midst," to "that of God" in all of us, we must address this separation. This present volume moves a great distance for me in my quest for the "beloved community" toward which Brooks, Green, Dunbar, and other Friends of color have guided us since the birth of Quakerism in the United States. We must hear their pain, their seeking for community, and our corporate need to bring us all into a religious community, which we currently share in theory but not always in practice. I am happy to be a part of this collection for my father and mother, for my neighbors in Buffalo, New York, for those I work with in movements for human and political justice, but most of all to make more real that Spirit of God's love in and between us all.

Preface III

by Stephen W. Angell

When I was attending Friends General Conference in 1962 and was all of nine years old, my father introduced me to Barrington Dunbar one day. I already loved Dunbar from afar; I perceived and treasured his quiet grace. And he certainly stood out in a crowd. As we stood on a street corner in Cape May, New Jersey, he greeted me very warmly, and as I craned my neck looking up at him, he talked to me for a few minutes in his lilting Caribbean accent. I cannot remember comprehending his heavily accented words, but that really did not matter. As the Native American Papunehang said, after John Woolman permitted his translator not to translate his prayer from English, I loved to feel where the words came from. My admiration of him grew. I resonated with his calls that we Quakers should listen to black power advocates like Stokely Carmichael, and I was glad when my yearly meeting at that time, New York Yearly Meeting, invited a Black Muslim, Warith Deen Muhammad, to speak to them in about 1980. Unfortunately, Dunbar had died a few years earlier, too soon to see our yearly meeting heed his counsel.

In 1973, I was part of a crowd of two hundred people who gathered to listen to Howard Thurman speak at another Friends General Conference gathering, this one at Earlham College in Richmond, Indiana. At age twenty, I was used to the adulation given to the performers at rock concerts, but I never had encountered anything quite like the electric buzz that filled this large room of mostly European American women. I really knew hardly anything about Thurman, but joined the hush when a dignified, elderly, dark-skinned man came into the room. He spoke that day about what we all have in common at the heart of our humanness; he commended to us whatever had "the sound of the genuine" in our spiritual encounter. His delivery was brief, soft, and gentle.

As Quakers, we navigate many contradictions in the area of racial justice. We muddle through. Every year or two, we would schedule an

African American keynote speaker at the Friends General Conference gathering, always from the acceptable non-violent philosophic viewpoint—a James Farmer (1966) or Andrew Young (1972 and 1978), for instance. Yet the audience on such occasions was virtually all European American. At Westtown School, where I attended from 1967 to 1970, students like myself volunteered to tutor African American children in nearby West Chester, or signed up for the inaugural course in African American history in the 1968-1969 school year. But there was little or no attention or guidance given to helping an "integrated" school (yes, Westtown hired African American faculty and admitted African American students at the time) feel a true brotherhood and sisterhood among us in our one race, the human race, nor to achieve a true integration of heart, mind, or spirit. Perhaps that was too much to ask; the whole nation was boiling over with just such questions during the three years I was at Westtown. Yet Quakers, often bold in their critiques of United States war-making follies, often grow cautious when the subject of race relations and racial justice crops up. The Earlham School of Religion, where I now teach, has few African American students and no African American faculty. How can we do better?

One way is by listening to the voices of Barrington Dunbar, Howard Thurman, and other wise women and men, whose writings and thoughts are anthologized in this volume. We have so much to learn from our African American brothers and sisters—as I did from 1990 to 2001, when I taught religious studies at Florida A&M University (FAMU), a historically black university, and as I have since the 1980s through my participation in the Afro-American Religious History Group (AARHG) at the American Academy of Religion. At FAMU, I was fortunate to be a part of an extraordinary group of students and colleagues who brought out the best in each other, in large part because we were eager to look at what wisdom could be obtained by studying race relations and racial justice issues as something belonging at the center of the human experience, rather than as a subject that should just hang around on the margins. The AARHG is one of those associations all too rare in American society. Since our founding in the 1970s, we have consciously cultivated an interracial fellowship of scholars, of both genders, whose work is of high quality, to explore the past, with its tragedies and its glories, as well as opportunities for the present and the future scholarship discloses to us all.

These are the kinds of opportunities that I treasure and tha[t I] wish for all my friends, and Friends. May we all take the opp[ortunity] presented by the publication of this book, with the many pa[st,] sometimes joyful, sometimes anguished voices between its co[vers, to] spark many more discussions and to build many more fellowsh[ips. It] may help us to realize, in all of its difficulties and its triumphs, th[e glori]ous oneness of our human family.

Introduction

AFRICAN AMERICAN QUAKERS, women and men, have made major contributions to society, culture, education, life, arts, science, polity, and economy for over three hundred years. Yet little is known about their collective writings, let alone their identity or identification as Quakers. Scholars have expressed surprise when we revealed to them that we were working on an anthology of writings by African American Quakers. They admit to not knowing there are any such Quakers. Even fewer know that the international majority of the world's Quakers are of African descent. Over half of the world's Quakers live on the continent of Africa. Kenya has the largest number of Quakers of any country in the world. Yet, when people are asked to characterize Quakers, the dominant image, often revealed in free-association tests, is "white."

This anthology helps fill a longstanding gap. It features writings by some of the most inspirational and influential Quaker thinkers, writers, and activists of the twentieth century: **Jean Toomer**, **Bayard Rustin**, **Howard Thurman**, **Ira Reid**, and others of renown. It also includes earlier writings by pioneering Friends in the eighteenth and nineteenth centuries: philanthropist-abolitionist **Paul Cuffe**, self-taught scientist-mathematician-publisher **Benjamin Banneker**, activist-educator **Sarah Mapp Douglass** (ancestor of twentieth century artist-activist-scholar Paul Robeson), and others. We have assembled this collection as a first step toward offering to readers both the light of spiritual insight and the heat of passion for justice expressed by African American Quakers in a body of writing we call *Black Fire*.

In making these selections, the editors had to consider the questions: who belongs in the category "African American Quakers," and how to capture a meaningful representation of writings on subjects ranging from an emphasis on religion and spirituality to an emphasis on justice and human rights?

Some of the authors included in this collection have held formal membership in the Religious Society of Friends; others are "friends of

Introduction

Friends," longtime participants in Friends worship and community who never formally joined. Some have held "living ties" with the Society through their activities and actions—such as activist **Bill Sutherland**, who served in several capacities for the American Friends Service Committee (AFSC), and theologian **Howard Thurman**, who wrote prolifically for Friends United Press.

Quaker insights, while providing an entry to a crucial core area of Christian, indeed human, spirituality for Howard Thurman, could never be entirely satisfying to him as long as a denominational tag dictated boundaries for the association of mystics, seekers, and finders. For Thurman, the only denomination that could be satisfying was one that transcended denominationalism and united sincere seekers drawn from every race, ethnicity, and creed. Hence Thurman's core affiliation was with the Church for the Fellowship of All Peoples, despite long and close relations with Friends.

By the mid-twentieth century, there was an option available to non-Friends who felt deeply attracted to the principles of the Religious Society of Friends. The Wider Quaker Fellowship, founded in 1937 by the second World Conference of Friends, provided an opportunity for another kind of relationship. Howard Thurman was one who availed himself of this option, and he became a member of the Wider Quaker Fellowship. This collection includes, even prior to 1937, African Americans who were so attracted to the principles of Friends that they might be thought of as part of a wider Quaker fellowship.

The writings included herein draw upon published works and historical archives. Among the Quaker publishers of pamphlets, articles, poetry, and books selected are Pendle Hill Publications, *Friends Intelligencer*, Friends United Press, Friends General Conference, and Philadelphia and New York Yearly Meetings, as well as unpublished American Friends Service Committee memoranda and other materials from such peace organizations as the Fellowship of Reconciliation. The archives at Haverford, Swarthmore, and Earlham Colleges have been especially good sources of documents, published and unpublished.

This anthology fills blind spots in Quaker literature and studies, Africana studies, and equality/racial justice studies. In addition we will introduce you to African American Quaker women who, during the eighteenth, nineteenth, and twentieth centuries, did not hesitate to write about the human rights mistreatment of African Americans. **Sarah Mapps Douglass** was one; the twentieth-century lawyer-activist-philanthropist **Mahala Ashley Dickerson** explicitly condemned the racial policies and practices within the Society of Friends. Yet, both retained their faith—their spirituality—in the Society of Friends and chose to fight human rights violations both within and outside Quakerism. Dickerson went so far as to migrate to Alaska as a homesteader with the hope of finding less racial discrimination and was instrumental in establishing a new meeting there. Poet **Helen Morgan Brooks** wrote searingly about human rights violations based on racial prejudice and lovingly about the peacefulness of Quaker worship. Their male counterparts, humanities scholar **Charles Nichols** and political activist **Bill Sutherland**, took their talents abroad for decades of exile, rather than face the continued frustration of the violation of human rights caused by inequality of opportunity in the United States.[1]

A number of African American Friends included in this volume made important contributions to social and political issues of their times. Pan-Africanist **Paul Cuffe**, a New England Friend of the late eighteenth and early nineteenth centuries, became an active leader of the Back-to-Africa movement as a means of resisting abusive treatment of African Americans. Through slave narratives, **Charles Nichols** was among the first scholars to publish a comprehensive treatment of enslaved Africans in the United States speaking for themselves about the nature of chattel slavery and their tools of resistance and rebellion. The impact of spirituality and religion on human rights, including the Civil Rights Movement of the 1950s and 1960s, is documented by **Bayard Rustin** and **Howard Thurman**, both mentors to Martin Luther King, Jr. Spirituality and the search for self are poetically and aesthetically explored by **Jean Toomer** in writings representing various aspects of his life. Toomer is acknowledged for his pioneering literary and artistic contributions to the Harlem Renaissance, yet few know him as an active Quaker during part of his life.

African American Quaker social scientists, humanists, and activists have contributed to the body of Quaker literature, Africana studies, and social science literature. Renowned Haverford sociology professor **Ira Reid** and Rutgers anthropologist **Vera Green** made important contributions to their respective disciplines and fields of study in the

Introduction

social sciences as well as to the Society of Friends. **Bayard Rustin**, a frequently quoted intellectual-activist, influenced the evolutionary shift "from protest to politics." AFSC activist **Bill Sutherland**, for whom AFSC named its training institute, the Bill Sutherland Institute for Training (no longer in existence), also brought major contributions to the evolving operational definitions of nonviolence and violence in the struggle for freedom in Africa. He is credited with pinpointing systemic violence—for him that meant capitalism, unemployment, racism, sexism, and other social problems—as more of a threat to a decent, humane society than is the individual violence against which society's efforts most often appear to be directed.

In defining the scope of this anthology, the editors made an extremely difficult decision to limit this collection to African American Quakers born prior to 1930. We do not want readers to take away the impression that there are no important, inspirational, or illuminating African American Quaker voices today. There are important works continuing to emerge from the pens of living Quaker writers of both African American and African nationalities, and we look forward to the publication of future collections that will give these contributions more of the recognition they deserve.

We hope our readers will be educated and enlightened by, and find enjoyable, the fresh and diverse Friends voices here, which have been too long ignored. We have selected these writings for the broadest audience possible: the general reader, as well as students and scholars in the social sciences and humanities. Among the fields of study where we think this material can be of great use are: Africana Studies, Religious Studies, History, Political Science, Quaker Studies, and other related fields.

Endnotes

1 See Ernest Dunbar, *Black Expatriates: A Study of American Negroes in Exile* (London: V. Gollancz, 1968) for gripping descriptions of Nichols's life as professor and scholar in Berlin and Europe and Sutherland's role as advisor to political leaders in various West, East, and Southern African colonies and independent nations.

I
The Early Period

edited by Stephen W. Angell

Benjamin Banneker

Benjamin Banneker (1731–1806) was a farmer, surveyor, and astronomer who lived in Maryland. He was born free; his father Robert was a freed slave. He had very little formal education, although he did attend a small Quaker interracial school for some years during his childhood. He never married. In addition to farming tobacco, he participated in surveying the ten-mile-square plot of land that would become the District of Columbia. Subsequently, he produced almanacs annually from 1792 to 1804, and he found publishers for his almanacs until 1797. In a 1793 edition of his almanac, he published Benjamin Rush's plan for a United States Peace Office, a text that, on both the author's and publisher's part, may reflect Quaker influence in its advocacy of pacifism, the disuse of oaths, and the abolition or reduction in use of the death penalty.[1] This edition of his almanac includes much reprinted

material relative to Banneker's peace and anti-slavery concerns, including an extract from William Pitt's speech against the slave trade in the British parliament, an extended quotation criticizing slavery from Thomas Jefferson's *Notes on Virginia*, and a comment from Phocion, an ancient Greek orator, highly critical of warfare.

Banneker never joined any denomination, but he frequently attended Quaker meetings. His almanacs included a schedule for Quaker yearly meetings throughout North America, from Rhode Island to North Carolina;[2] the Quakers were the only denomination for which Banneker provided such information in his almanac.

Copy of a Letter from Benjamin Banneker to Thomas Jefferson
Maryland, Baltimore County, August 19, 1791

SIR,

I AM fully sensible of the greatness of that freedom, which I take with you on the present occasion; a liberty which seemed to me scarcely allowable, when I reflected on that distinguished and dignified station in which you stand, and the almost general prejudice and prepossession, which is so prevalent in the world against those of my complexion.

I suppose it is a truth too well attested to you, to need a proof here, that we are a race of beings, who have long labored under the abuse and censure of the world; that we have long been looked upon with an eye of contempt; and that we have long been considered rather as brutish than human, and scarcely capable of mental endowments.

Sir, I hope I may safely admit, in consequence of that report which hath reached me, that you are a man far less inflexible in sentiments of this nature, than many others; that you are measurably friendly and well disposed towards us; and that you are willing and ready to lend your aid and assistance to our relief, from those many distresses, and numerous calamities, to which we are reduced.

Now Sir, if this is founded in truth, I apprehend you will embrace every opportunity, to eradicate that train of absurd and false ideas and opinions, which so generally prevails with respect to us; and that your sentiments are concurrent with mine, which are, that one universal Father hath given being to us all; and that he hath not only made us all of one flesh, but that he hath also, without partiality, afforded us all the same sensations, and endowed us all with the same faculties; and that however variable we may be in society or religion, however diversified in situation or color, we are all of the same family, and stand in the same relation to him.

Sir, if these are sentiments of which you are fully persuaded, I hope you cannot but acknowledge, that it is the indispensible duty of those who maintain for themselves the rights of human nature, and who profess the obligations of Christianity, to extend their power and influence to the relief of every part of the human race, from whatever burthen or oppression they may unjustly labor under; and to this I apprehend a full conviction of the truth and obligation of these principles should lead all to.

Sir, I have long been convinced that if your love for yourselves, and for those inestimable laws, which preserve to you the rights of human nature, was founded on sincerity, you could not but be solicitous that every individual, of whatever rank or distinction, might with you equally enjoy the blessings thereof; neither could you rest satisfied, short of the most active effusion of your exertions, in order to their [sic] promotion from any state of degradation, to which the unjustifiable cruelty and barbarism of men may have reduced them.

Sir, I freely and cheerfully acknowledge, that I am of the African race, and in that color which is natural to them of the deepest dye; and it is under a sense of the most profound gratitude to the Supreme Ruler of the Universe, that I now confess to you, that I am not under that state of tyrannical thraldom, and inhuman captivity, to which too many of my brethren are doomed, but that I have abundantly tasted of the fruition of those blessings, which proceed from that free and unequalled liberty with which you are favored; and which, I hope, you will willingly allow you have received, from the immediate hand of that Being, from whom proceedeth every good and perfect gift.

Sir, suffer me to recall to your mind that time, in which the arms and tyranny of the British crown were exerted, with every powerful effort, in order to reduce you to a state of servitude: look back, I entreat you, on the variety of dangers to which you were exposed; reflect on that time, in which every human aid appeared unavailable, and in which even hope and fortitude wore the aspect of inability to the conflict, and you cannot but be led to a serious and grateful sense of your miraculous and providential preservation; you cannot but acknowledge, that the present freedom and tranquility which you enjoy, you have mercifully received, and that it is the peculiar blessing of Heaven.

This, Sir, was a time when you clearly saw into the injustice of a state of slavery, and in which you had just apprehensions of the horrors of its condition. It was now that your abhorrence thereof was so excited, that you publicly held forth this true and invaluable doctrine, which is worthy to be recorded and remembered in all succeeding ages: "We hold these truths to be self-evident, that all men are created equal; that they are endowed by their Creator with certain unalienable rights, and that among these are, life, liberty, and the pursuit of happiness."

Here, Sir, was a time, in which your tender feelings for yourselves had engaged you thus to declare, you were then impressed with proper ideas of the great valuation of liberty, and the free possession of those blessings, to which you were entitled by nature; but how pitiable is it to reflect, that although you were so fully convinced of the benevolence of the Father of Mankind, and of his equal and impartial distribution of these rights and privileges, which he hath conferred upon them, that you should at the same time counteract his mercies, in detaining by fraud and violence so numerous a part of my brethren, under groaning captivity and cruel oppression, that you should at the same time be found guilty of that most criminal act, which you professedly detested in others, with respect to yourselves.

Sir, I suppose that your knowledge of the situation of my brethren is too extensive to need a recital here; neither shall I presume to prescribe methods by which they may be relieved, otherwise than by recommending to you and all others, to wean yourselves from those narrow prejudices which you have imbibed with respect to them, and as Job proposed to his friends, "put your soul in their souls' stead";[3] thus shall your hearts be enlarged with kindness and benevolence towards them; and thus shall you need neither the direction of myself or others, in what manner to proceed herein.

And now, although my sympathy and affection for my brethren hath caused my enlargement thus far, I ardently hope, that your candor and generosity will plead with you in my behalf, when I make known to you, that it was not originally my design; but having taken up my pen in order to direct to you, as a present, a copy of an Almanac, which I have calculated for the succeeding year, I was unexpectedly and unavoidably led thereto.

This calculation is the production of my arduous study, in this my advanced stage of life; for having long had unbounded desires to become acquainted with the secrets of nature, I have had to gratify my curiosity herein, through my own assiduous application to Astronomical Study, in which I need not recount to you the many difficulties and disadvantages, which I have had to encounter.

And although I had almost declined to make my calculation for the ensuing year, in consequence of that time which I had allotted therefor being taken up at the Federal Territory, by the request of Mr. Andrew Ellicott, yet finding myself under several engagements to printers of this state, to whom I had communicated my design, on my return to my place of residence, I industriously applied myself thereto, which I hope I have accomplished with correctness and accuracy; a copy of which I have taken the liberty to direct to you, and which I humbly request you will favorably receive; and although you may have the opportunity of perusing it after its publication, yet I chose to send it to you in manuscript previous thereto, that thereby you might not only have an earlier inspection, but that you might also view it in my own hand writing.

And now, Sir, I shall conclude and subscribe myself, with the most profound respect, Your most obedient humble servant,

Benjamin Banneker.

To Mr. BENJAMIN BANNEKER.

Philadelphia, August 30, 1791

SIR,

I THANK you, sincerely, for your letter of the 19th instant, and for the Almanac it contained. Nobody wishes more than I do to see such proofs as you exhibit, that Nature has given to our black brethren talents equal to those of the other colors of men; and that the appearance of the want of them is owing merely to the degraded condition of their existence, both in Africa and America. I can add with truth, that nobody wishes more ardently to see a good system commenced, for raising the condition, both of their body and mind, to what it ought to be, as far as the imbecility of their present existence, and other circumstances which cannot be neglected, will admit.

I have taken the liberty of sending your Almanac to Monsieur de Condorcet,[4] Secretary of the Academy of Sciences at Paris, and Member of the Philanthropic Society, because I considered it as a document to which your whole color had a right for their justification against the doubts which have been entertained of them.

I am with great esteem, Sir, Your most obedient Humble Servant,

Thomas Jefferson.

Source

Benjamin Banneker, *Benjamin Banneker's Pennsylvania, Delaware, Maryland, and Virginia Almanack and Ephemeris for the Year of our Lord 1793* (Baltimore: William Goddard and James Angell, 1793), unnumbered pages. The correspondence with Jefferson is the first item in this edition of the almanac.

William Boen

William Boen (1735–1824) was a farmer and former slave. He lived near Mount Holly, New Jersey. He was extremely pious and became friends with John Woolman, also of Mount Holly. He married at age 28, and sometime shortly before or after his marriage, was granted his freedom, after which he came to own property and was able to live comfortably. He applied for membership in the Religious Society of Friends, but despite his exemplary life and religious profession, and suggestions by Woolman himself that Boen was suitable not only for membership but also to serve as an elder of the Mount Holly Meeting, his membership application was stalled for four decades. He was not accepted into membership until 1814.

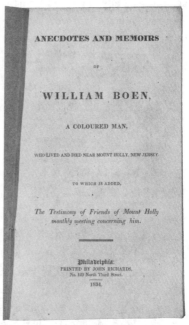

Memoirs and Anecdotes of William Boen

    William Boen was a coloured man, who resided near Mount Holly, New Jersey. Like many of his brethren of the African race, in those days, he was from his birth held as a slave. But though poor and ignorant, in his early days, he was cared for, as all others are, by the universal Parent of the human family. He became a pious, sober, temperate, honest, and industrious man; and by this means, he obtained the friendship, esteem, and respect of all classes of his fellow-men, and the approbation and peace of his heavenly Father.

    His industry, temperance, and cleanliness, no doubt, contributed much to his health and comfort; so that he lived to be a very old man, with having but little sickness through the course of his life. His character being so remarkable for sobriety, honesty, and peace, that it induced some younger people to inquire by what means he had arrived to such a state, and attained such a standing in the neighbourhood where he lived. Ever willing to instruct, counsel, and admonish the youth, he could relate his own experience of the work of grace in his heart, which led him into such uprightness of life and conduct. For his memory did not appear to be much impaired by reason of old age.

To a friend who visited him in the eighty-sixth year of his age, he gave the following account of his early life, and religious experience. On being asked, whether he could remember in what way, and by what means, he was first brought to mind and follow *that*, which had been his guide and rule of faith and life, and which had led and preserved him so safely along through time? William answered as follows: "Oh! yes; that I can, right well. In the time of the old French war, my master (for I was a poor black boy, a slave) my master sent me to chop wood, on a hill-side, out of sight of any house; and there was a great forest of woods below me; and he told me to cut down all the trees on that hill-side. When I went home, in the evenings, I often heard them talking about the Indians killing and scalping people: and sometimes, some of my neighbours would come in, and they and my master's family talked of the Indians killing such and such,—nearer and nearer to us. And so, from time to time, I would hear them tell of the Indians killing, and scalping people, nearer and nearer: so that I began to think, like enough, by and by, they would kill me. And I thought more and more about it; and again would hear tell of their coming still nearer. At length, I thought, sure enough they will get so near, that they will hear the sound of my axe, and will come and kill me. Here is a great forest of woods below me, and no house in sight:—surely, I have not long to live. I expected every day would be my last;—that they would soon kill me, a poor black boy, here all alone."

"A thought then came into my mind, whether I was fit to die. It was showed me, and I saw plain enough, that I was not fit to die. Then it troubled me very much, that I was not fit to die; and I felt very desirous,—very anxious that I might be made fit to die. So I stood still, in great amazement; and it seemed as if a flaming sword passed through me. And when it passed over, and I recollected myself (for I stood so, some time) it was showed me how I should be made fit to die: and I was willing to do any thing, so I might be made fit to die."

"Thus, I was brought to mind and follow *that*, that has been the guide and rule of my life,—*that within me*, that inclined me to good, and showed and condemned evil. Now I considered I had a new master—I had two masters; and it was showed me (in my mind) by my new Master, a certain tree on the hill-side, that I must not cut down. I knowed the tree well enough. I had not come to it yet. But I did not know what I *should* do; for my old master had told me to cut all the trees down, on that hill-side. My new master forbids me to cut a certain one. So I thought a good deal about it. I cut on; and by and by I came to the tree. I cut on by it, and let it stand. But I expected, every day, my old master would come, and see that tree standing, and say, 'What did thee leave that tree standing for? Did I not tell thee to cut all the trees down, as thee went? Go, cut that tree down.' Then, I didn't know what I *should* do. But he never said any thing to me about it. I cut on, and got some distance by it; and one day my old master brought out his axe, and cut the tree down himself; and never said, William, why didn't thee cut that tree down? never said anything to me about it. Then I thought, surely my new Master will make way for me, and take care of me, if I love him, and mind him, and am attentive to this my guide, and rule of life. And this seemed an evidence and proof of it, and strengthened me much in love, and confidence in my Guide."

After the respectable and goodly old man, had given this interesting account of the way and manner in which he was brought to follow the guide of his life, the following question was put to him: "Well, William, has thee, from that time, till now, been so careful and attentive to thy guide, as never to say or do amiss?" To which he replied, "Oh! no: I have missed it—I have several times missed it." He was then asked, "Well, William, in that case, how *did* thee get along?" He answered, "Oh! when I missed it,—when I found I had said, or done wrong, I felt very sorry. I tried to be more careful, for time to come;—never to do so any more: and I believe I was forgiven."

Another inquiry was made of William, how he and his old master got along together, after his change. He said, "Very well. Some time afterwards, one of his neighbours said to me, one day, 'William, thy master talks of setting thee free.' I didn't think much about it—didn't expect there was any thing in it; though I heard others say he talked of setting me free;—till, after some time, as my master was walking with me, going to my work, he said, 'William, wouldn't thee like to be free?' I didn't say any thing to it. I thought he might know I should like to be free. I didn't make him any answer about it, but then I thought there was something in it. So after awhile, sure enough, he did set me free."

There is no doubt his old master observed a great change in him; for his guide taught him to be dutiful, industrious and diligent in his business, careful in his words and actions, and sober, steady, and exemplary in all he said, and in all his conduct.

William Boen's guide, and rule of life and conduct, his *new Master*, as he called him, that did so much for him, and raised him from the state of a poor slave, to be a free man, in good esteem—thro' habits of temperance, sobriety, honest industry and integrity,—whereby he was enabled to become the respectable head of a family, and to acquire a house, and property of his own, sufficient for the comfortable accommodation of himself and his family;—and who forsook him not when he became old, and grey-headed;—his new Master was the same Light that appears unto all; and it would guide every one in the right way, as it did him, if they would take it for their Master, and mind and obey it, as he did. It was the guide of his youth,—because his Lord and Master,—preserved him from evil,—and conducted him safely through the trials of life, to a good old age.

William Boen's new Master was, and is the same thing that the apostle Paul, in his Epistle to Titus, bears testimony to, in these words: "the grace of God, that bringeth salvation, hath appeared to all men;—teaching us, that, denying all ungodliness and worldly lusts, we should live soberly, righteously, and godly in the present world." Now, surely, if we don't take it for our master, and mind its teachings, we cannot *know* it to bring our salvation, or *save us* from *all ungodliness* and *worldly lusts*, as he did, and as all do, that are obedient to this grace of God, *the Light of Christ, within.*

In William Boen's simple account of the way and means, by which he was showed how he should be made fit to die;—that is, by minding and following *that within* him, which inclined him to good, and that showed and condemned him for evil,—the goodness, mercy, and condescending care of the Almighty Father, are strikingly manifest. How graciously he suits his dispensations to the weak and ignorant states of his children, who sincerely seek him, and inquire what they shall do to be saved! When William Boen thought of death, something showed him he was not fit to die. He "saw it plain enough," and was troubled. In his anxiety to be prepared to die, he became still and quiet—and then he felt condemnation, as a flaming sword, pass through him. When this had its effect to bring him to a state of humility and watchfulness, the Divine Light in his soul showed him the way in which he should walk, in order to become fit to die. He became willing to do any thing required of him: so, to prove his obedience, it was showed him, by his new Master, that he must leave a certain tree standing, where he was felling timber. He began to reason upon consequences, but resolved to obey his new Master, in preference to his old one. It was sufficient to test his faith and love; and though a simple circumstance, it was probably of great use to him ever after; as by it he was taught to be faithful in little things, and thus became ruler over more.

It may be useful to survivors, who, like William, are desirous so to live, as that they may become fit to die,—to bring into view some anecdotes of his life, that show the principles by which his mind and conduct were regulated.

In his conversation among men, he was very careful to keep to the plain language,—the language of truth and sincerity—yet, through the help of his guide, he detected himself in deviation from it, in the following circumstances. A wealthy neighbour, a white man, frequently availed himself of William's obliging dispositions, by using his grindstone, instead of procuring one for himself. On an occasion of this kind, his neighbour told him he was obliged to him for the use of his grindstone: to which, William returned the usual compliment of saying he was welcome. After the man was gone, William became uneasy in his mind, with his reply, as being insincere. He therefore went to his neighbour, and made an acknowledgment, that although he had told him he was welcome, yet it was only in conformity with custom, and was not the case; for he thought his neighbour was better able to keep a grindstone of his own, than he was.

How many customary compliments, by-words, and common expressions, would be dispensed with, as idle words, for which we must give an account in the day of judgment,—if a strict regard to truth and sincerity, were the ruling principle or guide of all our words and actions!

William Boen appears to have been as strictly careful in his adherence to the principles of justice, and the rights of property, as he was in regard to truth and sincerity in his communications. Being employed, with several others, to mow the meadows attached to the place called Breezy Ridge, on Lomberton creek,—William, with his scythe, accidentally struck a partridge that was concealed from his view, in the grass, and killed it. As it appeared to be in good order, his companions proposed that he should take it home, for his own use. William, however, was not easy to do so: he said the partridge did not belong to him, but to the owner of the meadow.

On another occasion, he manifested the acuteness of his feelings, in regard to the rights of property. With other labourers, he was employed to cut timber in the pines, at a distance from the settlements. They took provisions with them, to encamp for a week or two in the woods; and, finding an empty cabin on lands that did not belong to their employer, they made use of it. William's mind, however, was not quite satisfied. He had been using the property of another, without leave. So, after his return, he took an early opportunity to represent the case to the owner of the cabin, who lived some miles distant from him.

William Boen believed in Christ, as the Prince of peace; and that those who professed to be Christians, and lived in his peaceable spirit, could have nothing to do with war, in any shape. He therefore had a testimony to bear against the spirit of war, and the love of money that stands in connexion with it. Not far from William's habitation, there lived a storekeeper, a man of considerable note, who had been an officer in the army, during the time of the American revolution. Some time after the peace was concluded, this storekeeper traded largely in buying up soldiers' certificates, for much less than their nominal value. By this means, he made considerable profits to himself, with which he engaged in building a large and fine house. While thus employed, William Boen called on him, and told him he had been much concerned for him, on account of his traffic in what he considered no better than the price of blood, and that the money with which he was building his house, was unrighteousness gain.

He also quoted that passage of scripture, as applicable to the case, respecting Judas, who betrayed his Master for the sake of money; and mentioned the manner of his death.

His reproof and admonition were delivered with so much honesty and tender feeling, and the kind and friendly motives that influenced him thereto, were so apparent, that his neighbour, though a high-spirited man, received his communication, in a respectful manner;—and, on a subsequent occasion, upon hearing some persons remark, that they wondered that William was not ridiculed by boys, and light, vain persons, on account of his singular appearance, and wearing his beard so long,—he stated, that William Boen was a religious man; and that his well known piety impressed the minds of such people with awe and respect towards him; and thus they were prevented from manifesting that levity which the singularity of his dress and appearance might otherwise have produced.

For it is to be observed, that he thought it right to have all his clothing of the natural colours, and made very plain and simple. As he was very clean in his person, his wearing apparel became very white, by washing—his hair and beard also became white through age: and these, contrasted with his dark skin, gave him a very venerable appearance. He was affable, modest, and respectful, in his manners and deportment; while the mildness and gravity of his countenance, indicated a mind governed by the precepts of the gospel, and often impressed lessons of serious reflection on those who beheld him;—especially in the solidarity and reverence, with which he sat in religious meetings.

It was probably on account of his dress, that some person remarked to him, that he appeared to be endeavoring to walk in the footsteps of John Woolman, —a Friend with whom he had been intimately acquainted. After a pause, he said, "I am endeavouring to follow the footsteps of Christ."

William Boen, by attending to his Guide, and faithfully following Christ, his *new Master*, was brought to believe in his doctrine, in relation to gospel ministers: "Freely ye have received, freely give." He therefore did not approve of hireling ministry, or paying men for preaching. This testimony to a free gospel ministry, he carried so far, in order to keep a pure conscience towards his Divine Master, that on one occasion, after he had sold some woods to a person, who was called a clergyman,—he felt scrupulous about receiving money from him, which was obtained by preaching: as it would not be, in his apprehension, bearing a faithful testimony against hireling ministry. So he went to the man, and asked him whether he got his money by preaching. On being answered in the affirmative, William told him, he was not free to take his money in pay for the wood, as he did not approve of making money by preaching, contrary to the command of Christ.

Yet his mind was clothed with Christian charity towards his fellow-creatures, who had not been brought to see and walk in the way which he apprehended to be required of him. William was not free to use any thing either in food or clothing, that he knew to be produced through the labour of slaves. On its being asked him, whether he thought so well of his friends that used the products of slavery, as he would do, if they did not use such articles; he replied, "*Obedience is all, with me.* I believe it is required of me, not to use these things: and if it has never been required of them, not to use these things, then they are as much in the way of their duty, in using them, as I am in the way of my duty, in not using them."

When William was drawing near the close of his long and exemplary life, his bodily powers failed through weakness, and the decay of nature; but his mind was preserved clear and tranquil. At this season, he was frequently visited by a friend, who, on one occasion, made some remarks respecting the calm and peaceful state of mind, which he appeared to enjoy, and inquired of him by what means he had attained to such a happy state. William, in accordance with his common expression of trying all things by the mind, gave this short and comprehensive answer: "By keeping the mind easy,—and resisting every thing that made it uneasy."

Soon after his death, the following obituary notice, appeared in one of the public papers: "Died, near Mount Holly, on the 12th instant, in the ninetieth year of his age, William Boen, (alias Heston) a coloured man."

Rare, indeed, are the instances that we meet with, in which we feel called upon to record the virtues of any of this afflicted race of people. The deceased, however, was one of those who have demonstrated the truth of that portion of scripture, that "of a truth God is no respecter of persons; but in every nation, they that fear him and work righteousness, are accepted with him."

He was concerned, in early life, "to do justly, love mercy, and walk humbly with his God;" and by a close attention to the light of Christ within, and faithfully abiding under the operation of that blessed spirit of Divine grace in his soul, he was enabled, not only to bear many precious testimonies faithfully, to the end of his days, but also to bring forth those fruits of the spirit which redound to the glory of God, and the salvation of the soul. He was an exemplary member of the Religious Society of Friends; and as he lived, so he died,—a rare pattern of a self-denying follower of Jesus Christ. He had no apparent disease,—either of body or mind; but, as he expressed himself a short time before his death, he felt nothing but weakness: which continued to increase, until he gently breathed his last; and is, no doubt, entered into his heavenly Father's rest.

"Mark the perfect man, and behold the upright: for the end of that man is peace."

6th month, 1824

Memorial of Mount Holly monthly meeting of Friends, concerning William Boen, a coloured man

[*Read in the Yearly Meeting of Friends, held in Philadelphia, 1829*]

As the memory of those who have followed the leadings of that Teacher which leadeth into all truth, and enables its votaries to become, by example, preachers to righteousness, is precious, we feel encouraged to give the following testimony concerning our deceased friend, William Boen, a coloured man.

He was born in the year 1735, in the neighbourhood of Rancocas. Being a slave from his birth, he had very little opportunity of acquiring useful learning; yet by his own industry and care, he succeeded in learning to read and write.

His mind became seriously impressed while very young, and he was induced in early life, to attend to the monitions of light and life in his own mind, being convinced from what he felt within him, of the existence of a Supreme Being; and also of the manner of his visiting the children of men, by the inward peace which he felt upon a faithful performance of what he thus apprehended to be his duty.

About the twenty-eighth year of his age, he contracted for his freedom; and having entered into marriage engagements with a woman in the neighbourhood, but not being, at that time, a member of our society, he was straitened in his mind how to accomplish it; as he was fully convinced of our testimony in that respect.

In this difficulty, he made known his situation to our friend, John Woolman, who, to relieve him, had a number of persons convened at a friend's house, where they were married after the manner of our society, and a certificate to that effect, furnished them by those present.

About this time he made application to become a member of our society; but way not opening in Friends minds, he was not received, but encouraged to continue faithful; which we believe he did, from the account we have of nearly his whole life.

He was concerned above all things, to walk in the path of truth and righteousness; and according to his measure, to be faithful to every opening of duty, by which means he obtained the esteem of all who knew him.

As he thus continued steadfast to the light in his own mind, he was favoured to see the necessity of a daily cross to all the gratifications of self, and that the cause of truth cannot grow in us, while we are governed by a worldly spirit.

By yielding full of obedience to that light, which it was his chiefest joy to follow, he became truly convinced of the necessity of maintaining the various testimonies which we, as a people, have been called upon to bear; and, in some respects, he had to bear a testimony against things in which many of his white brethren indulge, particularly in regard to slavery; refusing to wear, or use in any shape, articles which come through that corrupted channel. And, we believe, it was through dedication to the Lord, and an unreserved surrender of his will, to the Divine will, that he was brought to see these things in that light, which deceiveth not. Thus, evincing by his conversation and example, the truth of that scriptural declaration, "All thy children shall be taught of the Lord, and great shall be the peace of thy children; in righteousness shalt thou be established."

It appears, not only from his own words, but also from his weighty example, that his great concern was to keep his mind easy, believing that right and wrong actions would result either in peace or pain within; hence, his great care was to "try all things by the mind," as he expressed it, or the light of Christ within; with which he was, no doubt, through faithfulness, in a remarkable manner favoured; esteeming it right to be obedient to every manifested duty, however in the cross, or insignificant to the carnal mind, these small duties might appear; and as he was found, like the servant in the parable, "faithful in the little," he was strengthened to rule over the carnal propensities of his nature, bringing his words and actions into the obedience of Christ. His humility was such, that although in low circumstances, he appeared to be content, and even refused to indulge himself in rich food or clothing, saying that "bread and water was good enough for him." In 1814, he was, on application, received into membership with us, and continued to the last, when able, a steady attender of our meetings, both for worship and discipline.

He enjoyed reasonable health and strength until about his eighty-seventh year, when his strength began to fail, but the faculties of his mind remained good until his end.

Some weeks previous to his death, he spoke of it with the utmost composure, and recounting his past trials and experiences said, "he had thought he was alone with regard to his testimony against slavery." But, as though he had fresh evidence thereof, said, "he believed it would grow and increase among Friends." He appeared perfectly resigned to death, having no will therein; as he expressed himself, "that some died hard and others easy, but for himself, he had no wish for either, being fully resigned to the Divine will in all things."

To a friend present, the day previous to his death, he stated "that he felt himself going very fast; but that he had no wish to stay." His weakness increasing, and having no desire to take any nourishment, he was asked if he was sick, or felt any pain; to which he answered, "that he felt neither pain nor sickness, but weakness, and a total disrelish for every thing of this world." His weakness continued to increase until he passed quietly away, on the night of the 12th of the 6th month, 1824, in the ninetieth year of his age; and we doubt not, he has entered into his heavenly Father's rest.

The Early Period

Read in, and approved by, Mount Holly monthly meeting of Friends, held 11th month 6th, 1828.

Amos Bullock, Clerk.

Read in, and approved by, Burlington Quarterly meeting of Friends, held at Chesterfield, on the 25th of the 11th month, 1828, and directed to be forwarded to the Yearly Meeting.

Andrew C. Ridgway, Clerk.

SOURCE

William Boen. *Anecdotes and Memoirs of William Boen, a Colored Man, Who Lived and Died Near Mount Holly, New Jersey. To Which is Added, The Testimony of Friends of Mount Holly Monthly Meeting Concerning Him.* Philadelphia: J. Richards, 1834. Accessible at http://docsouth.unc.edu/neh/boen/menu.html

Paul Cuffe

Paul Cuffe (1759–1817) was a ship owner and early Pan-Africanist. The son of a freed slave brought from West Africa and a Wampanoag Indian mother, Cuffe grew to adulthood in Massachusetts during the Revolutionary War. He and his brother served jail time for refusing to pay taxes while deprived of the right to vote, protesting the American colonists' failure to include peoples of African descent in their vision of freedom and equality.

He constructed an interracial school on his property when the state refused to educate his children because they were black. He was very successful in his maritime business, eventually becoming the owner of several ships and one of the wealthiest African Americans of his time. Although he, his siblings, and his parents had a long association with Friends, it was not until 1808 that he joined the Friends Meeting in Westport, Massachusetts. He sought to encourage business between Sierra Leone in West Africa and the United States, attempting to enlist support in both the U.S. Congress and among British philanthropists, such as Quaker William Allen. (Legislation supporting Cuffe's African venture failed by seven votes in the U.S. House of Representatives.) Cuffe sponsored trips to Sierra Leone using his own fortune in 1811 and in 1815, but ill health and lack of reimbursement prevented any further trips. He endorsed the new American Colonization Society in 1817, shortly before his death.

Fragment of an Address to New York Methodists

Mercifull Father I humbly besech thee that thou wilt be pleased to enlighten my understanding that my mind may no longer be in doubt also all who have called on thy name, that they may be favored with the influence of thy holy spirit to see and understand the knowledge of the true light.

As a query was put to me by two Methodist preachers whither I understood English I answered them there was a part I did not understand viz that many persons who profess being enlightened with the true light, yet had not seen the evil of one brother professor making merchandize of, and holding his brother in bondage. This has often felt very trying to me, and in much love, I beg leave to lay my request before the beloved united society assembled for the Methodist conference in the city of New York that they through the devine assistance may be enabled to clear this stumbling bock and lighten the load that lays heavy on one who wishes well to all mankind.

Paul Cuffe
New York 5th mo 15th 1812

I felt Engaged that the above Should not miscary. I Went unto their Bishop and there Delivered him the above copied Request. I Was accompanied by my friend Thomas Eddy of New York.

Paul Cuffe's "Anadress"

To the Scattered Breatheren and fellow Countery men at Sierra Leone in Africa Grace unto you and peace be multiplied from God our father and from the Lord Jesus Christ[5] who hath Begotten in me a Lively hope[6] in Rememberence of you for which hope Sake I desire Ever to be humbled. World Without End, amen.[7]

Dearly Beloved friends and fellow Counterymen I Recommend to you that of assembeling yourselves together to Worship the Lord your God. For God is a

Spirit and they who Worship him Exceptely[8] must Worship in Spirit and in truth[9] the Substance of which Will beget that Living hope in us which hope Will be as an anchor to the Sole.[10] In this hope may Ethopia Soon Stretch out her hand unto God.[11] Come my African Breatheren and fellow Countery men Let us Walk in the Light[12] of the Lord this pure Light which Bringeth Salvation into the World hath appeared to all men[13] to Profit With all. I would Recommend to Saints Elders and all Sober peopel in the Colony of Sierra Leone to unite together and adopt the mode of meeting together once a month and at this meeting Converse with Each other for your mutual good, but above all things Let your meeting be owned of the Lord for he hath told us "Where there is 2 or 3 gethered in my name there am I in the midst of them,"[14] Saith our Lord Jesus Christ and that you may have a Record made of those meeting that it may be left on Record for the Encouragement of the young and Rising generations. In this meeting you may be favoured to institute all good institutions and in So doing I believe it Will prove for your temporal and Spiritual good. May the Prince of Peace[15] be your preserver is the Sincier Desires of one who Wishes Will to all men.[16]

Paul Cuffe
undated[17]

Advice to the Adress

Firstly,[18] may all faithfulness be Recommended with Sobriety and Stedfastness that all professors may be Careful to [be] good Examples in all things that may Walk humbley Deal justely and Love mercy.[19]

Secondly that Arly Care may be Extended towards the youths Whilst their minds are young and tender that they mey be Redeemed from corruptions of the World Such as nature is prone to (Viz) Swearing, following Lude Company Drinking of Spirituous Liquors and that they may be kept out of Idleness but be Encouraged in industry for this is good to Cultivate the minds and may you be good Examples there in your Selves.

Thirdely and Lastly may your Servents be Encouraged to Discharge their Duty with faithfulness, may they be brought up to industry, may their minds be Cultivated for the Reciption of the good Seed Which is promised to all that will Seek after it. I Wants that We Should be faithful in all things[20] that We may become a Peopel giveing Satisfaction to those who have born the heat and burthen of the Day in Liberating us from a State of Slavery.

I must Leave you in the hands of him who is Abel to preserve you through time and to Crown you With that Blessing that is prepared for all those whose faithfull unto Death. Farewell.

Paul Cuffe

SOURCE FOR ABOVE THREE SELECTIONS
Rosalind Cobb Wiggins, *Captain Paul Cuffe's Logs and Letters, 1808–1817: A Black Quaker's "Voice from within the Veil"* (Washington: Howard University Press, 1996), pp. 232–234.

Paul Cuffe's Petition to Congress

To the Presedent Senate and House of Representatives of the United States of America the memorial petition of Paul Cuffe of Westport state of Massachusetts respectfully showeth that your memorialist actuated by motives which he conceives are dictated by that philanthropy which is the offspring of Christian benevolence he is induced to ask the patronage of the Government of the United States in affording aid in the execution of a plan which he cherishes a hope may ultimately prove beneficial to his brethren of the African race within their native climate. In order to give a compleat view of the object in contemplation it may not be considered trespassing too much upon your time to premiss some of the leading Circumstances which have led to the present application.

Your memorialist being a decendant of Africa and early instructed in habits of solicity and industry has gratefully to acknowledge the many favors of bountifully Providence both in preserving him from many of the evils to which people of his colour have too often fallen into, but also by blessing his industry with such a partion of the comforts of Life as to enable him in some degree not only to communicate but to relieve the sufferings of His fellow creaters. And having early found implanted in his head the principles of equity and Justice he could not but view the practice of his brethren of the African Race in selling their fellow creatures into a state of slavery for life as very inconsistent with that Divine principal, and his mature age having been greatly [instructed or levelled, both crossed out] in the abundant Labours of many pious individuals both in this country and in England to produce a termination of the wrongs of Africa by prohibiting the slave trade and also to improve the condition of the degraded inhabitants of the Land of his ancestors. He conceived it a duty incombent upon him as a faithful steward of the mercies he had received to give up a portion of his time and his property in visiting that country and affording such means as might be in his power to promote the improvement to civilization of the Africans. Under these impressions he left his family and with the sacrafice of both time and money visited Sierra Leone and there gained such information of the country and its inhabitants as enable him to form an opinion of many improvements that appeared to him essential to the well being of that people.

These he had an oppertunity of personally communicating to several distinguished members of the Royal African Institution in London and he had the satisfaction at that time to find that his recommendations were approved by the celebrated philanthropists the Duke of Gloscester,[21] W. Wilberforce,[22] T. Clarkson,[23] Wm Allen[24] and others and has since Learned that the Institution have also so far acceded to his plans as to make some special provisions to carry them into effect. One of these objects was to keep up an intercourse with the People of Colour in the United States in the Expectation that some persons of reputation would feel industry sobriety and frugality amongst the nations of that country. These views having been communicated by your petition[er] to the People of Colour in Baltimore and Philadelphia, New York and Boston they with a Zeal becoming so important a concern have manifested a disposition to promote so laudable an undertaken. And several family whose characters promise influences have come to a conclusion if proper ways could be open to go to Africa for a Temporary residence in order to give their aid in promoting the objects already adverted to your petitioner still animated with a sincere desire of making the Knowledge he has acquired and the sacrifices he has all ready made more permanently useful in promoting the Civilization of Africa solicits your aid so far as to grant permission that a Vessel may be imployed if liberty can also be obtained from the British Government between this country and Sierra Leone to transport such persons and families as may be inclined to go, as also some articles of provisions together with impliments of husbandry and machinery for some michanic arts and to Bring back such of the Natives productions of that country as may be wanted. For Altho pecuniary profit does not enter into calculations in the object in contemplation nor does it afford any very promising prospects yet without a little aid from the trifling commerce of that country the expenses would fall too heavy upon your petitioner and those of his friends Who feel disposed to patronize the undertaking. Your petitioner therefore craves the attention of Congress to a concern which appears to him Very important to a portion of his fellow creaturs who have been Long much excluded from the common advantage of Civilized life and prays that they will afford him and his friends such aid as they in their wisdom may think best.

With much respect I am your ashured friend
Paul Cuffe
Westport 6th mo 1813

Source

Rosalind Cobb Wiggins, *Paul Cuffe's Logs and Letters*, pp. 252–253.

Elizabeth

Elizabeth (1766–1866) was a traveling Methodist minister and former slave. Her Maryland parents were Methodists, and her father read the Bible aloud regularly. She was separated from her family by sale at age eleven. She gained her freedom at age 30. Her role in ministerial leadership began shortly thereafter; she held her first service in Baltimore. Her ministerial travels took her to such locations as Michigan and Canada, and in her old age she settled in Philadelphia. She often attended Quaker meetings and received spiritual sustenance there. She felt support from Quakers for her assertion of a right to minister as a woman and for her stands in favor of equality. Her memoirs were dictated to a Quaker and published in 1863, in the midst of the Civil War, by a Quaker press.

Elizabeth: A Colored Minister of the Gospel, Born in Slavery.

"I visited many remote places, where there were no meeting-houses, and held many glorious meetings, for the Lord poured out his Spirit in sweet effusions. I also travelled in Canada, and visited several settlements of colored people, and felt an open door amongst them.

"I may here remark, that while journeying through the different States of the Union, I met with many of the Quaker Friends, and visited them in their families. I received much kindness and sympathy, and no opposition from them, in the prosecution of my labors.

"On one occasion, in a thinly settled part of the country, seeing a Friend's meeting-house open, I went in; at the same time a Friend and his little daughter followed me. We three composed the meeting. As we sat there in silence, I felt a remarkable overshadowing of the Divine presence, as much so as I ever experienced anywhere. Toward the close, a few words seemed to be given me, which I expressed, and left the place greatly refreshed in Spirit. From thence I went to Michigan, where I found a wide field of labor amongst my own color. Here I remained four years. I established a school for colored orphans, having always felt the great importance of the religious and moral agriculture of children, and the great need of it, especially amongst the colored people. Having white teachers, I met with much encouragement.

SOURCE

Electronic Edition, encoded from: Philadelphia: The Tract Association of Friends, 1889. http://docsouth.unc.edu/neh/eliza2/menu.html. [First Edition: Philadelphia: Collins, 1863.]

Sojourner Truth

Sojourner Truth (1799–1883) was an abolitionist and advocate for women's rights. She was born in slavery in Ulster County, New York. Her birth name was Isabella Baumfree. She married in 1815 while a slave and had five children. One of her sons, Peter, was sold to a man in Alabama in 1826, and she sued successfully in New York courts for his return. New York state law decreed the emancipation of all slaves by July 4, 1827, but she received her freedom late in 1826, slightly ahead of the legal deadline, with the help of Levi Roe, a Quaker, and others. She adopted her name of "Sojourner Truth" in 1843, and made her first speech at an anti-slavery meeting in New York two years later. She supported herself by selling copies of her portrait and of her autobiography (dictated to a fellow abolitionist), *The Narrative of Sojourner Truth*, the first edition of which was published in 1850.

She associated with members of many religious sects. After a Methodist conversion experience in 1827, she identified closely with Methodists. At one point she accounted for her preferring to join the Methodists rather than the Quakers by noting that the Methodists would let her sing, but the Quakers would not.[25] After 1856 she lived in Battle Creek, Michigan, among Progressive Quakers. In general, she seems to have had high regard for Progressive Quakers, an offshoot from the Hicksite branch of Quakers, and the branch of antebellum Quakers that had the closest ties to the abolitionist movement. She often dressed in the garb of Quaker women. She affirmed that "I have always loved the Quakers," and her latest biographer observes, "Sojourner's relationship with . . . Progressive Friends was as close as she came to a religious affiliation."[26] During the Civil War, she assisted southern African American refugees.

———•———

Sojourner Truth's Speech to the Women's Rights Convention, Akron, Ohio, 1851

Version One

One of the most unique and interesting speeches of the convention was made by Sojourner's Truth, an emancipated slave. It is impossible to transfer it to paper, or convey any adequate idea of the effect it produced upon the audience. Those only can appreciate it who saw her powerful form, her whole-souled, earnest gesture, and listened to her strong and truthful tones. She came forward to the platform and addressing the President said with great simplicity:

May I say a few words? Receiving an affirmative answer, she proceeded; I want to say a few words about this matter. I am a woman's rights [sic]. I have as much muscle as any man, and can do as much work as any man. I have plowed and reaped and husked and chopped and mowed, and can any man do more than that? I have heard much about the sexes being equal; I can carry as much as any man, and can eat as much too, if I can get it. I am strong as any man that is now.

As for intellect, all I can say is, if woman have a pint and man a quart—why can't she have her little pint full? You need not be afraid to give us our rights for fear we will take too much—for we won't take more than our pint'll hold.

The poor men seem to be all in confusion and don't know what to do. Why children, if you have woman's rights give it to her and you will feel better. You will have your own rights, and they won't be so much trouble.

The Early Period

I can't read, but I can hear. I have heard the Bible and have learned that Eve caused man to sin. Well if woman upset the world, do give her a chance to set it right side up again. The lady has spoken about Jesus, how he never spurned woman from him, and she was right. When Lazarus died, Mary and Martha came to him with faith and love and besought him to raise their brother. And Jesus wept—and Lazarus came forth. And how came Jesus into the world? Through God who created him and woman who bore him. Man, where is your part?

But the women are coming up blessed be God and a few of the men are coming up with them. But man is in a tight place, the poor slave is on him, woman is coming on him, and he is surely between a hawk and a buzzard.

SOURCE

Anti-Slavery Bugle (Salem, OH) June 21, 1851, reprinted in Judith Weisenfeld and Richard Newman, eds., *This Far By Faith: Readings in African-American Women's Religious Biography* (New York: Routledge, 1996), pp. 289–293.

Version Two

"Well, chillen, whar dar's so much racket dar must be som'ting out o' kilter. I tink dat 'twixt de niggers of de Souf and de women at de Norf, all talkin' 'bout rights, de white men will be in a fix pretty soon. But what's all dis here talkin' 'bout? Dat man ober dar say dat woman needs to be helped into carriages, and lifted ober ditches, and to hab de best place eberywhar. Nobody eber helps me into carriages, or ober mud-puddles, or gives me any best place!" And raising herself to her full height, and her voice to a pitch like rolling thunders, she asked "And ar'n't I a woman? Look at me. Look at my arm," and she bared her right arm to the shoulder, showing her tremendous muscular power. I have plowed and planted and gathered into barns, and no man could head me—And ar'n't I a woman? I could work as much and eat as much as a man (when I could get it) and bear de lash as well—And ar'n't I a woman? I have borne thirteen chillen, and seen 'em mos' all sold off to slavery, and when I cried out with my mother's grief, none but Jesus heard me! And ar'n't I a woman? "When dey talks 'bout dis ting in de head. What dis dey call it?" "Intellect," whispered some one near. "Dat's it, honey. What's dat got to do with woman's rights or niggers' rights? If my cup won't hold but a pint, and yourn holds a quart, wouldn't ye be mean not to let me have my little half-measure full?" And she pointed her significant finger, and sent a keen glance at the minister who had made the argument. The cheering was long and loud. "Den dat little man in black dar, he say woman can't have as much right as man 'cause Christ wa'n't a woman! *Whar did your Christ come from?*"

Rolling thunder could not have stilled that crowd as did those deep wonderful tones, as she stood there with outstretched arms and eyes of fire. Raising her voice still louder, she repeated,

"Whar did your Christ come from? From God and a woman! Man had nothin' to do with Him." Oh, what a rebuke she gave the little man. Turning again to another objector, she took up the defense of Mother Eve. I cannot follow her through it all. It was pointed and witty and solemn; eliciting at almost every sentence deafening applause; and she ended by asserting: "If de fust woman God ever made was strong enough to turn de world upside down all her one lone, all dese togeder," and she glanced her eye over us, "ought to be able to turn it back an git it right side up again, and now dey is asking to, de men better let 'em." (Long continuous cheering.) "Bleeged to ye for hearin' on me, and now old Sojourner ha'n't got nothin' more to say."

Amid roars of applause she turned to her corner, leaving more than one of us with streaming eyes, and hearts beating with gratitude. She had taken us up in her strong arms and carried us safely over the slough of difficulty, turning the whole tide in our favor.... I have never in my life seen anything like the magical influence that subdued the mobbish spirit of the day, and turned the jibes and sneers of an excited crowd into notes of respect and admiration. Hundreds rushed up to shake hands with her and congratulate the glorious old mother, and bid her "God-speed" on her mission of "testifyin' agin concerning the wickedness of this here people."

SOURCE

Francis Dana Gage, Letter, *Independent*, April 23, 1863, reprinted in Judith Weisenfeld and Richard Newman, *This Far By Faith: Readings in African-American Women's Religious Biography* (New York: Routledge, 1996), pp. 289–293.

Sojourner Truth's Song

[*Pennsylvania Yearly Meeting of Progressive Friends, 1853. Afternoon session, third day, May 24, 1853.*]

Sojourner Truth, an emancipated slave mother, after uttering a few impressive sentences, expressed herself as being deeply moved to sing, and she accordingly sung the following lines:

> I pity the slave mother, careworn and weary,
>   Who sighs as she presses her babe to her breast;
> I lament her sad fate, all so hopeless and dreary,
>   I lament for her woes, and her wrongs unredressed.
> O who can imagine her heart's deep emotion,
>   As she thinks of her children about to be sold;

You may picture the bounds of the rock-girdled ocean,
  But the grief of that mother can never be told.

The mildew of slavery has blighted each blossom,
  That ever has bloomed in her pathway below;
It has froze every fountain that gushed in her bosom,
  And chilled her heart's verdure with pitiless woe;
Her parents, her kindred, all crushed by oppression,
  Her husband still doomed in his desert to stay;
No arm to protect from the tyrant's aggression—
  She must weep as she treads on her desolate way.

O, slave-mother, hope! see—the nation is shaking!
  The arm of the Lord is awake to thy wrong!
The slaveholder's heart now with terror is quaking,
  Salvation and Mercy to Heaven belong!
Rejoice, O rejoice! for the child thou art rearing
  May one day lift up its unmanacled form,
While hope, to thy heart, like the rainbow so cheering,
  Is born, like the rainbow, 'mid tempest and storm.

SOURCE
Proceedings of the Pennsylvania Yearly Meeting of Progressive Friends, Held at Old Kennett, Chester County, Fifth Month, 1853. (New York: John F. Trow, 1853), pp. 8–9.27

I Am Pleading for My People

[*Sung to the tune of "Auld Lang Syne."*]

I am pleading for my people,
A poor, down-trodden race,
Who dwell in freedom's boasted land
With no abiding place.

I am pleading that my people
May have their rights astored;
For they have long been toiling,
And yet had no reward.

They are forced the crops to culture,
But not for them they yield,
Although both late and early
They labor in the field.

Whilst I bear upon my body
The scars of many a gash,
I am pleading for my people
Who groan beneath the lash.

I am pleading for the mothers
Who gaze in wild despair
Upon the hated auction block
And see their children there.

I feel for those in bondage—
Well may I feel for them;
I know how fiendish hearts can be
That see their fellow men.

Yet those oppressors steeped in guilt—
I still would have them live,
For I have learned of Jesus
To suffer and forgive.

I want no carnal weapons,
No enginery of death;
For I love not to hear the sound
Of war's tempestuous breath.

I do not ask you to engage
In death and bloody strife,
I do not dare insult my God
By asking for their life.

But while your kindest sympathies
To foreign lands do roam,
I would ask you to remember
Your own oppressed at home.

I plead with you to sympathize
With sighs and groans and scars,
And note how base the tyranny
Beneath the stripes and stars.

SOURCE

This is a song Sojourner Truth composed herself. Erlene Stetson and Linda David, *Glorying in Tribulation: The Lifework of Sojourner Truth* (East Lansing: Michigan State Univ. Press, 1994), pp. 203–204; see also Carleton Mabee and Susan Newhouse, *Sojourner Truth: Slave, Prophet, and Legend* (New York: New York University Press, 1993), pp. 90, 227.

Sarah Mapps Douglass

Sarah Mapps Douglass (1806–1882) was an educator, author, and abolitionist. She was part of a distinguished free African American Quaker family in Philadelphia with long ties to Quakers. She attended Friends Meeting with her mother, Grace Mapps, but they were seated on a segregated bench in an out-of-the-way corner of the meeting. Douglass became an eloquent opponent, not only of slavery, but also of racial prejudice wherever it manifested itself, even among groups with an anti-slavery reputation such as the Society of Friends. Sarah Mapps assisted in organizing the Female Literary Society of Philadelphia in 1831, and she published widely in anti-slavery journals. She developed a close friendship with abolitionists Sarah and Angelina Grimké. She married William Douglass in 1855, and it proved to be an unhappy marriage. She was a school teacher from 1825 onwards. For many years, she operated her own school, but she kept accruing financial losses, and in 1852, on better terms with Quakers, she closed her school and accepted a position as the head of the Girl's Preparatory Department of the Orthodox Quaker-sponsored Institute for Colored Youth (which later became Cheyney University). After the Civil War, she helped to raise money for the freed people in the South.

Society of Friends in the United States: Their Views of the Anti-Slavery Question, and Treatment of the People of Colour
Compiled from Original Correspondence

The following are extracts from a letter, received from a highly respectable correspondent in America:

***** A Female of Colour who has been for years convinced of the principles of Friends, has adopted their dress and language, and goes to their Meetings constantly, *has been advised not to apply to be received into Membership, as she would* *be* REJECTED. This advice has been given in tenderness, to spare her feelings; but I regret that she abided by it; because, I am willing we should *act out* our feelings toward this oppressed class. She has mentioned this to me, with deep feeling, and remarked, "The hardest lesson my Heavenly Father ever set me to learn, was to love Friends; and in anguish of spirit I have often queried why the Lord should require me to go among a people who despise me on account of my complexion; but I have seen that it is designed to humble me, and to teach me the lesson, 'Love your enemies, and pray for them who despitefully use you.'"

An aged man, of undoubted piety, who had lived many years in the family of an Elder of **** Meeting, requested to be received into Membership. *He was rejected.* An Overseer of that Meeting, told ****, that the *only* reason was, because *he was colored*: for his character, as a religious man, was unquestioned, and he was fully convinced of our principles. This thing was done privately, and elicited no condemnation that I know of.

*The following letter from the young woman referred to, addressed to **** furnishes an affecting corroboration of the truth of William Bassett's remarks:*

My dear ****

You ask me for some account of my beloved Brother, and his trials: it is a sadly pleasing theme, and I hasten to tell you what I can recollect. My brother Charles was naturally sensitive, and felt more keenly than any of us, the prejudice against color; but most of all, the conduct of professing Christians was a stumbling-block to him, particularly their behavior in their Meeting-Houses to our people. *It drove him to the very verge of Infidelity.* Many times, stung almost to madness by their contempt, he has been ready to curse them, and in the bitterness of his heart, exclaimed "there is no reality in religion, 'tis all a fable, or why do Christians act thus?" When quite a child, he, with the rest of the family, went to Friends' Meeting; but, as he grew to man's estate, the Cross, of being seated on the *back bench* on account of his complexion, was too heavy to bear, and with Mother's permission, he went to Meeting with Father, among the Presbyterians. It was manifest, however, that he did not grow in grace, and in the knowledge of our Lord and Savior Jesus Christ, and his constant reply, when spoken to on religious subjects, was, "'tis all a fable; if it is not, why do the people act thus?" He continued in this state of mind until his 19th year, when it pleased the Lord to lay on him the rod of affliction. As his health declined, his lion-like temper was subdued, and he became a little child in meekness. He no longer scoffed and jested at the conduct of Christians, but mourned in secret over their unkindness. The Church of which my Father was a member, was without a Pastor, and on Sabbath morning, a little company assembled in the Church to read the scriptures and to pray, and for the two last years of his life, my dear Charles was a constant attendant, kindly assisting the aged and illiterate of his own people, by reading the scriptures to them; and so carefully did he conceal from his left hand, what his right was doing, that many of his friends knew nothing of it until he had ceased to live and mourn. As his bodily strength decreased, his mind turned towards the Society of Friends to the religion of his childhood; but he stumbled at the Cross, and went away sorrowful. A few months before his death, Mother accompanied him to **** for change of air, and once or twice he went with her to Friends' Meeting, and found comfort in going, and remarked, "if they did not despise me so, I should like to go always." Oh! If Friends only knew the anguish this one common expression of theirs, *"this bench is for the black people:"* —*"This bench is for the People of Color,"* inflicts on the sensitive and tender amongst us: if they knew how it shuts up the springs of life, and causes us to turn away from their Meetings, weary and unrefreshed, they would not, they could not use it so often. Oh! Surely the darkness that might be felt, has enveloped their minds on this point.

I had been at home just one week, when Charles was stretched on his sick bed, never to leave it in life. He said, he was quite willing to die, if he could see his way clear. He felt that he was a great sinner. Mother told him, "Not the righteous, *Sinners*, Jesus came to save;" and recommended him to cast his burden on Him, and, blessed be God, he was enabled so to do. I had been deeply concerned for my brother, and pleaded earnestly with the Lord for a satisfactory evidence of his acceptance, promising to give him up freely, if I could have this; and He was mercifully pleased to grant it. He bore his intense sufferings without a murmur. Our beloved friend and physician, ***** said, that he had never in the course of his long practice, seen but one person who endured pain with so much patience and fortitude. He received every thing we gave him, even the disagreeable medicines, with so much thankfulness, that we all felt it a privilege to be near him, and to administer to his wants. A few evenings before his decease, the doctor ordered fresh applications of mercurial ointment. When he was gone, Charles said pleasantly, "Mother, doctor will not let me go *home* to night." The next day, as he lay groaning with weakness, he turned his dear, languid eyes on Mother, and said, "Is Christ in the vessel?" She replied, "Yes, my dear son, and though the tempest rages, and hides His face, He does not slumber, He is watching over thee." When almost fainting with pain, he said, "Oh Lord Jesus, take me to thine everlasting arms of love." The day following, the adversary of souls was permitted to buffet him, and to fill his mind with doubts, and he prayed fervently, "Oh Lord, let not the enemy of souls pluck this little lamb from thy fold." That evening, when at prayers, I kneeled beside him with his hand clasped in mine. At the conclusion of the prayer, he raised his head from his pillow, and said, "I have had some doubts; but, glory to God, all is clear *now*;" and throwing his arms around my neck, he pressed his lips to my forehead, and prayed, "Oh, Lord, grant my dear brothers and sister as full an assurance of *their* acceptance." The next day, this passage of scripture was given him, "Neither heights nor depths, principalities nor powers, things present nor things to come, shall ever be able to separate us from the love of God in Christ Jesus." No cloud arose after this, to hide his Lord, for one moment, from his eyes; and, on the morning of the 1st of September, 1835, he fell asleep, sweetly murmuring, "Come, Lord Jesus, come quickly."

During the whole of his illness, his intellect shone out strong and clear, so that our neighbors and friends did greatly marvel: and when the cold grave had hidden him from our view, testimonials of his moral worth, his cultivated understanding, and affectionate disposition, poured in upon us daily; and we could not but rejoice, that one so young, so beloved, and so respected, had escaped from the suffering inflicted by scorn and prejudice, and the varied trials which belong to humanity. Still his death has left an aching void, and nature demands her tears.

> We miss him when the board is spread;
> We miss him when the prayer is said;
> Upon our dreams, his dying eyes,
> In still and mournful fondness rise.

Please excuse inaccuracies, as I have been interrupted frequently. Your sympathy is invaluable. May the Lord bless you and our beloved *****.

SOURCE

Writttten but not signed by Sarah Mapps Douglass. "Printed" by Elizabeth Pease. London, 1840, pp. 23-26. Available at: http://digital.library.cornell.edu/m/mayantislavery/browse.html.

Robert Purvis

Robert Purvis (1810–1898) was an abolitionist. He was born in Charleston, South Carolina. His father was a cotton broker, and his mother, of partly African heritage, was the daughter of a flower merchant. When Purvis was age nine, the family moved to Philadelphia. He received a substantial inheritance at the time of his father's death, when Purvis was age 16.

Purvis was a close associate of William Lloyd Garrison, and was present at the founding convention of Garrison's American Anti-Slavery Society in 1833. Purvis was extremely active in the anti-slavery movement. When his house was attacked in riots occurring in 1842, Purvis moved his family to Byberry, outside Philadelphia. Purvis chaired the General Vigilance Committee in the 1850s, the main organization in Philadelphia coordinating actions of the Underground Railroad. He recruited African American soldiers during the Civil War.

He was a cradle Episcopalian, a connection that he relinquished as a young man, and shortly prior to his death, he was counseled by a Unitarian clergyman. In the many decades between, he had numerous ties with Quakers. He was a close friend of James and Lucretia Mott. His children attended Quaker schools. Like Sojourner Truth, he was associated with the Progressive Friends movement in Pennsylvania, which met first at Longwood in 1853. His second wife, Tacie Townsend Purvis, was a Quaker before she married Purvis, although she resigned her membership shortly thereafter. Margaret Hope Bacon, through close examination of membership records, has gone far toward disproving Henry Cadbury's conjecture that Purvis had probably been a member of the Society of Friends. Purvis could be critical of Quaker stances in the area of race relations (indeed, his curmudgeonly demeanor sometimes found him in conflict with other abolitionists, including for a time, Garrison himself). Perhaps his reluctance to embrace pacifism, when it was unclear how African Americans were going to be liberated from slavery and race prejudice, was more determinative than criticism of some Quaker stands on racial issues in his decision not to join the Society of Friends, despite his numerous close ties.

Speech given against the idea of the colonization of Africa by freed people of color

Robert Purvis, of Pennsylvania, said he was grateful to God for the day. He felt to pour out speaking gratitude of his soul to the Convention, for the spirit they had manifested during the session, and especially during the pending of this resolution. He most heartily concurred in such a vote, and had no doubt but that it would pass unanimously. The name of William Lloyd Garrison sounded sweet to his ear. It produced a vibration of feeling in his bosom, which words could but too feebly sound forth. It was a feeling of love and hearty confidence, which none but a conscientious abolitionist could know.

Three years ago, he had watched the progress of Mr. Garrison with extreme solicitude. The nation was then sound asleep on this subject. The colonization scheme—that scheme of darkness and delusion—was then making its wide havoc among the persecuted people of color. It was the cholera to our ranks. But Garrison arose. His voice went up with a trumpet tone. The walls of Baltimore prison could not confine its thunders. The dampness of his cell did not repress the energy of his spirit. Free and unfettered as the air, his denunciations of tyranny rolled over the land. The Liberator speedily followed. Its pages flashed light and truth far and wide. Darkness and gloom fled before it. The deep, unbroken, tomb-like silence of the church gave way. The tocsin of righteous alarm was sounded. The voice of God-like liberty was heard above the clamor of the oppressors. The effect of these efforts is seen and felt this moment, in this interesting Convention. It is, indeed, a good thing to be here. My heart, Mr. President, is too full for my tongue. But whether I speak to them my feelings as they exist in my inmost soul or not, the friends of the colored American will be remembered. Yes, Sir, their exertions and memories will be cherished, when pyramids and monuments shall crumble. The flood of time, which is rapidly sweeping to destruction that refuge of lies, the American Colonization Society, is bearing on the advocates of our cause to a glorious and blessed immortality.

SOURCE

Abolitionist, December 1833, UDM Black Abolitionists Archive. University of Detroit (Mercy). Available at: http://research.udmercy.edu/find/special_collections/digital/baa/. This is an online archive available to any researcher.

Appeal of Forty Thousand Citizens, Threatened with Disfranchisement, to the People of Pennsylvania, 1837

[*The Pennsylvania Constitutional Convention, meeting from May 1837 to February 1838*[28] *inserted the word "white" prior to "freeman" in delineating voting qualifications, overturning decades of precedents dating back to the Declaration of Independence and the state's gradual emancipation statute of 1780 that had previously been interpreted as permitting African American males to vote. The "Forty-Thousand Citizens, Threatened with Disfranchisement," then, were African American males, and this appeal, whose primary writer was Robert Purvis, eloquently and immediately pled their case for retaining their suffrage. We reprint the rousing conclusion to this appeal.*]

Are we to be disfranchised, lest the purity of the *white* blood should be sullied by an intermixture with ours? It seems to us that our white brethren might well enough reserve their fear, till we seek such alliance with them. We ask no social favors. We would not willingly darken the doors of those to whom the complexion and features, which our Maker has given us, are disagreeable. The territories of the commonwealth are sufficiently ample to afford us a home without doing violence to the delicate nerves of our white brethren, for centuries to come. Besides, we are not intruders here, nor, were our ancestors. Surely you ought to bear as unrepiningly the evil consequences of your fathers' guilt, as we those our fathers' misfortune. Proscription and disfranchisemnt are the last things in the world to alleviate these evil consequences. Nothing, as shameful experience has already proved, can so powerfully promote the evil which you profess to deprecate, as the degradation of our race by this oppressive rule of yours. Give us that fair and honorable ground which self-respect requires to stand on, and the dreaded amalgamation, if it take place at all, shall be by your own fault, as indeed it always has been. We dare not give full vent to the indignation we feel on this point, but we will not attempt wholly to conceal it.

We ask a voice in the disposition of those public resources which we ourselves have helped to earn; we claim a right to be heard, according to our numbers, in regard to all those great public measures which involve our lives and fortunes, as well as those of our fellow citizens; we assert our right to vote at the polls as a shield against that strange species of benevolence which seeks legislative aid to banish us—and we are told that our white fellow citizens cannot submit to an *intermixture of the races!* Then let the indentures, title-deeds, contracts, notes of hand, and all other evidences of bargain, in which colored men have been treated as men, be torn and scattered on the winds. Consistency is a jewel. Let no white man hereafter ask his colored neighbor's *consent* when he wants his property or his labor; lest he should endanger the Anglo-Saxon purity of his descendants? Why should not the same principle hold good between neighbor and neighbor, which is deemed necessary, as a fundamental principle, in the Constitution itself? Why should you be ashamed to act in private business, as the Reform Convention would have you act in the capacity of a commonwealth? But, no! we do not believe our fellow citizens, while with good faith they hold ourselves bound by their contracts with us, and while they feel bound to deal with us only by fair contract, will ratify the arbitrary principle of the Convention, howmuchsoever they may prefer the complexion in which their Maker has pleased to clothe themselves.

We would not misrepresent the motives of the Convention, but we are constrained to believe that they have laid our rights a sacrifice on the altar of slavery. We do not believe our disfranchisement would have been proposed, but for the desire which is felt by political aspirants to gain the favor of the slaveholding States. This is not the first time that northern statesmen have "bowed the knee to the dark spirit of slavery," but it is the first time that they have bowed so low! Is Pennsylvania, which abolished slavery in 1780, and enfranchised her tax-paying colored citizens in 1790, now, in 1838, to get upon her knees and repent of her humanity, to gratify those who disgrace the very name of American Liberty, by holding our brethren as goods and chattels? We freely acknowledge our brotherhood to the slave, and our interest in his welfare. Is this a crime for which we should be ignominiously punished? The very fact that we are deeply interested for our kindred in bonds, shows that we are the right sort of stuff to make good citizens of. Were we not so, we should better deserve a lodging in your penitentiaries than a franchise at your polls. Doubtless it will be well pleasing to the slaveholders of the South to see us degraded. They regard our freedom from chains as a dangerous example, much more our political freedom. They see in everything which fortifies our rights, an obstacle to the recovery of their fugitive property. Will Pennsylvania go backward towards slavery, for the better safety of southern slave property? Be assured the South will never be satisfied till the old "Keystone" has returned to the point from which she started in 1780. And since the number of colored men in the commonwealth is so inconsiderable, the safety of slavery may require still more. It may demand that a portion of the white tax-payers should be unmanned and turned into chattels—we mean those whose hands are hardened by daily toil.

Fellow citizens, will you take the first step towards reimposing the chains which now have rusted for more than fifty years? Need we inform you that every colored man in Pennsylvania is exposed to be arrested as a fugitive from slavery? and that it depends not upon the verdict of a jury of his peers, but upon the decision of a judge on summary process, whether or not he shall be dragged into southern bondage? The Constitution of the United States provides that "no person shall be deprived of life, liberty, or property, without due process of law"—by which is certainly meant a trial by jury. Yet the act of Congress of 1793, for the recovery of fugitive slaves, authorizes the claimant to seize his victim without a warrant from any magistrate, and allows him to drag him before "any magistrate of a county, city, or town corporate, where such seizure has been made," and upon proving, by "oral testimony or affidavit," to the satisfaction of such magistrate that the man is his slave, gives him a right to take him into everlasting bondage.

Thus may a free-born citizen of Pennsylvania be arrested, tried without counsel, jury, or power to call witnesses, condemned by a single man, and carried across Mason and Dixon's line, within the compass of a single day. An act of this commonwealth, passed in 1820, and enlarged and re-enacted in 1825, it is true, puts some restraint upon the power of the claimant under the act of Congress; but it still leaves the case to the decision of a single judge, without the privilege of a jury! What unspeakably aggravates our loss of the right of suffrage at this moment is, that, while the increased activity of the slave-catchers enhances our danger, the Reform Convention has refused to amend the Constitution so as to protect our liberty by a jury trial! We entreat you to make our case your own—imagine your own wives and children to be trembling at the approach of every stranger, lest their husbands and fathers should be dragged into a slavery worse than the Algerine[29]—worse than death! Fellow citizens, if there is one of us who has abused the right of suffrage, let him be tried and punished according to law. But in the name of humanity, in the name of justice, in the name of the God who you profess to worship, who has no respect of persons,[30] do not turn into gall and wormwood the friendship we bear to yourselves by ratifying a Constitution which tears from us a privilege dearly earned and inestimably prized. We lay hold of the principles which Pennsylvania asserted in the hour which tried men's souls—which Benjamin Franklin and his eight colleagues, in name of the commonwealth, pledged their lives, their fortunes, and their sacred honor to sustain: We take our stand upon that solemn declaration; that to protect inalienable rights "governments are instituted among men, deriving their just powers from the consent of the governed," and proclaim that a government which tears away from us and our posterity the very power of consent, is a tyrannical usurpation which we will never cease to oppose. We have seen with amazement and grief the apathy of white Pennsylvanians while the "Reform Convention" has been perpetrating this outrage upon the good old principles of Pennsylvania freedom. But however others may forsake these principles, we promise to maintain them on *Pennsylvania soil*, to the last man. If this disfranchisement is designed to uproot us, it shall jail Pennsylvania's fields, valleys, mountains, and rivers; her canals, railroads, forests, and mines; her domestic altars, and her public, religious and benevolent institutions; her Penn and Franklin, her Rush,[31] Rawle,[32] Wistar,[33] and Vaux;[34] her consecrated past and her brilliant future, are as dear to us as they can be to you. Firm upon our Pennsylvania Bill of Rights, and trusting in a God of Truth and justice, we lay our claim before you, with the warning that no amendments of the present Constitution can compensate for the loss of its foundation principle of equal rights, nor for the conversion into enemies of 40,000 friends.

SOURCE

Richard Newman, Patrick Rael, and Philip Lapsansky, eds. *Pamphlets of Protest: An Anthology of Early African-American Protest Literature, 1790–1860.* (New York: Routledge, 2001), pp. 140–142.

Call for a General Religious Conference, with a view to the establishment of a Yearly Meeting in Pennsylvania

[*This Call was presented at the Pennsylvania Yearly Meeting of Progressive Friends in 1853. Robert Purvis and his wife, Harriet Forten Purvis, were two of the 58 signers.*][35]

The various religious denominations in the land are arrayed against the progressive spirit of the age, and by their very structure, assumptions, and regulations, cannot occupy a co-operative position, because they impose fetters upon freedom of speech and of conscience, by requiring a slavish conformity in matters of abstract faith and sectarian discipline. This has led and is leading to extensive secessions from such organizations in all parts of the country, leaving the seceders generally in a scattered and isolated condition, whose talents, influence and means might be profitably concentrated for the advancement of the world-embracing cause of Human Brotherhood, and who are yearning for some form of association at once simple, free and attractive.

The abuse of a good thing is not a reason for its utter rejection; and organization, in itself considered, is not only proper, but may be rendered powerfully efficacious as an instrument in the hand of Reform, without impairing the liberty, detracting from the independence, or limiting the conscience of any individual; though from the nature of things its perpetuation is not to be expected or desired, but it is at all times to be regarded as a means to an end, and to be discarded whenever it becomes an impediment to the progress of truth.

The Society of Friends has been a theatre of agitation for years, growing out of ecclesiastical domination on the one hand, and the demand for practical righteousness on the other; a domination entirely at variance with the spirit of primitive Quakerism, seeking to suppress free thought and to exclude from membership those whose lives are without blemish, whose example in word and deed is as a burning and shining light, and who are seeking to know and do the will of God at whatever sacrifice; a domination which has been deemed so intolerable, that in the States of *New-York, Ohio* and *Michigan,* Yearly Meetings have been formed, two of which have taken the name of Congregational Friends, and two others that of Progressive Friends, and which invited to membership "all those who look to God as a Universal Father, and who regard as one Brotherhood the whole family of man."

In view of facts like these, and believing there is an extensive preparation of mind for such a movement, we cordially invited not only the members of the Society of Friends, but all those who feel the want of social and religious co-operation, and believe that a Society may be formed, recognizing the *Progressive Element* which will divorce Religion from *Technical Theology,* to meet with us in general conference at Friends' Meeting House, at Old Kennett, in Chester

County, Pennsylvania, on First day, the 22d of Fifth month, 1853, to deliberate upon such plan of organization as may commend itself to the judgment of those assembled, and to take action upon such subjects pertaining to Human Duty and Welfare, as may appear to demand the attention of the assembly.

Source

Proceedings of the Pennsylvania Yearly Meeting of Progressive Friends, Held at Old Kennett, Chester County, Fifth Month, 1853. (New York: John F. Trow, 1853), pp. 3-4.

Speech on December 3, 1864

Mr. Chairman, Ladies and Gentlemen: . . . This is a proud day for the "colored" man. For the first time since this Society was organized, I stand before you a recognized citizen of the United States (applause). And let me add, for the first time since your government was a government is it an honor to be a citizen of the United States! Sir, old things are passing away, all things are becoming new. Now a black man has rights, under this government, which every white man, here and everywhere, is bound to respect (applause). The damnable doctrine of the detestable Tancy[36] is no longer the doctrine of the country. The Slave power no longer rules at Washington. The slaveholders and their miserable allies are biting the dust, and Copperhead Democracy has come to grief. The black man is a citizen, all honor to Secretary Bates,[37] who has so pronounced him. The black man can take out a passport and travel to the uttermost parts of the earth, protected by the broad aegis of the government; all honor to Secretary Seward,[38] who was the first to recognize this right. The black man is a citizen, soldier, standing on an equality in the rank and file with the white soldier; all honor to Secretary Stanton[39] and the rest of the Administration. Sir, I know very well that this government is not yet all that it ought to be, I know that Mr. Bates is not considered a progressive man, and that Mr. Seward has incurred the severe displeasure of loyal anti-slavery people. But, sir, these gentlemen have in a signal manner recognized my right, and the rights of my oppressed countrymen. They have officially invested us with the prerogatives of which we had been basely robbed, and I would be false to my nature, false to my convictions, false to my best feelings, did I not thus publicly testify my sense of respect and heartfelt gratitude. Say what you please of Mr. Seward, condemn as you may his shortcomings and his failures—I make no apology for either; but it must always be owned, to his immortal honor, that he has from the beginning, been the fast friend of the "man of color." From the time when, as Governor of this Empire State, he refused to deliver up to the Governor of Virginia certain black refugees, to the day, when, as a lawyer, he defended the idiotic black culprit Freemen, and from that day till the present time, Mr. Seward has been the unprejudiced respector of the black man's equal rights, and as such, I feel bound here and everywhere to honor him. I have said that I consider it an honor to be a citizen of this Republic, and I repeat it. I am proud to be an American citizen. You know, Mr. Chairman, how bitterly I used to denounce the United States as the basest despotism the sun ever shone upon; and I take nothing back that ever I said. When this government was, as it used to be, a slaveholding oligarchy; when such imbecile and heartless cravens as our Buchanan and your Pierce were its nominal rulers; when its powers were used and abused by slaveholding, slave-breeding traitors, such as Jefferson Davis and Howell Cobb, and Thief Floyd and Isaac Toucey,[40] and when the old Jesuit Taney was unshorn of his power as Chief President in his Temple of Justice; then, sir, I hated it with a wrath which words could not express, and I denounced it with all the bitterness of my indignant soul (applause). My friends would urge me to moderate my tone, but it was impossible; out of the bitterness of the heart the mouth would speak. I was a victim, stricken, degraded, injured, insulted in my person, in my family, in my friends, in my estate; I returned bitterness for bitterness and scorn for scorn. I am the same man still, and I must be allowed, as some would say, though I do not, to err on the other extreme. I forget the past; joy fills my soul at the prospect of the future. I leave to others the needful duty of censure. But, I hear some of my hearers saying, "It is too soon to begin to rejoice; don't hallo till you are out of the woods; don't be too sure of the future—wait and see." No, sir, I will not wait—I cannot be mistaken. My instincts, in this matter at least, are unerring. The good time which has so long been coming is at hand. I feel it, I see it in the air, I read it in the signs of the times; I see it in the acts of Congress, in the abolition of slavery in the District of Columbia, in its exclusion from the Territories, in solemn treaties for the effectual suppression of the infernal foreign slave trade, in the acknowledgment of the black republics of Hayti and Liberia. I see it in the new spirit that is in the army; I see it in the black regiment of South Carolina (applause); I see it in the 54th Regiment of Massachusetts; I see it in the order of Adjt. General Thomas, forming a Black Brigade at Memphis;[41] I see it, above all, and more than all, in the *glorious and immortal* imperishable incident the three million of slaves in the rebel States were legally and irrevocably free! (the opinion of Mr. Greeley, of *The Tribune*, to the contrary notwithstanding). By that immortal document all the remaining slaves of the country are in effect promised their freedom. In *spirit* and in *purpose*, thanks to *Almighty God!* This is no longer a slaveholding republic. The fiat has gone forth which, when this rebellion is crushed—and it will be crushed as sure as there is a God in heaven—the fiat has gone forth which, in the simple but beautiful language of the President, "will take all burdens from off all backs, and make every man a freeman."

The Early Period

Sir, this is a glorious contest. It is not simply and solely a fight about the black man. It is not merely a war between the North and the South. It is a war between freedom and despotism the world over. If this government had only the South to contend with, their work would soon be done. But it is with the South, backed up by pro-slavery Europe and pro-slavery England, that this government has to contend. It is pro-slavery England that furnishes to the rebels the arms, ammunition, ships, encouragement and money with which to carry out the base slaveholding, slave-breeding conspiracy. I say pro-slavery England, for, Mr. Chairman, I need not tell you there are two Englands—anti-slavery England, that manumitted her 800,000 slaves, and the England that opposed, as long as there was any hope of success, that glorious act; the England which now speaks in our favor in the voice of John Bright and William R. Forest, and that noble man and unequalled orator, George Thompson,[42] and the England which holds the reins of power in its hands and uses that power, as far as it *dares*, to break down this government. Sir, the former England I honor and admire; the latter, the England which now uses and abuses the great power of that country, I abhor and repudiate. When I was in England, many years ago, it was my fortune to be introduced to Ireland's great Liberator, the eminent Daniel O'Connell.[43] Before extending his hand to me he said "that he would never take the hand of an American, unless he knew him to be an anti-slavery man." Thanking him for his noble resolution, and declaring myself at the same time to be an Abolitionist, he grasped me warmly by the hand and shook it heartily. It was a striking circumstance, and left a deep impression on my mind. Mr. Chairman, I am prepared now to practice in the lesson I then learned. O'Connell has gone, and alas! his spirit has gone with him. If hereafter any one coming from Great Britain, be he Saxon or Celt, should seek an introduction to one so humble as myself, I think, before extending my hand, I would feel bound to say, What sort of an Englishman or Irishman are you? Are you of the herd that support the slaveholding rebels, and that build Alabama corsairs and Florida pirates to prey on the commerce of Freedom? If you are, I will have nothing to do with you, I regard you as an enemy of God and of the human race. But if your sympathies are with struggling freedom, and your hatred toward its enemies, then give me your hand.

Mr. Chairman, I had intended to say something about the Copperhead Democracy, but these dastards don't trouble me now. They are as malignant, as venomous, as traitorous as ever, and perhaps more so, but their power is gone, and their days are numbered. They are

"Their country's curse, their children's shame,
Outcasts of virtue, peace and fame."[44]

They may, in their baseness and pusillanimity, denounce the black man as inferior, as do your Vallandighams (I trust he has got his deserts at last), Morses and Coxes, or they may hound on a mob, as do your Fernando Woods[45] and Bobby Brookses (applause) in your streets; but I repeat it, sir, their power is gone.

Mr. Chairman, I end as I began: This is a proud day for the "colored man," and a day of glorious promises for the country. Our work as Abolitionists is not finished. Much remains to be done. But we have thousands upon thousands of helpers. Anti-slavery societies and anti-slavery agents are numerous and powerful. The United States Senate and House of Representatives, the State Legislature, the "Union Leagues" are anti-slavery societies; the Cabinet at Washington is a great Executive Committee, and thousands of its civil and military officers are its agents. Our country is not yet free, but thank God for those signs of the times that unmistakably indicate that it soon will be. With a future so glorious before us, may we not, in the eloquent language of Curran, say, "to the stranger and the sojourner," who sets his foot on the soil of America, "he treads on ground that is holy and consecrated by the genius of universal emancipation. No matter in what language his doom may have been pronounced; no matter what complexion, incompatible with freedom, an Indian or an African sun may have burned upon him; no matter in what disastrous battle his liberty may have been cloven down; no matter with what solemnities he may have been devoted upon the altar of slavery, the first moment he touches the sacred soil of [America] the altar and the god sink together in the dust, his soul walks abroad in her own majesty, his body swells beyond the measure of his chains, that burst from around him, and he stands redeemed, regenerated and disenthralled by the irresistible Genius of *Universal Emancipation*" (enthusiastic applause).[46]

SOURCE

Speeches and Letters of Robert Purvis, Published by the request of the Afro-American League, pp. 6–11. UDM Black Abolitionists Archive.

ENDNOTES

1 Benjamin Banneker, *Banneker's Almanac and Ephemeris for the Year of our Lord 1793* (Philadelphia: Joseph Crukshank, 1793), unnumbered pages (the fourth, sixth, and eighth pages after the title page).

2 See, e.g., *Benjamin Banneker, Benjamin Banneker's Pennsylvania, Delaware, Maryland, and Virginia Almanack and Ephemeris for the Year of our Lord 1794* (Baltimore: James Angell, 1794), pp. 44–45. Both 1793 editions of the almanac also have this material.

3 Job 16:4.

4 Marquis Jean-Antoine-Nicolas de Caritat Condorcet (1743–1794), philosopher and political theorist, was a a supporter of the American Revolution, an opponent of slavery, and an advocate of universal education as a means to enlightenement.

5 This document has numerous Biblical allusions. This phrase is a standard opening phrase for many of the New Testament epistles attributed to the apostle Paul, including 1 and 2 Corinthians and Galatians.

6 I Pet. 1:3.
7 "World without end, amen": Eph. 3:21.
8 Wiggins supplies the correction "acceptably" for "exceptely."
9 John 4:24.
10 Heb. 6:19.
11 Psalm 68:31 in the King James Version reads "Princes shall come out of Egypt; Ethiopia shall soon stretch out her hands to God." Albert Raboteau comments that this was the most commonly cited verse in nineteenth-century African American churches: "The Black Experience in American Evangelicalism" in Timothy E. Fulop and Albert J. Raboteau, eds., *African-American Religion: Interpretive Essays in History and Culture* (New York: Routledge, 1997), p. 104.
12 "Walk in the light": I John 1:7; Rev. 21:24.
13 Here Cuffe appears to synthesize John 1:9 and Titus 2:11; if that is the case, he sees God's light and God's grace as the same thing.
14 Matt. 18:20.
15 Isa. 9:6.
16 As in the letter to the Methodists, Cuffe probably means that he "wishes well to all men."
17 Wiggins believes, from evidence of style, that Cuffe may have written this document in the fall of 1812.
18 Wiggins identifies this passage as a continuation of the "anadress."
19 Micah 6:8.
20 "faithful in all things:" I Tim. 3:11.
21 Prince William Frederick (1776–1834), an advocate of slavery's abolition both during his service in Parliament and as president of the African Institution.
22 William Wilberforce (1759–1833) was a Member of Parliament from 1780 to 1825, an evangelical Anglican, and an eloquent opponent of slavery. He was the major force behind the enactment of legislation ending Britain's involvement in the international slave trade in 1807.
23 Thomas Clarkson (1760–1846), a leading anti-slavery writer, researcher, and activist. He also wrote important works on the history of Quakerism.
24 William Allen (1770–1843), Quaker chemist, anti-slavery activist, and philanthropist.
25 Carleton Mabee and Susan Mabee Newhouse, *Sojourner Truth: Slave Prophet, Legend* (New York: New York University Press, 1993), pp. 219–220.
26 Margaret Washington, Sojourner Truth's America (Urbana, IL: University of Illinois Press, 2009), pp. 151, 251.
27 This song was written by "Mrs. Price." It apparently was originally published in William Lloyd Garrison's *Liberator*, and was to be sung to the tune of "Araby's Daughter." Adin Ballou, *The Hopedale Collection of Hymns and Songs: For the Use of Practical Christians* (Hopedale, Mass: n.p., 1850), hymn no. 202; William W. Brown, *The Anti-Slavery Harp: A Collection of Songs for Anti-Slavery Meetings* (Boston: n.p., 1848). See http://www.fullbooks.com/The-Anti-Slavery-Harp.html (access date: March 16, 2010).
28 Article III, Section 1, Duquesne University Law School, Pennsylvania Constitution Website, http://www.paconstitution.duq.edu/PAC_CC_1837.html (access date: March 1, 2009).
29 The longstanding practice by North African powers (Barbary States) of enslaving citizens of European or American nations that did not pay tribute was a major cause of the Barbary Wars fought by the United States between 1801 and 1815. See Donald K. Pickens, "Tribute," in *Dictionary of American History*, Stanley I. Kutler, ed. (New York: Charles Scribner's Sons, 2003.)
30 God "has no respect of persons," Acts 10:34.
31 Benjamin Rush (1746–1813), signer of the Declaration of Independence and advocate for the U.S. Constitution during Pennsylvania's ratification process; physician; lifelong opponent of

slavery and friend to many of Pennsylvania's black founders, including Richard Allen and Absalom Jones. See *American National Biography Online*, s.v. "Benjamin Rush," by Robert B. Sullivan.

32   William Rawle (1759–1836), Quaker attorney, District Attorney for Pennsylvania from 1791 to 1799, abolitionist, first president of Historical Society of Pennsylvania. See http://www.archives.upenn.edu/people/1700s/rawle_wm.html (access date: March 16, 2010).

33   Most likely he refers to Caspar Wistar (1761–1818), Quaker physician and anti-slavery activist. See http://www.archives.upenn.edu/people/1700s/wistar_caspar.html (access date: March 16, 2010).

34   Roberts Vaux (1786–1836), Quaker anti-slavery activist, and reformer of the criminal justice system and of educational institutions; humanitarian. He campaigned effectively for free education for everyone. See *American National Biography Online*, s.v. "Vaux, Roberts," by Donald Brooks Kelley. Note that Rawle and Vaux had died just prior to the Constitutional Convention.

35   Although there is no evidence that Purvis had a hand in crafting this Call, it is included here as a good example of what there was about Quakerism that Purvis could affirm. It is interesting that Progressive Quakerism was the one branch of Quakerism that downplayed the whole concept of membership. That may be one factor that made it hospitable to persons like Robert Purvis and Sojourner Truth, who were connected to Friends without ever becoming members officially.

36   Roger Taney (1777–1864), Chief Justice of the U.S. Supreme Court from 1836 to 1864, was author of the 1857 *Dred Scott* decision, which drastically curtailed what few rights African Americans may have had at that time. See *American National Biography Online*, s.v. "Taney, Roger Book" by Sandra F. VanBurkleo, Bonnie Speck.

37   Edward Bates (1793–1869) was the Attorney General of the United States from 1861 to 1864.

38   William Henry Seward (1801–1872) was the Secretary of State from 1861 to 1869. Seward and Bates had both campaigned for the Republican nomination for the U.S. presidency that Lincoln won in 1860, and Lincoln put them both in his cabinet. See Doris Kearns Goodwin's *Team of Rivals: The Political Genius of Abraham Lincoln* (New York: Simon and Schuster, 2005).

39   Edwin M. Stanton (1814–1869) was Secretary of War from 1862 to 1868.

40   All of these men served in the cabinets of President Lincoln's two immediate predecessors, Franklin Pierce and James Buchanan. Jefferson Davis was Secretary of War from 1853 to 1857; Howell Cobb was Secretary of the Treasury from 1857 to 1860; and John Floyd was Secretary of War from 1857 to 1861. All three were southerners and actively supported the Confederacy (Jefferson Davis, of course, was its president; Floyd and Cobb became Confederate generals.) Floyd had sought, during his service to the United States, to enrich himself by allowing contractors to borrow from government funds, and many politicians called unsuccessfully for his resignation; hence the appellation of "thief" used by Purvis. Isaac Toucey, the sole northerner on this list (and presumably not a slaveowner), supported the Union during the Civil War, but had been criticized for his slowness in resupplying Fort Sumter while he was still Secretary of the Navy in Buchanan's cabinet. See *American National Biography Online*, s.v. "Floyd, John Buchanan" by William G. Shade; "Toucey, Isaac" by Frederick J. Blue; "Cobb, Howell" by Brooks D. Simpson.

41   The 1st Regiment, South Carolina Volunteer Infantry (African descent) mustered in refugees from slavery in South Carolina and Florida; it was the first official African American military unit, formed in January 1863, within a month of the Emancipation Proclamation, allowing for African American troops. It participated in military action, but not in any major engagement. The 54th Massachusetts Regiment was an African American regiment that was most famous for its determined assault on the Confederate stronghold of Fort Wagner, South Carolina, on July 18,

1863, a battle in which it took over 40% casualties. That battle did much to convince northerners of African Americans' courage and ability to fight. Adjutant General Lorenzo Thomas (1804–1875), not noted for his battlefield ability, was, however, distinguished in his ability to recruit African American troops in Tennessee and adjacent states, and in his work to promote the welfare of his recruits and their families. His efforts led to the recruitment of 76,000 African American troops. See Joseph T. Glatthaar, *Forged in Battle: The Civil War Alliance of Black Soldiers and White Officers* (New York: Free Press, 1990), pp. 36–38, 135–141, passim. Also see *American National Biography Online*, s.v. "Thomas, Lorenzo" by Edward Hagerman.

42 John Bright (1811–1889) was a Quaker and an eminent British M.P. In the early years of the American Civil War, he was one of the most vigorous supporters of the North. William R. Forest is obscure. George Thompson (1804–1879) was a brilliant anti-slavery orator. See Miles Taylor, "Bright, John (1811–1889)," and W. A. S. Hewins, "Thompson, George Donisthorpe (1804–1878)," rev. Matthew Lee, *Oxford Dictionary of National Biography* (Oxford University Press, 2004).

43 Daniel O'Connell (1775–1847) was an Irish M.P. influential both in the anti-slavery struggle and in the struggle for Catholic emancipation in the United Kingdom. He was a tireless advocate for any whose civil rights were denied to them. See R. V. Comerford, "O'Connell, Daniel (1775–1847)," *Oxford Dictionary of National Biography* (Oxford University Press, 2004).

44 Thomas Moore, "The Fire Worshippers," in *Lalla Rookh: An Oriental Romance* (Buffalo: George H. Derby and Co., 1850), p. 187 (originally published 1817; available through Google Books).

45 Clement L. Vallandigham (1820–1871), former U.S. Congressman from Ohio, was by 1863 a "Peace Democrat" (also known as "Copperheads"). In 1863 he was arrested, tried, and convicted of treason. Lincoln changed his prison sentence to a sentence of exile to the Confederacy, but Vallandigham fled to Canada after only a few weeks in the Confederacy. Samuel S. Cox (1824–1889), an Ohio Democratic congressman, was a friend of Vallandigham and a vocal opponent of racial equality; Samuel F. B. Morse (1791–1872), artist and inventor, was a nativist, anti-Catholic, and staunch defender of slavery; Fernando Wood (1812–1881) was a New York congressman and Peace Democrat. See *American National Biography Online* (http://www.anb.org/articles/04/04-01009.html), s.v. "Vallandigham, Clement Laird" by William G. Andrews; "Cox, Samuel Sullivan" by Allen Peskin; "Wood, Fernando," by Phillis F. Field. Also see, for Morse: http://www.yaleslavery.org/WhoYaleHonors/morse.html (accessed March 17, 2010).

46 These words are quoted from a masterful speech by lawyer and Irish liberal John Philpot Curran, in which he sought to summarize the meaning of a 1772 court decision in a case brought by James Somerset, a Jamaican who had been stolen from Africa as an eight-year-old child. That court rejected the claims of ownership by the man who had been holding him as a slave, and the Somerset decision is commonly seen as establishing the principle that slavery can never exist on the British Isles themselves—this, 68 years prior to the abolition of slavery in British colonies, such as Jamaica. Many nineteenth-century American abolitionists, including Frederick Douglass, Harriet Beecher Stowe, and Benjamin Lundy, lovingly quoted the passage used here by Purvis. See Curran's 1794 oration, "In Behalf of Rowan and Free Speech" at http://www.bartleby.com/268/6/7.html (accessed March 16, 2010). On the Somerset case, see Steven M. Wise, *Though the Heavens May Fall: The Landmark Trial That Led to the End of Human Slavery* (Cambridge, MA: Da Capo Press, 2005).

II

N. Jean Toomer
(1894–1967)
edited by Paul Kriese

Jean Toomer was born in Washington, DC, and given the name Nathan Pinchback Toomer. He was a poet, essayist, novelist, and a pioneer of the Harlem Renaissance. He was also a lifelong spiritual seeker who believed that for the sake of Christ's work on earth, for the sake of others and of ourselves, that we are obligated here and now to do all we can do to dispel the stuff of darkness. Religion must be rooted in the whole lives of people and not just what they do on the Sabbath. Toomer joined Friends in 1940, where he provided leadership at the monthly and yearly meeting levels, because he felt that Quakers emphasized direct experience, not to take Jesus's teaching secondhand, but to live in direct contact with the Spirit that guides all teachers. Toomer believed that religious bodies such as Quakers were life-centered, not book- or church-centered. Friends worship arose from the well of life within the individual. According to the faith of Friends, all people have within them something of the very spirit that created the scriptures and which makes religion the action of the spirit. Our every act is a prayer; our whole life is continuous worship.

―――――•―――――

The Basis of Friends Worship and Other Inward Practices

Some people believe that whereas God's nature is divine, man's nature is depraved. God is good, but men are evil. God, according to this view, exists in heaven, remote from us. We exist in sin, remote from Him, in hell or next door to it. Human beings are completely separated from the Divine Being. The only possible connection between men and God is that brought about by the mediation of the church and its authorized officials. Friends have never held this view.

Friends, beginning with George Fox, realize that something of God dwells *within* each and every human being, and that, therefore, He is reachable by us through direct contact, and we are within His reach, subject to His immediate influence. This is the well-known basis of Friends worship.

Since God is within us, Friends turn inward to find Him. This is not a matter of choice or inclination; it is a matter of necessity. Turning inward, we turn away from all externals. Friends practice inwardness. Rufus Jones writes, "The religion of the Quaker is primarily concerned with the culture and development of the inward life and with direct correspondence with God."

Some number of Friends in the early days of the movement not only sought God but found him, though it would perhaps be better to say were found by him. It was because they found God that they had such living worship, such vital meetings. It was because they truly worshiped and had vital meetings that they progressively discovered God and came increasingly within his power. The one led to the other. Without the one we cannot have the other.

That there is that of God in every man was, as already implied, more than a belief or a concept with the early Friends. It was an experience. It was a recovery of the living Deity. As he made and continued to make this recovery in himself, George Fox went about his apostolic work and laid the foundation of what came to be the Society of Friends. What did Fox aim for? How did he regard his ministry? Let him answer in his own words. "I exhorted the people to come off from all these things (from churches, temples, priests, tithes, argumentation, external ceremonies, and dead traditions), and directed them to the spirit and grace of God that they might come to know Christ, their free Teacher."

Pointing as they do to the basis of Friends worship, these several considerations do not, of themselves, throw light on the reason for certain other inward practices. The basis of these other practices is, unfortunately, less simple and less well-known. Why is there need of particular occasions for prayer and worship? Why need we gather together and sit quietly? Why practice waiting before God? If He is in us, why does He not manifest to us continually, why does His power not always motivate our actions? Why do we have to practice His presence, and why is this practice, so difficult? To answer these questions we are forced to adopt a somewhat complex and non-habitual view of the situation.

Suppose we are approached by a person of inquiring mind who says, "You say that there is that of God in every man. All right, I am prepared to accept that as truth. But precisely where in us does the divine spark exist? Is it in our bodies? Is it in our ordinary minds and everyday thoughts and emotions? Do you mean to say that God exists in ignorance, in man's prejudices and hatreds, in human evil?" How will we reply? Obviously God does not exist in our trivial actions, nor in our godless thoughts and feelings. Certainly He does not exist in our ignorance and evil. But these things exist in us. They constitute a part of us. This part of us, then, is separated from God, while another part is related to Him. Insofar as we identify with the separated part and believe it to be ourselves, we exist divorced from that of God in us.

The attitude, in brief, is this. There is that of God in every man. Therefore man, in his entirety, is not separated from God. But man is divided within, and against, himself, into two different and opposing aspects, and one of these aspects is separated from God. This is my view of the situation. If I understand the writings of the early Friends, this was their view of the situation.

The early Friends had names for the part of us that is separated from God. They called it the "natural man," the "earthly man." I shall sometimes refer to it as the "body-mind" or the "separated self." The early Friends called the part of us that is related to God in which God dwells the "spiritual man," the "new birth," the "new creation." I shall sometimes call it the "inner being," the "spiritual self."

It is of course the separated self that presents the problem. It obstructs our attempts to relate ourselves to God and to our fellow men. It interferes with worship as well as with love. It is because of this self that we do not pray and love as naturally as we breathe. The separated self stands in the way. Therefore it must be overcome. For divine as well as genuinely human purposes it must be subdued and eventually left behind. Every real religious practice, whether of Friends or of others, either directly or indirectly aims to enable human beings to transcend the separated self in order that we may be united with the spiritual self or being which is near God because He dwells therein.

In the light of these facts we can understand the need and the purpose of certain specific inward practices, such as the practice of contending with oneself (Isaac Penington called it "lawful warring") and the practice of gathering silently and waiting upon God. Since the separated self exists, and is an obstruction, we must contend with it. We contend with it so as to remove it and, at the same time, activate the spiritual nature. Gathering in silence and waiting upon God is necessary for the same reason, and is another means to the same end. More will be said of this presently.

The early Friends, while proclaiming the good news that there is a spiritual man in each and all of us, that God dwells in this part of human beings and is, for this very reason, close even to the earthly man, regarded the earthly man as unregenerate, sinful, blind and dead to the things of the spirit. Only by rising above the earthly aspect of ourselves can we pass from sin into righteousness, from death to life, from that which exists apart from God into that which exists as part of God. Only by yielding to God's power can the earthly man be regenerated. To the degree that this happens, we are unified with our spiritual natures.

Thus we are mended and made whole. What formerly was a separated and contrary part, becomes the instrument of expression of the resurrected spiritual being.

If the earthly man is dead to the things of the spirit, then, as long as he remains so, he obviously can neither truly pray nor truly worship. Nor can we, as long as we remain identified with him. Should he try to pray, he but prays according to his own ignorant and faulty notions. Should he try to worship, he but worships in his own will, not according to the will of God. Robert Barclay called this kind of worship "will-worship."

Will-worship was what the Friends condemned and tried to avoid. They aimed for true spiritual worship. They wanted to worship God by and through the workings of His spirit and power in their spiritual beings. How were they to fulfill this aim? What, specifically, were they to do? Try, by all available means, to quiet and subdue the earthly man, to lay down his will, to turn the mind to God. But, having done this, they found that something more was wanted. They discovered, as you and I have or will, that it is one thing to still our habitual thoughts and motions, but quite another to cause the spiritual self to arise. By our own efforts we can subdue the body-mind to some extent. Few of us, by our efforts alone, can activate our spiritual natures in a vital and creative way. We need God's help. We need the help of one another. But God's help may not come at once. Our help to each other, even though we are gathered in a meeting for worship or actively serving our fellow men outside of the meeting, may be and often is delayed as regards our kindling one another spiritually. What are we to do in this case? There is only one thing we can do—wait. Having done our part to overcome the separated self, we can but wait for the spiritual self to arise and take command of our lives. Having brought ourselves as close as we can to God, we can but hold ourselves in an attitude of waiting for Him to work His will in us, to draw us fully into His presence.

So the early Friends engaged in silent waiting, humble yet expectant waiting, reverent waiting upon the Lord, that they might be empowered by Him to help one another and to render to Him the honor and adoration which, as Robert Barclay said, characterizes true worship; that His power might come over them and cover the meeting; that He might bring about the death of the old, the birth of the new man.

Friends waited, both in and out of meeting. They waited for God to move them, quicken them to life, make them His instruments. They waited for the power of God to do its wonder-work, lifting up the part of them that was akin to Him, gracing them with the miracle of resurrection. Waiting preceded worship. Waiting prepared for worship, and the springing up of new life. By waiting they began worshiping. The stillness of the meeting house, the silence of the lips, the closed eyes and composed faces were the tangible signs of the preliminary period of waiting.

It is instructive and reassuring to note how frequently, among the early Friends, the practice of waiting did have the desired sequel. This seeming inactivity led to spiritual action. Out of this chrysalis what a life was born! God found them in the silence. Blessed and renewing experiences came to Friends, experiences which enabled them to be agents of the divine spirit in every situation of human life. It is instructive because it points us, of this day, to a religious practice that is effective. It is reassuring because from it we may have sound hope that, if we rightly and faithfully engage in this and other inward practices, we may reach and even surpass the high level of religious experience and service attained by Friends in the days when the Quaker movement really moved. In our present-day lives and meetings there can be soul-shaking events. The Light can invade us. Truth can take hold of us. Love may gather us. Above all, God himself may become real to us as the supreme Fact of the entire universe.

We of this modern age are inclined to be more lenient in our views of the earthly man. We are disposed to consider him a moderately decent fellow except when under the active power of evil. This makes us more tolerant, less intense. It makes us more likely to indulge our fondness for the earthly world and its things and pleasures, less moved to seek God and His Kingdom. Nevertheless if we examine our experience we shall recognize characteristics of the earthly man that are similar to those seen by the early Friends. The outside world has changed considerably in three hundred years, but man's constitution is much the same now as then in all essential respects.

The earthly man, whether we regard him as good, bad, or indifferent, is evidently an exile from God's Kingdom. Our body-minds, namely our every-day persons, are out of touch with our spiritual natures most of the time, hence out of touch with God. We, as ordinary people, are not by inclination turned towards God, but, on the contrary, are turned away from Him. Day in and day out we do not even think of the possibility of loving God and doing His will, but think of ourselves, and are bent to enact our own wills, have our own way. Whether we, as earthly men, can truly pray and worship is a question about which there is likely to be disagreement. But who will deny that when we are absorbed in our affairs, as we are most of the time, we do not pray or worship? Recognition of these several facts will lead us to a position similar to that of the early Friends, and point us to the same needs as regards what we must do if we would truly pray and worship, and, indeed, truly live. We too must endeavor to subdue the body-mind and turn the mind Godwards. We too must try to overcome the separated self and re-connect with our spiritual natures. We too must practice waiting. We too must strive to attain the Quaker ideal so well expressed by Douglas Steere, "to live from the inside outwards, as *whole* men."

When compared with bodily action, what could seem more inactive than waiting upon God? The modern world asks, "Where will that get you?" Young people say, "We want action." Yet, as we have seen, it was precisely through this and other apparently inactive means that the early Friends came into a power of whole action that surpasses anything that we experience today. We say we are activists, but often lack the spiritual force to act effectively. They said they were waiters, and frequently acted as moved by God's light and love. I think that we in this age of decreasing inner action, of ever increasing outer activity, have a profound lesson to learn from the early Friends. We had best learn it now, and quickly, lest the faith and practices of the Friends become so watered that they lose their character and flow into the activities of which the world is full, and are absorbed by them, and Friends cease to be Friends. I do not say we should go back to the old days. That is impossible. Let us move forward, as we must if we are to move at all. But let us build upon those foundations, not scrap them. Let those past summits show us how high men can go, with God's help.

Friends are by no means the only ones who realize that the body-mind presents a problem; that, in its usual state, it is an obstacle to worship and to all forms of the religious life. Friends are not alone in recognizing that when the separated self is uppermost and active, the spiritual self is submerged and passive, and that we are called upon to reverse this. All genuine religious people, whatever the religion, have recognized the problem and have endeavored to solve it in one way or another. Generally speaking, there are two ways of dealing with the situation. One way consists of the attempt to lift the body-mind above its usual condition, so that it may be included in the act of worship. The body-mind is presented with sight of religious symbols. It is given sound of religious music and of specially trained speakers called priests or ministers. It participates in rituals, ceremonies, sacraments. This way may be effective. When it is, the body-mind actually is lifted above its usual state, the spiritual nature is evoked. But when this way is not effective it merely results in exciting the body-mind and gives people the illusion that this excitation is true worship. Or it may result in a sterile enactment of outward forms.

The other way is just the opposite. It consists of the effort to reduce the body-mind below its usual state, so that it will not interfere with worship. All externals are dispensed with. No religious symbols are in view. No music is provided, no rituals, no appointed speakers. The external setting is as plain as possible, so that the body-mind may be more readily quieted. Internally, too, the attempt is to remove all causes of excitement, all of the ordinarily stimulating thoughts, images, desires. The one thought that should be present is the thought of turning Godwards, seeking Him, waiting before Him. This way may be effective. When it is, the body-mind is subordinated and ceases to exist as the principal part of man. The spiritual nature is activated and lifted up. When, however, this way is not effective, it merely produces deadness.

In both cases the test is this: Does the spiritual nature arise? Friends have chosen the way of subduing the body-mind, of excluding it from worship except insofar as it may act as an organ of expression of the risen spirit. Having chosen this way, we are called upon to do it effectively, creatively. If we succeed—and we sometimes do—our inner life is resurrected, the whole man is regenerated, and a living worship connects man with God. But if we fail—and we often do—the spiritual nature remains as if dead, and, on top of this, we pile a deadened body-mind. What should be a meeting for worship, a place where man and God come together, becomes a void. There is no life, only a sterile quietism. Sterile quietism is as bad as sterile ritualism.

Sterility, in whatever form, is what we want to avoid. Creativity is what we must recover—aliveness, growth, moving, wonder, reverence, a sense of being related to the vast motions of that ocean of light and love.

Source

"An Interpretation of Friends Worship" (Philadelphia: Committee on Religious Education of Friends General Conference, 1947), pp. 11–19.

What to Do in the Meeting for Worship

Definite periods for worship should be established because, constituted as we are, worship does not occur as naturally as it might, and at all times. Unless we set aside regularly recurring times, many of us are not likely to worship at any time. We appoint times and places so that we may do what something deep in us yearns to do, yet which we all too rarely engage in because most often we are caught up in the current of contrary or irrelevant events. Set times of worship not only aid us to worship at those times but at others too; and, of course, the more often we try to worship at other times, the more able we become to make good use of the established occasions.

Among the people of our day, Mahatma Gandhi is an outstanding example of applied religion. It might seem that he, of all people, would feel no need of special times of prayer; yet this is not the case. There are appointed times each day when he and those around him engage in prayer. Whenever possible he attends a Friends meeting for worship. The following quotation from the *Friends Intelligencer* gives his view of this matter. "Discussing the question whether one's whole life could not be a hymn of praise and prayer to one's

Maker, so that no separate time of prayer is needed, Gandhi observed, 'I agree that if a man could practice the presence of God all the twenty-four hours, there would be no need for a separate time of prayer.' But most people, he pointed out, find that impossible. For them silent communion, for even a few minutes a day, would be of infinite use."

Each of us individually should daily prepare for worship and, now and again, go off by himself in solitude. Fresh stimulus and challenge are experienced when a man puts himself utterly on his own and seeks to come face to face with his God. Aloneness may release the spirit. So may genuine togetherness. Group or corporate worship is also necessary because, as already mentioned, we need each other's help to quiet the body-mind, to lay down the ordinary self, to lift up the spiritual nature. Many a person finds it possible to become still in a meeting for worship as nowhere else. Peace settles over us. Many a person is inwardly kindled in a meeting for worship as nowhere else. The creative forces begin to stir. When a number of people assemble reverently, and all engage in similar inward practices with the same aim and expectancy, life-currents pass between them; a spiritual atmosphere is formed; and in this atmosphere things are possible that are impossible without it. More particularly, we may have opportunity in a meeting for coming close to a person more quickened than we are. By proximity with him or her we are quickened. It is true that in a Friends meeting the responsibility for worship and ministry rests upon each and every member; but it is also true that Friends, like others, must somewhat rely for their awakening upon those who are more in God's spirit and power than the average. We minimize an essential feature of our meetings if we fail to recognize the role of the sheer presence of men and women who are spiritually more advanced than most and are able to act as leaven.

The meeting for worship should begin outside the meeting house, on our way to it. As we enter the house, we would do well to remind ourselves of the meaning of worship, the significance of corporate worship, the possibility of meeting with God. Be expectant that this may happen in this very gathering. Lift up the mind and heart to the Eternal Being in whom we have brotherhood. The hope is that by these initial acts we will put ourselves in the mood of worship for the meeting and give spiritual meaning to all subsequent efforts.

Settle into your place as an anonymous member of an anonymous group. If you have come to have a reputation among people, forget this and become anonymous. If you have not made a name for yourself, forget this. The opportunity to practice anonymity is a precious one. The meeting for worship would be of great value if it did no more than make this practice possible. If you are accustomed to feel yourself important in the eyes of men, lay it down and feel only that you and others may have some importance in the eyes of God. If you feel unimportant, lay this down. If articulate or inarticulate, forget this. Lay aside all your worldly relationships and your everyday interior states. In fine, forget yourself. Surrender yourself. Immerse yourself in the life of the group. This is our chance to lose ourselves in a unified and greater life. It is our opportunity to die as separated individuals and be born anew in the life and power of the spirit. Seek, in the words of Thomas Kelly, to will your will into the will of God.

Quiet and relax the body. We should try to quiet its habitual activity, to relax it from strain, yet not over-relax it. Though relaxed it should not become limp or drowsy. It must be kept upright, alert, wakeful. What we desire is a body so poised and at rest that it is content to sit there, taking care of itself, and we can forget it.

Still the mind, gather it, turn it steadfastly towards God. This is more difficult. It is contrary to the mind's nature to be still. It is against its grain to turn Godwards. Left to itself it goes on and on under its own momentum, roaming, wandering. It thinks and pictures and dreams of everything on earth except God and the practice of His presence. Even those who developed great aptitude for taking hold of the mind and turning it to God found it difficult and even painful in the beginning. If we expect it to be easy and pleasant we shall be easily discouraged after a few trials. Brother Lawrence warns us that this practice may even seem repugnant to us at first.

The mind of an adult is more restive and all over the place than the body of a child. How are we to curb its incessant restlessness and stay it upon prayer and worship? How restrain its wanderings and point it to the mark? How take it away from its automatic stream of thoughts and focus it on God? Only by effort, practice, repeated effort, regular practice. It requires life-long preparation and training. We cannot hope to make much progress if we attempt to stay the mind only on First-days during meeting. We must make effort throughout the week, daily, hourly.

It is by stilling the body-mind that we center down. Put the other way, it is by centering down that we still the body-mind. I would judge that all Friends have in common the practice of centering down. This is our common preparation for worship. From here on, however, each of us is likely to go his individual way, no two ways being alike. This is the freedom of worship which has ever been an integral part of the Friends religion. We are not called upon to follow any fixed procedure. This is creative. The individual spirit is set free to find its way, in its own manner, to God. Yet it leaves some of us at a loss to know what to do next. Some of us are not yet able to press on. We are unsure of the inward way, and our available resources are not yet adequate to this type of exploration. We need hints from others, suggestions, guides. To meet this need, a number of Friends have written of what they do after they center down. Among these writings may be mentioned Douglas V. Steer's *A Quaker Meeting for Worship*, and Howard E. Collier's *The Quaker Meeting*. In the same spirit I would like to indicate what I do.

Once I have centered down I try to open myself, to let the light in. I try to open myself to God's power. I try to open myself to the other members of the meeting, to gain a vital awareness of them, to sense the spiritual state of the gathering. I try so to reform myself inwardly that, as a result of this meeting, I will thereafter be just a little less conformed to the unregenerate ways of the world, just a little more conformed to the dedicated way of love.

I encourage a feeling of expectancy. I invite the expectation that here, in this very meeting, before it is over, the Lord's power will spring up in us, cover the meeting, gather us to Him and to one another. Though meetings come and go, and weeks and even years pass, and it does not happen, nevertheless I renew this expectation at every meeting. I have faith that some day it will be fulfilled. We should be bold in our expectations, look forward to momentous events. We should not be timid or small but large with expectancy, and, at the same time humble, so that there is no egotism in it.

I kindle the hope that, should the large events not be for me and for us this day, some true prayer will arise from our depths, some act of genuine worship. I hope that at the least I will start some exploration or continue one already begun, make some small discovery, feel my inward life stir creatively and expand to those around me.

Having aroused my expectancy, I wait. I wait before the Lord, forgetting the words in which I clothed my expectations, if possible forgetting myself and my desires, laying down my will, asking only that His will be done. In attitude or silent words I may say, "I am before thee, Lord. If it be thy will, work thy love in me, work thy love in us."

"O wait," wrote Isaac Penington, "wait upon God. Be still a while. Wait in true humility, and pure subjection of soul and spirit, upon Him. Wait for the shutting of thy own eye, and for the opening of the eye of God in thee, and for the sight of things therewith, as they are from Him."

Sometimes, while waiting, a glow steals over me, a warmth spreads from my heart. I have a chance to welcome the welling up of reverence, the sense that I am in the presence of the sacred. Sometimes, though rarely, the practice of waiting is invaded by an unexpected series of inner events which carry me by their action through the meeting to the end. I feel God's spirit moving in me, my spirit awakening to Him.

More often I come to have the sense that I have waited long enough for this time. To forestall the possibility of falling into dead passivity, I voluntarily discontinue the practice of waiting and turn my attention to other concerns. I may summon to mind a vital problem that confronts me or one of my friends, trying to see the problem by the inward light, seeking the decision that would be best. I may bring into consciousness someone I know to be suffering. This may be a personal acquaintance or someone whose blight I have learned through others, or people in distress brought to my attention by an article in a newspaper or magazine. I call to him or them in my spirit, and suffer with them, and pray God that through their suffering they will be turned to Him, that by their very pain they may grow up to Him.

Hardly a meeting passes but what I pray that I and the members of the meeting and people everywhere may have this experience: that our wills be overcome by God's will, that our powers be overpowered by His light and love and wisdom. And sometimes, though again rarely, I find it possible to hold my attention, or, rather, to have my heart held, without wavering, upon the one supreme reality, the sheer fact of God. These are the moments that I feel to be true worship. These are the times when the effort to have faith is superseded by an effortless assurance born of actual experience. God's reality is felt in every fibre of the soul and brings convincement even to the body-mind.

I would not give the impression that what I have described takes place in just this way every time, or that it happens without disruptions, lapses, roamings of the mind, day-dreams. Frequently I must recall myself, again still the mind and turn in Godwards, again practice waiting. All too often I awake to find, no, not that I have been actually sleeping, but that I might as well have been, so far have I strayed from the path that leads to God and brotherhood. And I must confess, too, that during some meetings I have been buried under inertia and deadness and unable to overcome them. Having meant nothing to myself, it is not likely that my presence meant anything to the others. My body was but an object, unliving, filling space on a bench. It would have been better for others had I stayed away. A dead body gives off no life; it but absorbs life from others, reducing the life-level of the meeting.

As I am one of those who are sometimes moved to speak in meetings, I may indicate how this happens in my case. First let me say what I do not do. I never try to think up something to say. I am quite content to be silent, unless something comes into my mind and I am moved to say it, or unless I sense that the meeting would like to hear a few living words. In this latter case, I may search myself to see what may be found; and by this searching I may set in motion the processes which discover hidden messages.

I never go to the meeting with an "itch" to speak, though it sometimes happens to me, as to others, that I am moved to speak before arriving at the meeting house. Even so, I usually restrain the urge until we have had at least a short period of silent waiting before God. One is vain indeed if he thinks that his words are more important than this waiting. If I have not been moved to speak before arriving, such an impulse, if it comes at all, is likely to arise after I have been waiting a while. It arises within my silence. An insight or understanding flashes into my mind. A prayer or a pleading or a brief exhortation comes upon me. I hold it in mind and look at it, and at myself. I examine it.

Is this a genuine moving that deserves expression in a meeting for worship, or had I best curb and forget it? May it have some real meaning for others, and is it suited to the condition of this meeting? Can I phrase it clearly and simply? If it passes these tests, I regard it as something to be said but I am not yet sure it should be said here and now. To find out how urgent it is, I press it down and try to forget it. If time passes and it does not take hold of me with increased strength, I conclude that it is not to be spoken of at this time. If, on the other hand, it will not be downed, if it rebounds and insists and will not leave me alone, I give it expression.

If it turns out that the words were spoken more in my own will than in the power, I feel that egotistical-I has done it, and that this self-doing has set me apart from the other members of the meeting. I am dissatisfied until again immersed in the life of the group. But if it seems that I have been an instrument of the power, I have the feeling that the power has done it and has, by this very act, joined those assembled even closer. Having spoken, I feel at peace once again, warmed and made glowing by the passage of a living current through me to my fellows. With a heightened sense of fellowship with man and God, I resume my silent practices.

I never speak if, in my sense of it, spoken words would break a living silence and disrupt the life that is gathering underneath. But I have on occasion spoken in the hope of breaking a dead silence. Spoken words should arise by common consent. The silence should accept them. The invisible life should sanction them. The members of the meeting should welcome them and be unable to mark exactly when the message began and when it ends. The message should form with the silence a seamless whole.

If the message be a genuine one, the longer I restrain it the better shaped it becomes in my mind and the stronger the impulse to express it. A force gathers behind it. Presently, however, I must either voice it or put it from my mind completely, lest it dominate my consciousness overlong and rule out the other concerns which should engage us in a meeting for worship. It is good when a message possesses us. Our meetings need compelling utterances. But it is not good when a message obsesses us to the exclusion of all else. This is a danger which articulate people, particularly those like myself who have much dealing with words, must avoid. We miss our chance if we do not use the meeting for worship as an opportunity to dwell in the depths of life far below the level of words, rising to the surface only when we are forced to by an upthrust of the spirit which seeks to unite the surface with the depths and gather those assembled into a quickened sense of creative wholeness—each in all and all in God.

SOURCE
"An Interpretation of Friends Worship" (Philadelphia: The Committee on Religious Education of Friends General Conference, 1947), pp. 20–27.

Keep the Inward Watch

Said William Penn to his children, "Be free; live at home—in yourselves, I mean—where lie greater treasures hid than in the Indies." The treasures referred to were, of course, those of man's deep spiritual resources: the inner light and love and power, and, as Penington expressed it, a "rejoicing of soul from and before the Lord." Penn could give this advice with authority because he knew, by experience, where it led. He, together with other early Friends, had made the momentous discovery that under the surface of man's ordinary life there is a divine deposit.

Surely all of us want to make the same discovery in our own experience. We too aim to come closer to and eventually center in the wonderful powers. Our aim to deepen the spiritual life, and the concern expressed by Rufus Jones, that under God we have a new birth of life and power—these will be fulfilled only to the extent that we effectively uncover and recover the immeasurable riches of inner reality.

The question is, how to do it. How may we overcome whatever obstructs us? The early Friends knew how. They used certain means—and passed on to us indications as to what they were.

The example of George Fox may be misleading in this connection. Fox, once he began to open, seemed to experience no great difficulty in so doing. But in this respect as in so many others he was an exceptional human being. Penn, Penington, and others testified to having prolonged difficulties. Indeed, they encountered their most stubborn obstacles *after* experiencing their original openings. They are better examples for us. They warn us to take a sober yet hopeful view of what we are up against. It is deceptive optimism to believe that it is easy.

Why is it so difficult for us to go in and become able, in the words of Douglas Steere, "to live from the inside, outwards, as *whole men*?" The way in is blocked—and this, I think, is why we turn out and become so externalized. With the inner way obstructed, some see no choice but to live from the outside outwards, as divided and partial men. In many cases the obstruction is so dense as to seem an impenetrable wall with nothing back of it. Thus many a human being lives and dies without ever coming upon even a token of the light and life and power that dwell on the other side of the "great divide."

This barrier consists, without doubt, of certain properties in us: greed, vanity, prejudice, hate, hardness, etc. In so far as we harbor these, we literally stand in our own way. What we are called upon to do is to make openings in ourselves.

This effort, like so many others of the religious life, calls for new sight. Usually we look outward and see the mote in the other person's eye. Now we must see it also in our own. When people of good will do see evil in themselves, they usually so evaluate it because of its bad effects upon others. Now each one must also realize that the evil in him is a constant handicap to himself. In general it may be said: If we would find and live by that of God in us, we must contend with and overcome that of the devil in us—and it is as necessary that our eyes be opened to that of the devil as to that of God.

First of all, then, there must be awareness. We must see the bad properties, the impediments, the snares. Each one must bring himself to see them in himself. Next, we must squarely face and honestly evaluate them. If we disguise their real nature or rationalize about them, we might as well be blind. Having seen, faced, and honestly evaluated them, we will be aroused to overcome them. We will actively deny them, struggle against them, suffer them to be burnt out of us. The method as indicated so far may be summarized in the following five steps.

1. See them, one by one, of course. We cannot see them all at once.
2. Face them.
3. Honestly evaluate them.
4. Deny, that is, oppose them.
5. Struggle against them.

This fifth step, an active contending with our own impediments, is what Isaac Penington called "lawful warring." A sixth step may be mentioned: Suffer them. We must be willing to undergo whatever suffering is involved in our efforts to open, overcome and purify ourselves. Suffering itself, properly experienced, is a powerful purifying force.

William Penn wrote: "Oh, children! Love the grace, harken to this grace; it will teach you, it will sanctify you, it will lead you to the rest and kingdom of God; as it taught the saints of old, first, what to deny, viz: To live soberly, righteously and godly in this present world.... Truth in the inward parts is of great price with the Lord. And why called Truth? Because it tells man the truth of his spiritual state; it shows him his state, deals plainly with him, and sets his sins in order before him." In another place Penn wrote, "Repentance from dead works to serve the living God comprehends three operations; first, a sight of sin; secondly, a sense and godly sorrow for it; thirdly, an amendment for the time to come. This was the repentance they (the Friends) preached and pressed, and a natural result from the principle (the Light within) they turned all people unto. For of light came sight; and of sight came sense and sorrow; and of sense and sorrow came amendment of life."

We who read Penn's words, though we may not yet have had the full experience he writes of, can readily understand that if Grace is actively operating in us it will teach us what to deny and what to affirm; and if Truth is manifest in us it will show us our state; and if the Light is shining into us it will illumine us and enable us to see clear through to our most hidden faults, weaknesses, vices, impediments. The trouble is that Grace, Truth, and Light are foremost among the very treasures we aim to uncover by use of the method under consideration. What are we to do in their absence, what available faculty are we to use?

There can be but one answer. We must use such light and truth as we may have—in short, our available awareness. We must increase our present consciousness and train it to see, to face, to evaluate, to deny or affirm what we find in ourselves. This is just what the early Friends did. When the Light was not illumining them, they tried to illumine themselves. To themselves and to others they repeatedly stressed the need of being alert and vigilant. Though they seldom or never used the term awareness or stated that we must increase our consciousness, this is just what they meant. Their word was *watch*. Be watchful was their injunction. Said Penn, "Keep the inward watch." Said Penington, "There must be a daily watching against that which deceives and hardens." Said Fox, "Be careful and watchful. . . . And so here is the good man's watching against sin and evil without: And here is also a watching against sin and evil within, and a waiting to receive Christ the Lord at his coming."

Exercise such consciousness daily. Train yourself to see yourself. Focus your alertness, in order to see your impediments *as they arise in you*. If seen only in retrospect they will be dim and remote; you will have missed your chance, until the next time. See them in action. In this way you will be able to take hold of and struggle against them. By removing them from yourself you will have removed all possibility of their harming others.

This method, properly employed, does not involve introspection, but an active *inspection* of ourselves as we react and behave in life situations. It necessitates a real detachment from, instead of immersion in, our ordinary persons. It calls for a life of active experience in which our harmful properties are brought to the surface, for, as we have already noted, it is then that we can best contend with them. The best time to overcome prejudice, egotism, fear, hardness, and all the rest is when they show their faces. Temptations to do evil are seen as opportunities to overcome evil. Use of the method enables us to make the most of these opportunities.

What we have considered so far is but one arm or branch of a two-armed practice. It calls for Right Denying, Right *Struggle Against*. There is a second arm as essential as the first. This other calls for Right Affirming, Right *Struggle For*. It calls for the effort to increase our spiritual forces as these manifest. For, of course, they do sometimes manifest, and we should be prepared to make the most of these opportunities, too. Thick though the wall may be, the inner powers occasionally come through. Something of that inner light and love breaks in upon us. These are moments of real being. These are periods, usually all too short, when the invisible reality is palpable, God is near, and we expand to the whole of his creation.

We are not to be blind or indifferent to these outcomings of the inward source. Certainly we are not to deny them fearing that they will upset our little lives. We are to be alert for them, to sense them, as they arise and move. We are to affirm, further, and struggle for them, endeavoring to strengthen them that they may increase and remain with us as long as possible. We may express them. By expression we develop them and offer their fruits to other human beings. We may speak, write, teach, and above all live them in our human relationships and let them guide our worship. The several steps of this arm of the method can be summarized:

1. See or sense the creative powers.
2. Recognize and properly evaluate them.
3. Actively affirm them.
4. Further them by struggling for them.
5. Express them.

Here too a sixth step may be mentioned! Enjoy them.

The two arms taken together, each to be used as required, constitute the complete method. Both arms are capable of still further development. More might be said, but those who practice and explore the first steps will in time discover the further ones.

Keep the inward watch. Keep the watch for both sides of yourself. It is this effort which underlies the method from first to last. Penn's words, though not covering the entire practice, indicate what it is, and may be used by us as a reminder to employ it daily.

Source

Originally published in *Friends Intelligencer*, vol. 102 (June 1945), pp. 411–412.

III

Howard Thurman
(1899–1981)
edited by Stephen W. Angell

Howard Thurman was born in segregated Daytona Beach, Florida, the son of a railway worker, Saul Thurman, who died when Howard was seven. The major influence in his childhood was his maternal grandmother, Nancy Ambrose, who inspired his love for education. Thurman graduated from Morehouse College in 1923 and from Colgate Rochester Seminary with a ministerial degree in 1926; his lifelong connection with Quakers began in 1929, when he undertook a semester of special study with Rufus Jones at Haverford College. He was part of a YMCA- and YWCA-sponsored Negro Friendship delegation to India in 1935 and 1936, during which he met with Mohandas Gandhi. In 1944, he resigned his tenured position as university chaplain and professor at Howard University to undertake the leadership of the fledgling Church for the Fellowship of all Peoples in San Francisco. Nine years later, he became the first African American university chaplain and professor at Boston University. Thurman was a prolific author, a very highly regarded preacher (*Life* magazine in the early 1950s designated him as one of America's twelve best), and a much sought after speaker. His main commitment was to the "search for common ground," religiously and in other ways, but he did maintain a membership in the Wider Quaker Fellowship, served as a guest professor one term (Winter of 1966) for the Earlham School of Religion, and served as a keynote speaker both at Friends United Meeting and at Friends General Conference; in each case, he spoke twice.[1]

During Thurman's lifetime, Quaker periodicals (such as *Friends Journal* and *Quaker Life*) frequently republished his essays of African American interest (see our last two selections). It is our contention that, while his contributions in that area are of great interest, Thurman is most relevant to Friends for his careful and probing analysis of the nature of the Light and of "centering down." In his profound insight into our interior spiritual lives, he continued the tradition of Rufus Jones as meaningfully as did Thomas Kelly and Douglas Steere.[2]

His influence as a mystic and social activist has not diminished since his death in 1981. Friends United Press continues to keep in print many of his books. The University of South Carolina Press, under the lead editorship of Walter Fluker, has recently published the first volume of a projected four volumes of his papers.[3]

The selections below represent, in order, the following themes from Thurman's body of work: familiar Quaker phrases as a path to deep spiritual truth, prayer and worship, the Light of Christ and Jesus, mysticism and service, the universal element in religious thought and service, peacemaking, and African American Christianity. Also included is Thurman's eulogy for Martin Luther King, Jr.

The Angel with the Flaming Sword

[This selection, and the four that follow, include short essays using quotations from Quakers as a path into deep spiritual truths.]

The Angel with the Flaming Sword[4] is a striking figure of speech as well as a very accurate bit of symbolism. George Fox used it to symbolize the guardian angel placed at his post by divine order. We are all of us brought into direct contact with the Angel. He works in many strange and well-nigh mysterious ways. There are times when we adopt a particular course of action in accordance with a series of powerful, urgent and right desires. Step by step, we make our way; one thing leads to the next, and on and on until at last we are brought face to face with the fateful moment, the climactic act. Then, time stands still, the whole pattern of one's life is brought to bear upon the crucial act; something happens; we do not go through with it; the Angel with the Flaming Sword has made his presence known. It is more than conscience, more than mere conflict between right and wrong, more than simple violation of what one was taught to hold true. The Angel is the symbol of the Eternal sitting in judgment upon the temporary and the passing; the combination of rushing wind, flashing lightning and still small voice. No man can go past the Angel and remain as he was before the searching encounter. Dreadful indeed would it be if the Angel were withdrawn from your life. He is the guardian of all your ultimate values, the keeper of the seal of your spirit, the guarantor of all your meanings. When your decisions are finally made, the Angel says "Yes" or "No" and, upon his nod or frown, turns your destiny. Of course, he can seem to be ignored, but every man knows deep within him that he cannot escape his tryst with the Angel. It is well to be full of thanksgiving that the Angel with the Flaming Sword guards the ultimate treasure and secret of the life of man. He is sustainer of the essence of your life and mine and our final protection against the dissolution of the integrity of life. It is small wonder that George Fox felt that, when he came up past the Angel with the Flaming Sword, all the world had a new smell. There is no more graphic meaning put into the word *hell* than this—the Angel with the Flaming Sword is on the war path in the human spirit—the Angel with the Flaming Sword is on the war path in the soul of a people—eternal guardian, great contender, mighty bulwark, God's wall of fire in and for the life of man.

SOURCE

Howard Thurman, *Deep Is the Hunger* (Richmond, IN: Friends United Press, 1978), pp. 17–18. (Reprint of 1951 edition by Harper. Subtitle supplied by editor.)

"Be Still and Cool in the Mind"

In the diary of George Fox there appears this very significant sentence: "Be still and cool in thy own mind and spirit, from thy own thoughts, and then thou wilt feel the principle of God to turn thy mind to the Lord from whence cometh life; whereby thou mayest receive the strength and power to allay all storms and tempests."[5] This is an important result of the habitual use of the quietness that a man can carry around inside of him. It is a central stillness of spirit that is so vital that it can tame the wildness out of almost any tempest, however raging it may be. Of course the individual must desire this to happen. Sometimes there are ragings of anxiety, of hurts that we do not want to see disappear. They provide excellent opportunities to bolster up our own ego or own sense of faltering security. This fact must not blind us to the great power that there is in what is here referred to as the central stillness. For it is in the quiet which invades us and which becomes a characteristic of our total respiration that we are most acutely aware of the operation of the Presence of God. Here is the "mercy seat" of God before which all things are stripped to their true essence and their real character revealed. The plans and purposes of our times, the primary and secondary levels of our desiring, the fateful issues of our loves and hates, the ground of our own faith are established and confirmed. There is a wonderful lift to the spirit in knowing that the way is always channeled so that it may have free access to the mind and the cleansing power.

SOURCE

Howard Thurman, *Meditations of the Heart* (Richmond, IN: Friends United Press, 1976), pp. 24–25. (Reprint of 1953 edition by Harper.)

If I Knew You

William Penn wrote, "Neither despise, nor oppose, what thou dost not understand."[6] He might have added "'nor approve' what thou dost not understand." It is very easy to pretend to understand what one does not understand. Often the degree to which we oppose a thing marks the degree to which we do not understand it. Sometimes we use our opposition to an idea to cover up our own ignorance. We express our dislike for things, sometimes for people, when we do not understand the things we pretend to dislike; when we do not know the people for whom we have the antagonism.

> If I knew you and you knew me,
> And each of us could clearly see
> By that inner light divine
> The meaning of your heart and mine;
> I'm sure that we would differ less
> And clasp our hands in friendliness,
> If you knew me, and I knew you.

One has to pay a price for understanding. In the realm of facts, one has to work hard and carefully, weighing and sifting and testing before one arrives at an understanding of them. This takes time as well. There must be a *will* to understand which informs the integrity of one's desire to understand. How much "more true" is it in the understanding of ideas, of experiences, yes, of the complexities of human beings. It takes time and effort and imagination. It does not come merely for the asking. One has to "fool around" the edges of another's life, getting closer and closer to the central place. Where this is lacking, it is easy to cover up one's own lacks by making a negative attitude into a positive appraisal. The basis of one's strength in understanding is the vast and unlimited understanding of God, who is the source and ground of all our being.

SOURCE
Thurman, *Meditations of the Heart*, pp. 115–117.

Miracles in the Spirit

"There are miracles in the spirit of which the world knows nothing."[7] Such is the testimony that comes to us from the lips of George Fox. Our lives are surrounded day by day and night after eventful night by the stupendous revelations of what man is discovering about the world around him. Each day we seem to penetrate more deeply into the process of nature. Thousands of men and women with utter devotion give themselves to the pursuit of secret disclosures from the chamber of mysteries of which they themselves are a part and from which they have come forth. It is as if there is a mighty collective and individual effort to remember what they were before the mind became mind and the body became flesh and blood. So successful has been the appropriation of the knowledge of the mysteries of air and wind and earth that what a decade ago would have startled and frightened the most matured adult is today taken for granted by the simplest child. We speak of going to the moon not as denizens of the shadows where unrealities tumble over one another in utter chaos. Rather we speak of going to the moon and back again with voices that are brimming over with an arrogance that even a god may not command.

But let one arise in our midst to speak of secrets of another kind. Let one say that the world of the spirit has vast frontiers which call to us as our native heath. At once the deep split in our spirits reveals itself. Out of our eyes, as we listen, there leaps the steady glow of recognition while our lips speak of superstition and delusion. Can the miracles in the spirit be real, true? Because they seem always to be personal and private, does this not add to their unreality?

The miracles in the spirit? What are they? The resolving of inner conflict upon which all the lances of the mind have splintered and fallen helplessly from the hand; the daring of the spirit that puts to rout the evil deed and the decadent unfaith; the experiencing of new purposes which give courage to the weak, hope to the despairing, life to those burdened by sin and failure; the quality of reverence that glows within the mind, illumining it with incentive to bring under the control of Spirit all the boundless fruits of knowledge; the necessity for inner and outer peace as the meaning of all men's striving; the discovery that the "Covenant of Brotherhood" is the witness of the work of the Spirit of God in the life of man and the hymn of praise offered to Him as Thanksgiving and Glory!

SOURCE

Howard Thurman, *The Inward Journey* (Richmond, IN: Friends United Press, 1971), pp. 48–49.

Power from Great Quakers

The other day we read in the headlines that the Nobel Peace Prize had been awarded to the Quakers for the work done by the American Friends Service Committee and the similar agency in Great Britain. Who are these Quakers and what do they stand for? In this series for a week now we are to concentrate upon great Quakers.

Dr. Henry Seidel Canby, Editor of *The Saturday Review of Literature*, says this about the Quakers: "Quietly, and without slogans or campaigns, the Quakers have become the most trusted agents of humanity in an inhuman age.

They carry relief where no others are permitted to go. They win the confidence of violent and dictatorial men because it is evident that they have freed their hearts of both violence and hatred. They have made a successful adjustment between what they believe to be the will of God and what they regard as the proper will of man. They are not afraid to have confidence in a disciplined human nature."

In their early days the Quakers were not so regarded. Listen to this description from the pen of Mary Agnes Best: "Carrying their message of freedom and equality, Fox and his intrepid band of outlaws, without respect of person, held up and admonished czars, kings, and sultans, princes and prelates, convicts and pirates, within and without the law.... In its time the Quaker uprising was regarded as extreme left-wing radicalism, subversive of law and order, threatening the overthrow of the government; and it was therefore considered a pious and patriotic duty to suppress it by fair means or foul.... Compared with the primitive Quakers, the I.W.W. in the oil fields of Oklahoma lead a sheltered and protected life. Far from being drab, their lives were lurid. They reached out toward danger as plants toward the sun. They trekked the whole world, challenging all the autocratic powers and potentates of their time.... In Old and New England vivisection was practiced on them—tortures too brutal to repeat to sensitive modern ears. They glutted English jails, and the convict ships on which they were deported afforded them hardly more than standing room only. Too frequently their sufferings were relieved by a martyr's death, and the history of their adventurous lives reads like an invasion of the realm of Teutonic legendary tales."[8]

SOURCE
Howard Thurman, Papers, Box 109. Boston University.

Prayer and Silence

[*This selection and the four that follow are from Thurman's writings on prayer and worship.*]

Meditation

Whither shall I go from Thy Presence?
From Thee is there some hiding place?[9]

The deed is a thing so private
So inside the perfect working of desire
That its inward part seems known to me,
To me alone.

Howard Thurman

The ebb and flow of thoughts
Within my hidden sea,
The forms that stir within the channels of my mind,
Keep tryst with all my intimate hopes and fears.
The ties that hold me fast to those whose
Life with mine makes one,
The tangled twine that binds my life
With things I claim as mine
Seem cut off from all else but
My embrace.

The great stillness that walls around
The heartaches and the pain
Is sealed against aught else that would invade.

The awe-filled contrition emptied of all violence and all sin
Keeps watch with the spent loneliness
Of my deserted soul.

The joy crowding to the quivering brim the heights and uppermost reaches of vast delight
Gives room to nothing but itself alone.

And yet,
Always I know that Another
Sees and understands—
Every vigil with me keeps watch—
The door through which He comes no man
Can shut—
He is the Door!

I cannot go from Thy Presence.
There is no hiding place from Thee.

Reading
La Vie Profonde

Hemmed in by petty thoughts and petty things,
Intent on toys and trifles all my years,
Pleased by life's gauds, pained by its pricks and stings,
Swayed by ignoble hopes, ignoble fears;
Threading life's tangled maze without life's clue,
Busy with means, yet heedless of their ends,

Lost to all sense of what is real and true,
Blind to the goal to which all Nature tends:—
Such is my surface self: but deep beneath,
A mighty actor on a world-wide stage,
Crowned with all knowledge, lord of life and death,
Sure of my aim, sure of my heritage,—
I—the true self—live on, in self's despite,
That "life profound" whose darkness is God's light.

— *Edmond G. A. Holmes*

To get at the core of God at his greatest, one must first get into the core of himself at his least, for no one can know God who has not first known himself. Go to the depths of the soul, the secret place of the most high, to the roots, to the heights; for all that God can do is focused there.

and

In limpid souls God beholds his own image; he rests in them and they in him. . . . I like best those things in which I see most clearly the likeness of God. Nothing in all creation is so like God as stillness.

— *source unknown*

Prayer and Silence. We are continuing the interpretation of prayer as the experience in which the individual draws upon resources beyond himself in behalf of himself, and on behalf of the interests by which that self is defined. The point of contact, the opening, through which these resources become manifest in human life is deep within human life. The process by which we work ourselves from the periphery, from the outside of ourselves, on the long journey to the floodgate within ourselves, is a part of what we mean by meditation. Quietness, stillness, silence, become very important. It is in the climate of quietness, stillness, silence, that we get release from the involvements which keep us defocused, scattered, entangled.

There is, of course, the immediate place that external quiet holds in this process. We must have a peaceful place where the physical, tangible environment can be at rest, so that the other dimensions of our lives can be brought into focus. Let me illustrate this.

Some years ago, one of my university students, who had been a deep-sea diver, wrote a very interesting sketch. In it he described one of his experiences on the Caribbean Sea. He was on the ocean bottom. It was very beautiful down there. The water was clear, and he was in the midst of a coral rock garden. Since he was in no particular hurry, he sat down to look around. He sat; he looked.

Occasionally, a fish would swim up to take a close look at him and would pass the word along to his friends, who were also curious. After an indefinite time, he lost track of all time awareness. Then he discovered that he was sitting in the midst of a very beautiful flower garden. There were plants of many shapes, and things that looked like blossoms. It was wonderful. He could enjoy the beauty for a long while; but he realized that he couldn't stay there forever, so he stirred to go about his business. And, as soon as he moved, every plant disappeared. Apparently these were living things that were in mid-passage between the vegetable and animal world. They emerged only when he was completely still. That's what I mean. Take the idea. Apply it!

Now we are ready for the second step. The physical silence needs a place that doesn't even look noisy. We must now turn within to see if the noises, the confusion, the churning that are going on inside us can be quieted. Otto calls this "the numinous silence of waiting." It is the silence of preparation when the individual is readying himself for the movement of the spirit of the living God. This waiting mood may be encouraged in various ways, sometimes by reading a great paragraph, sometimes by repeating over and over again some significant affirmation of the human spirit. Little by little we begin to settle down, to focus within. The Quakers have developed this ability to a very marked degree—this waiting. Many of you have been to Friends' meetings, or perhaps have had a similar experience elsewhere. At first, even though no one is moving, and there is no noise anywhere, the inner ear seems to hear confusion. You hear it. Then more and more... more and more... more and more... things begin to settle, to shake down. At what point, you don't know, but you do become involved in the stillness, in the quietness. Something begins breathing through the stillness, communicating to your mind and to your spirit, meeting your individual need at the level of your need. Let me illustrate this.

Once I traveled several hundred miles to speak on a Sunday morning at a Friends' meeting. In some way I wanted to share in the quality of the religious experience upon which their whole spiritual encounter was projected. I made no preparation. I gave no thought to what I should say. No subject or text was selected. I sat with the leader of the meeting on the facing bench. We settled down into the quietness. Little by little, I became still within. That stillness merged with the stillness of the meeting. Then a very strange thing happened. There began turning up in my mind words, words which were a part of a sentence. I had to wait for each word to be spelled out slowly and gradually. Finally the sentence spelled itself out. I read it! It formed a statement that had once come from the lips of Jesus. My mind seized upon it. I began wrestling with the idea that it gave me until it seemed that there was something within me that was ripe for expression. I moved my right foot back and my left foot just ahead and put my hands on the rail in front of me and was in the act of standing, when I heard behind me a woman's voice quoting that passage. She talked about it! All over the meeting, people arose, talking on the point, so that I began to wonder if I would have my chance at all. I had come many miles just to speak to these people. Only just before the hour was up, I had the opportunity to give my witness. During the waiting silence the traffic within me had stopped, the floodgate had opened, and there had begun to flow through me the spirit, the infinite resources of the living God.

The moment when this takes place becomes a sacramental moment, a moment that marks the step between the final act of meditation and the awareness of prayer. It is a moment when God appears. The waiting, the readying, the focusing, the centering down; then the spirit seems to pass over an invisible line of consciousness. The awareness of God bursts through all the corridors, all the reaches of the spirit.

I remember a rather interesting dramatization of this experience. Some of you may remember a play called *The Fool* in which the hero is the Christian. He has befriended a girl who is confined to a wheel chair. In one scene the girl in the wheel chair is on one side of the stage and on the other side, there is the "fool" himself along with a group of agitated workers. They accuse the fool of betraying their interests contrary to his profession and protestation. The leader of the group loses his temper, hits the fool on the chin, and knocks him down. When he falls, the crippled girl, who has never walked, gets out of her wheel chair, and walks across the stage. She kneels to help this man who has helped her and loved her. The leader of the group sees what has happened and cries: "Look, she walks! Down on your knees! God is in this room." It has been more than a quarter of a century since I saw this play in the theater. Even now as I relive it, I am caught up in the push of that moment, the sense of sacrament.

Less dramatic, but just as poignant and effective, is the experience of the individual, privately and personally, as he waits, readying his spirit in the quietness. The sacramental moment emerges within him. When it does, he prays. It may be that he prays for the first time in his life, because Something in him prays.

If I were to put into words what happened, it would be something like this: There is in every one of us an inward sea. In that sea there is an island; and on that island there is a temple. In that temple there is an altar; and on that altar burns a flame. Each one of us, whether we bow our knee at an altar external to ourselves or not, is committed to the journey that will lead him to the exploration of his inward sea, to locate his inward island, to find the temple, and to meet, at the altar in that temple, the God of his life. Before that altar, impurities of life are burned away; before that altar, all the deepest intent of your spirit stands naked and revealed; before that altar, you hear the voice of God, giving lift to your spirit, forgiveness for your sins, renewal for your commitment. As you leave that altar within your temple, on your island, in your inward sea, all the world becomes different and you know that, whatever awaits you, nothing that life can do will destroy you.

> O Sabbath rest by Galilee!
> O calm of hills above,
> Where Jesus knelt to share with Thee
> The silence of eternity
> Interpreted by love![10]

SOURCE

Howard Thurman, *The Growing Edge* (Richmond, IN: Friends United Press, 1974), "Part II: Concerning Prayer," pp. 37–45. (Reprint of 1956 edition by Harper & Row.)

How Good to Center Down!

How good it is to center down!
To sit quietly and see one's self pass by!
The streets of our minds seethe with endless traffic;
Our spirits resound with clashings, with noisy silences,
While something deep within hungers and thirsts for the still moment and the resting lull.
With full intensity we seek, ere the quiet passes, a fresh sense of order in our living;
A direction, a strong sure purpose that will structure our confusion and bring meaning in our chaos.
We look at ourselves in this waiting moment—the kinds of people we are.
The questions persist: what are we doing with our lives?—what are the motives that order our days?

SOURCE

Thurman, *Meditations of the Heart*, pp. 28–29.

Some Centering Moment

We wait in the quietness for some centering moment that will redefine, reshape, and refocus our lives. It does seem to be a luxury to be able to give thought and time to the ups and downs of one's private journey while the world around is so sick and weary and desperate. But, our Father, we cannot get through to the great anxieties that surround us until, somehow, a path is found through to the little anxieties that beset us. Dost Thou understand what it is like to be caught between the agony of one's own private needs and to be tempest-tossed by needs that overwhelm and stagger the mind and paralyze the heart? Dost Thou understand this, our Father?

For the long loneliness, the deep and searching joy and satisfaction, the boundless vision—all these things that give to Thee so strong a place in a world so weak—we thank Thee, Father. For whatever little grace Thou wilt give to Thy children even as they wait in confidence and stillness in Thy presence, we praise Thee. O love of God, love of God, where would we be without Thee? Where?

SOURCE
Howard Thurman, *The Centering Moment* (Richmond, IN: Friends United Press, 1980), p. 85.

"Still Dews of Quietness"

> "Drop Thy still dews of quietness
> Till all our strivings cease."[11]

"Drop Thy still dews of quietness." "Still dews of quietness" is a happy phrase which suggests a mood, an atmosphere, rather than an idea or a concept. It is a feeling tone of peace, of tranquillity, that settles down over one's spirit. It is the thing that can happen only when one somehow manages to "stay put" for a spell. How wonderful to sit alone, with one's own life parts gathered together, and sense the whole of one's interior landscape's being invaded by a blanket of calm—by the still dews of quietness. This I must cultivate more and more and with ever greater frequency.

"Till all our strivings cease." How deep and often bitter are the strivings within me! The conflicts of indecision, the conflicts of loyalty, the struggle between good and evil courses of conduct, all this and much more makes of my spirit a battleground, a citadel of tempests raging. All of this is a part of me; all of this must be stilled—must be settled. Oh, how my soul cries out for moments when the battle does not rage, when I hear the whisper of the still small voice giving me reassurance and renewal. After which I can go forward without fear but with confidence that the way I take is *The Way* for me.

> "Drop Thy still dews of quietness
> Till all our strivings cease."

SOURCE
Thurman, *Meditations of the Heart*, pp. 172–173.

The Power of Meditation

Douglas Steere[12] defines meditation as a voluntary act of the mind. Of course there are times when the mind slips involuntarily into meditation. The experience is like becoming aware of a tune in the mind without knowing precisely at what moment one began to hum it. Nevertheless, it is true that meditation is a deliberate and voluntary act of the mind. Out of the welter of ideas to which one is exposed, a particular idea is selected, quarantined, and subjected to careful and sustained scrutiny. It may be compared to what must have been true in the early stages of the development of human speech. There were many sounds beating ceaselessly upon the eardrums, but certain sounds were separated, charged with unique and perhaps personal meaning, again and again, until at last these sounds became symbols of meaning that in turn were the common coins of communication among people who lived together in one family, tribe or community. To return to the art of meditation—one phrase is selected, or one idea, complete in itself, embodied in a simple sentence or paragraph. All other ideas are rigidly excluded, and the mind is made to attend to it. The idea may set up a "chain reaction" which opens up a whole vista of thought or enlightenment. Once the idea is held at dead center in the mind, one must probe for its meaning. Once the meaning is clear, then one must proceed with a series of interpretive applications to one's own life situation and to one's world. The possibility of application or testing may open up for examination and exploration various aspects of one's own life that are not congenial to the acceptance of the idea. This may lead to a recognition of one's limitations, one's impotency, or one's stubbornness. It is often possible that such considerations reveal the need for a deeper commitment, a profounder earnestness, or a more sensitive spirit. In fine, a sense of sinfulness may be the direct result of meditation. This sense of sin may inspire a conscious need of strength and a seeking for sources of power to enable one to apply the insight to one's life. The search for personal power in this sense will eventually bring one face to face with Him who is recognized as the Source of all strength, God. We need not be distressed over the label; it may or may not be important. Sometimes, the awareness of the meaning of an idea or thought that is the selected subject of meditation will itself cause a fresh inrush of energy which so floods the life that much rubbish is swept away and a clean inner feeling fills one's being. Coming back to the daily round refreshed and renewed is one of the simple, but critically practical results of authentic meditation. Try it for yourself.

SOURCE

Thurman, *Deep is the Hunger*, pp. 173–175. (Subtitle supplied by editor.)

The Light that is Darkness
[*This selection and the three that follow address themes of the Light of Christ and Jesus.*]

Meditation

How good it is to enter together into the fellowship of silent waiting, joined by one another's presence and by a great invisible host whose languages we cannot speak, whose knowledges we cannot grasp, but who, after the pattern of their own lives, their own needs, their own urgencies, are waiting somewhere in their own silence.

Each of us has the smell of life upon him, each of us has his problems, his needs—problems and needs which seem utterly personal and unique. Each of us has his joys—joys which seem utterly personal and unique. Each of us, in his own way, is trying to find answers to crucial questions. For some of us, the seeking has been long and hard, sometimes terrifying, sometimes heartbreaking. For some, the finding has frightened us and given us an overbearing sense of responsibility and fear that dries up the springs of our activities and paralyzes our hopes. It is good to know that none is alone. It is good to feel the presence of others surrounding one's own privacy, spilling over into one's personal needs their strength and courage and hope.

To Thee, our Father, we expose the inward parts of our minds, holding back nothing, including in our offering the bad and the good, our failures and our successes, the things of which we are ashamed and the things in which we rejoice. Just as we are, without pretense, we expose to Thy light and Thy love, O God, our Friend and Redeemer.

Reading

"Let not thy will be set to sin."[13] These searching words are from the book of Tobit. The attitude toward wrongdoing depends upon the character of the individual conscience. Conscience is rooted in the sense of value which is a part of the working equipment of personality. This sense of value is given; the content varies. Here the results of training, of observation, of social heritage, of religious experience and instruction, are made manifest. The judgment which says of a deed that it is wrong is always a reflection of the content of the individual's sense of value. So often such a judgment concerning wrongdoings does not involve the will of the individual. There seems to be an automatic, unreflective element in conscience. A man says: "I do not know why this is wrong, all that I know is, this is the way I feel about it." Or he may say: "I know my feeling of guilt for what I have done does not make sense, except to me."

Again and again we find ourselves reacting to the events and situations of our lives apart from our wills in the matter. It is the way we are trained, conditioned, taught. But this does not alter the fact of our responsibility for our acts and our reactions. An important part of living is the process by which the individual Will brings under its private jurisdiction the behavior of the individual. This is an essential element in any doctrine of self-mastery or, more accurately, of self-knowledge.

How many things have you done during the past week for which you have an after-the-event sense of responsibility, reflected in guilt, hostility, or pride—deeds which did not express your conscious intent because the doing of the deed did not come before your will for review: it was automatic, the result of long-established habits, training, conditioning? But once the deed was done and you were faced with the consequences, you realized that this kind of behavior was not your intent. The common cry is: I did not know. I did not understand.

It is important to make the full conquest of one's life pattern to the end [that] the deeds of one's life will move more and more from the center of one's intent. Perhaps this is a goal that is never reached, but to work at it is to become increasingly mature and responsible. Meditation and prayer are helpful in providing a climate in which the deeds of one's life may be exposed and the character of the deeds understood. In such a climate, the most natural desire of the heart is the quiet utterance to God—

Let not my will be set to sin.

An elderly lady nearing the end of her life paused to look back and recall some of its great moments. She wrote, among other things, about an occasion when she was walking in the country. She had been under great strain but suddenly the strain snapped like the breaking of a cord. To quote her own words: "I was flooded with an ineffable soul light which seemed to radiate from a great personality with whom I was in immediate touch. I felt it to be the touch of God. The ecstasy was beyond description. I was passing through a patch of beggar's grass with its wiry stems ending in feathery heads. Every head shone and glistened like pearls. I could hardly walk for the overwhelming sense of the Divine Presence and its joy. I almost saw God."

A little dog that had been walking quietly beside her looked up into her face at this point and began to bark in great excitement. I do not doubt that he saw in her face the great effulgence that she saw in the grass. I am glad to think that the glory of God is at the heart of beggar's grass as well as at the heart of men and that little dogs as well as human beings may see and rejoice.

The Fourth Gospel refers to the light that lighteth every man that cometh into the world. This light is the very ground of all being, the ground of creativity. Every creative thing has within it the signature of the Creator—His imprint, His stamp. You may think of the light in every man as that seal of the Creator. There no one is devoid of that light. Every man is born with it. We do not deserve any credit for having it. In truth we cannot get rid of it; it is an inherent part of our nature. There is something very consoling and refreshing about light in that sense, which perhaps in essence is metaphysical.

Jesus also refers to a light of another kind, light that is understanding, light that is meaning, light that is value. If that be darkness, then what a darkness it is! This is the light that we see in the dawning conscience and oh, how often we try to short-circuit that light. I have been watching the developing conscience in a puppy that has just come into our household. He has been told not to climb in a certain chair. It has been demonstrated to him that to do so is to find that the world is not friendly. So, when he gets up into this place that is forbidden, and I ask him to get down, he pretends that he does not hear me. He looks away from me. But because he remembers a time when we had an encounter about this matter, his eye steals slowly around to pick me up in his field of vision. He hears my voice and quickly swings his head back. He is trying to put his light out, but he cannot quite do it. Finally, with great reluctance, he jumps down from the chair.

Now that is the way we all behave, isn't it? We develop a certain knowledge, and the more skilled we become in the use of this knowledge, the greater becomes the strength of experience. But also, the more likely are we to disassociate ourselves from the responsibilities that are involved in having knowledge. This is the crucial peril of any kind of professionalism; for instance, I am a minister; again and again I am impressed with the fact that it is not easy to grow in sympathy and understanding of other people. It is very easy to become professionally a religious person, professionally a minister, and let my knowledge of the Bible, my knowledge of the history of the Church, my knowledge of the psychology of religion, become a substitute for getting on my knees, seeking forgiveness of my sins, wrestling with my spirit in the presence of God. If I let my knowledge become a substitute for my understanding, then the light that is in me becomes darkness. If the light that is in me becomes darkness, what a darkness!

Sometimes a man's light becomes darkness when he knows distinctly what he ought to do; he looks his duty, his responsibility, clearly in the face, calls every aspect of it by its right name, and then refuses to do it When that happens, his light becomes darkness.

Just before he died, Hugh Price Hughes, celebrated Congregational minister of England, wrote an allegory which illustrates what I have in mind. He calls it "The City of Everywhere."

It is the tale of a man who might have been I, for I dreamed one time of journeying to that metropolis. I arrived early one morning. It was cold, there were flurries of snow on the ground and as I stepped from the train to the platform I noticed that the baggageman and the red cap were warmly attired in heavy coats and gloves, but oddly enough, they wore no shoes. My initial impulse was to ask the reason for this odd practice, but repressing it I passed into the station and inquired the way to the hotel. My curiosity, however, was immediately enhanced by the discovery that no one in the station wore any shoes. Boarding the streetcar, I saw that my fellow travelers were likewise barefoot, and upon arriving at the hotel I found the bellhop, the clerk and the habitues of the place were all devoid of shoes.

Unable to restrain myself longer, I asked the ingratiating manager what the practice meant.

"What practice?" said he.

"Why," I said, pointing to his bare feet, "why don't you wear any shoes in this town?"

"Ah," said he, "that is just it. Why don't we?"

"But what is the matter? Don't you believe in shoes?"

"Believe in shoes, my friend! I should say we do. That is the first article of our creed, shoes. They are indispensable to the well-being of humanity. Such chilblains, cuts, sores, suffering, as shoes prevent! It is wonderful!"

"Well, then, why don't you wear them?" I asked, bewildered.

"'Ah," said he, "that is just it. Why don't we?"

Though considerably nonplused I checked in, secured my room and went directly to the coffeeshop and deliberately sat down by an amiable-looking gentleman who likewise conformed to the conventions of his fellow citizens. He wore no shoes. Friendly enough, he suggested after we had eaten that we look about the city. The first thing we noticed upon emerging from the hotel was a huge brick structure of impressive proportions. To this he pointed with pride.

"You see that?" said he. "That is one of our outstanding shoe manufacturing establishments."

"A what?" I asked in amazement. "You mean you make shoes there?"

"Well, not exactly," said he, a bit abashed, "we talk about making shoes there and believe me, we have got one of the most brilliant young fellows you have ever heard. He talks most thrillingly and convincingly every week on this great subject of shoes. He has a most persuasive and appealing way. Just yesterday he moved the people profoundly with his exposition of the necessity of shoe-wearing. Many broke down and wept. It was really wonderful!"

"But why don't they wear them?" said I, insistently.

"Ah," said he, putting his hand upon my arm and looking wistfully into my eyes, "that is just it. Why don't we?"

Just then, as we turned down a side street, I saw through a cellar window a cobbler actually making a pair of shoes. Excusing myself from my friend I burst into the little shop and asked the shoemaker how it happened that his shop was not overrun with customers. Said he, "Nobody wants my shoes. They just talk about them."

"Give me what pairs you have already," said I eagerly, and paid him thrice the amount he modestly asked. Hurriedly, I returned to my friend and proffered them to him, saying "Here, my friend, some one of these pairs will surely fit you. Take them, put them on. They will save you untold suffering."

But he looked embarrassed; in fact, he was well-nigh overcome with chagrin.

"Ah, thank you," said he, politely, "but you don't understand. It just isn't being done. The front families, well, I—"

"But why don't you wear them?" said I, dumbfounded.

"Ah," said he, smiling with his accustomed ingratiating touch of practical wisdom, "that is just it. Why don't we?"

And coming out of the "City of Everywhere" into the "Here," over and over and over that query rang in my ears: "Why don't we? Why don't we? Why don't we?"

"Why call ye me, 'Lord, Lord,' and do not the things I command you?"

If I know what I ought to do in a given situation, if I see the action that I should take in order to be true to the deepest thing in me, if I look it steadily in the eye and see not, the light that is in me becomes darkness. If the light becomes darkness, what a darkness!

Are you putting out the light? Just think about it. In your own life this past week, did your light become darkness? Think about it without becoming morbid, depressed, or sentimental, but with a chastened spirit. Are you thinking right now about some decision that is waiting, about something that you know that you ought to do? And have you decided that you are not going to do it? When you made that decision, did the lights go out one by one and did you wonder what had happened to you? If the light that is in you be darkness, nothing outside of you can turn the light on again. Only you yourself can do that. Even God can't unless you give Him a hand.

Teach us, our Father, that if we nourish within ourselves those things that turn us away from the light, we shall spend our years stumbling through the darkness. Teach us, our Father, that if we be true to the light that is within us, we shall become like Thee, and to become like Thee is the be-all and end-all of our desiring.

SOURCE

Thurman, *The Growing Edge*, "Part VI: Concerning Christian Character," pp. 139–147.

Thy Light Within Me

Kindle Thy light within me, O God!

Kindle Thy light within me, that all my darkness may be clearly defined. It is so easy for me to recognize and respond to the darkness in others. Far more conscious am I of the error of others than of my own. The temptation is ever present to compare my strengths with another's weaknesses—to my own advantage, to my own self-glory. Searchingly, there wells up in my mind the terrible thought: "I thank thee that I am not as other men."

Kindle Thy light within me, O God, that I may be guarded against self-deception and the vanity that creeps into my spirit where a shadow is cast between me and Thy scrutiny. I must know through all the reaches of my spirit that my light at its best is dim and clouded with shadow! Teach me the technique by which I can lay bare not merely my failures, my shortcomings, my sin; but also my successes, my strengths and my righteousness.

Kindle Thy light within me, O God, that Thy glow may be spread over all of my life; yea indeed, that Thy glow may be spread over all of my life. More and more, may Thy light give radiance to my flickering candle, fresh vigor to my struggling intent, and renewal to my flagging spirit. Without Thy light within me, I must spend my years fumbling in my darkness.

Kindle Thy light within me, O God!

SOURCE

Thurman, *Meditations of the Heart*, pp. 159–160.

Jesus of Nazareth

O sabbath rest by Galilee!
O calm of hills above,
Where Jesus knelt to share with Thee
The silence of eternity,
Interpreted by love![14]

In so many ways, ways beyond our own calculation and reflection, our lives have been deeply touched and influenced by the life and character, teaching and spirit, of Jesus of Nazareth. He moves in and out on the horizon of our days like some fleeting ghost. At times when we are least aware and often least prepared, some startling clear thrust of his mind moves in upon us, upsetting the normal tempo of our ways, reminding us of what we are, and what life is, giving to us sometimes judgment, sometimes a wistful murmur of the possibilities that lie before us, stirring within us resolutions, activating ancient desires, kindling anew dead hopes, giving to leaden spirits wings that sweep. We owe so much to the spirit which he let loose in the world. We think about it now in our meditation, gathering up all the fragments of our lives to see if for us there can be some creative synthesis, some wholeness, some great healing that will still our tempests and give to us the quiet trust that God is our Father, and we are His children living under the shadow of His spirit.

Accept our lives, O God; we ourselves do not know what to do with them. We place them before Thee as they are, with no suggestions, no hints, no attempts to order the working of Thy spirit upon us. Accept our lives, our Father.

SOURCE
Thurman, *The Centering Moment*, p. 30.

The Work of Christmas

When the song of the angels is stilled,
When the star in the sky is gone,
When the kings and the princes are home,
When the shepherds are back with their flock,
The work of Christmas begins:
    To find the lost,
    To heal the broken,
    To feed the hungry,
    To release the prisoner,
    To rebuild the nations,
    To bring peace among brothers,
    To make music in the heart.[15]

SOURCE
Thurman, *The Mood of Christmas* (Richmond, IN: Friends United Press, 1973), p. 23.

Mysticism and Service

[*"Mysticism and Service" is the theme of the next two selections.*]

The mystic is forced to deal with social relations because, in his effort to achieve the good, he finds that he must be responsive to human need by which he is surrounded, particularly the kind of human need in which the sufferers are victims of circumstances over which, as individuals, they have no control; circumstances that are not responsive to the exercise of an individual will, however good and however perfect. This brings up for discussion the question of service. Canon Kirk writes, "Disinterested service is the only service that is serviceable."[16] Now, what is disinterested service? Kirk further defines selfishness as "a lack of due regard to the well-being of others" and unselfishness as "the payment of due regard to the well-being of others." It would seem to me that disinterested service is a kind of service in which the person served is not a means to some end in which he does not share and participate directly. There are at least two levels of disinterestedness. In one, the individual is free from exploiting the need of others for purely narrow interest or gratification. An American novelist of the last century puts it this way: "No man may say I have smiled on him in order to use him, or called him my friend that I may make him do for me the work of a servant." In a second level of service, the individual would be interested in relieving human need, because he sees it, in some definite sense, crowding out of the life of others the possibility of developing those qualities of interior graces that will bring them into immediate candidacy for the vision of God. It is in this latter sense that we come upon the mandatory *raison d'etre* of the mystic's interest in social change and in social action.

Source

Thurman, *Deep is the Hunger*, pp. 44–45. Subtitle supplied by editor.

She Practices Brotherhood

The telephone rang at seven-fifteen in the morning. And on the other end was a lady whose voice seemed full of years, soft but strong. What she had to say was profoundly stirring: "I am sorry to disturb you so early in the morning, but I wanted to call you before you left the hotel for the day. About ten years ago (I am now sixty-nine) I decided to examine my life to see what, if anything, I could do to put into practice my own convictions about brotherhood. Why I decided this, and not suddenly, I need not say. But I did. The first thing I discovered was that I knew almost nothing about other races in my own city, particularly about Negroes. I went to the library and was given a small list of books and magazines. I began to work. The things I learned! When it seemed to me that I had my hands on enough facts (and I discovered you don't need too many facts, because they get in your way), I plotted a course of action. Then I was stumped. What could I do? I had no particular abilities, very little energy, and an extremely modest income. But I did like to talk with people as I met them on the buses and in the stores. I decided that I would spread the facts I had and my own concern among all the people whose lives were touched by mine in direct conversation. It took me some time to develop a simple approach that would not be an intrusion or a discourtesy. For several years, I have been doing this on the bus riding into town each week, in a department store where I have made my purchases for two decades, and in various other places. Occasionally, I run into a person in the street who stops to introduce himself and to remind me of a previous meeting. One such person said, 'I guess you have forgotten, but about four years ago I sat by you on a bus, and I don't know how the question came up but we talked about the Negroes; and you started me thinking along lines that had never occurred to me. You even gave me the name of a book which I noted and purchased. Since then, I have been instrumental in changing the whole personnel practice of our business on this question. Thanks to you!'"

Continuing, she said "I know that this is not very much and I guess many people are doing much more. But I thought I would tell you this so that, in your moments of discouragement, you may remember what one simple old lady was doing to help in little ways to right big wrongs. Good-by and God bless you." She did not give me her name, nor her address; she merely shared her testimony and gave her witness.

SOURCE

Thurman, *Meditations of the Heart*, pp. 127–129.

The Desert Dweller

[*This selection and the next one touch on the universal element in religious thought and service.*]

He has lived in the desert so long that all of its moods have long since become a part of the daily rhythm of his life. But it is not that fact that is of crucial importance. For many years, it has been his custom to leave a lighted lantern by the roadside at night to cheer the weary traveler. Beside the lantern, there is a note which gives detailed directions as to where his cottage may be found so that if there is distress or need, the stranger may find help. It is a very simple gesture full of beauty and wholeness. To him, it is not important who the stranger may be, it is not important how many people pass in the night and go on their way. The important thing is that the lantern burns every night and every night the note is there, "just in case." Years ago, walking along a road outside Rangoon, I noted at intervals along the way a roadside stone with a crock of water and, occasionally, some fruit. Water and fruit were put there by Buddhist priests to comfort and bless any passerby—one's spiritual salutation to another. The fact that I was a traveler from another part of the world, speaking a strange language and practicing a different faith, made no difference. What mattered was the fact that I was walking along the road—what my mission was, who I was—all irrelevant.

In your own way, do you keep a lantern burning by the roadside with a note saying where you may be found, "just in case?" Do you place a jar of cool water and a bit of fruit under a tree at the road's turning, to help the needy traveler? God knows the answer and so do you!

SOURCE

Thurman, *Meditations of the Heart*, pp. 90–91.

Religious Dialogue in India

[*During his visit to India, Thurman visited Shantiniketan, a university associated with the poet Rabindranath Tagore, a recipient of the Nobel Prize for Literature.*]

It was important for us to see Tagore because he was a poet of India who soared above the political and social patterns of exclusiveness dividing mankind. His tremendous spiritual insight created a mood unique among the voices of the world. He moved deep into the heart of his own spiritual idiom and came up inside all peoples, all cultures, and all faiths.

However, my chief concern was to have some time with Dr. [Kshiti Mohan] Singh, who was the head of the division of Oriental studies in the university. One glorious morning we sat on the floor in searching conversation about the life of the spirit, Hinduism, Buddhism, and Christianity. When lunchtime came, I had to keep an appointment with some students. Getting up from the floor, massaging my usual charley horse, I looked at him.

He remarked, "I see you are chuckling."

I replied that he was doing the same. "Perhaps we are reacting to the same thing," I said.

"Suppose you tell me first," he remarked.

I said we had spent the entire morning sparring for position—"you from behind your Hindu breastwork, and I from behind my Christian embattlement. Now and then, we step out from that protection, draw a bead on each other, then retreat."

"You are right. When we come back this afternoon, let us be wiser than that."

That afternoon I had the most primary, naked using of total religious experience with another human being of which I have ever been capable. It was as if we had stepped out of social, political, cultural frames of reference, and allowed two human spirits to unite on a ground of reality that was unmarked by separateness and differences. This was a watershed of experience in my life. We had become a part of each other even as we remained essentially individual.

I was able to stand secure in my place and enter into his place without diminishing myself or threatening him.

SOURCE

Howard Thurman, *With Head and Heart: The Autobiography of Howard Thurman* (San Diego: Harcourt Brace Jovanovich, 1979), pp. 128–129.

Blessed Are the Peacemakers; for They Shall Be Called the Children of God

[Peacemaking is the theme of the next three selections.]

Blessed are the peacemakers.[17] Am I a peace maker? Do I make peace in my home? This is my desire. I have a will to peace—or do I? I must see that no man gives all nor takes all but rather that, by yielding and affirming, wholeness of living in community *becomes* the way of life. Of course I do not wish war in myself, in my private circle, in the wide world of men. Yet the seeds of war are in me. Deep is the conflict within. "When I would do good, evil is present," or "I want to do what is right, but wrong is all that I can manage." One slight injury to my pride, to my feelings, and I let it ferment until it sends a temperature all through my spirit—a false sense of honor. Sometimes I like to nurse my wounds. Whole nations do this.

Blessed are the peacemakers. This means that I must possess and create a will that is good toward myself, toward my fellows, toward life and living. This good will must constantly be fed by facts and a careful understanding of them—facts concerning myself, concerning my fellows, concerning life. There must be an energized imagination. In my mind, I must play with all manner of creative possibilities in my relations with others, familiarizing myself with the flavor of people and their potentiality. This I must do until there is revealed in them the very essence of what I know of myself. Then I will understand their understanding, feel their feeling, "sit where they sit." My judgment will be tenderized, my hardness will be softened, my justice will be merciful. I will be a peacemaker.

They shall be called the children of God. The peacemaker is so like what men are seen to be at their best that they remind men of what God must be like. They recall to men's minds the thought of the best and the highest. They warm men with the thought of God. They breathe His promise to the spirit of men. They bring to mind the assurance that all stand in immediate candidacy to achieve in fact what they are in essence—children of God.

SOURCE

Thurman, *Deep is the Hunger*, pp. 189–190.

Needed Adjustment of Human Mind and Spirit

Years and years ago—farther back than the records of history reveal—early man learned how to use a club in self-defense and thus to extend his control over an area farther than his arm unaided could reach. When he learned to throw this club with precision and power, it meant that the control of his environment was farther extended. So the story goes; as man developed—extending his arm through club, bow and arrow, gun powder, gasoline engine, through various kinds of vehicles and machines up to and including the jet-propelled plane and the atomic bomb—he has required a complete adjustment of his mind and spirit to his new power. He has been forced to fit his new powers, with each development, into a scheme of life that would keep him from destroying himself. Difficult as this adjustment has been for man's mind, it has been infinitely more difficult for his spirit and conscience. A bow-and-arrow conscience finds itself paralyzed in the presence of the cannon and the rifle. A sense of social responsibility in the use of the arrow finds itself paralyzed by the tremendous moral demands of gun powder. The dilemma of modern man is to match spiritual and moral maturity with the amazing power created by his mastery over nature. He has learned a part of the secret of energy by unlocking the door of the atom, and yet he continues to be moved by prejudice, greed and lust! He has devised a machine that can keep pace with the speed of the earth through the heavens, and yet he has not learned how to walk the earth in the midst of his fellows with simple reverence and grace. Today we stand on the verge of a brave, startling era which can yield the end of poverty, of war, and of all the breeds of hate that have made the earth a hell for countless millions. Oh, for how many years, by our deeds, shall we curse God and die, when we could reflect Him and live?

SOURCE
Thurman, *Deep is the Hunger*, pp. 33–34. Subtitle supplied by editor.

The Limits of Violence

A cursory glance at human history reveals that men have sought for countless generations to bring peace into the world by the instrumentality of violence. The fact is significant because it is tried repeatedly and to no basic advantage. The remark which someone has made, that perhaps the most important fact we learn from history is that we do not learn from history, is very much to the point. Violence is very deceptive as a technique because of the way in which it comes to the rescue of those who are in a hurry. Violence at first is very efficient, very effective. It stampedes, overruns, pushes aside and carries the day. It becomes the major vehicle of power, or the radical threat of power. It inspires fear and resistance. The fact that it inspires resistance is underestimated, while the fact that it inspires fear is overestimated. This is the secret of its deception. Violence is the ritual and the etiquette of those who stand in a position of overt control in the world. As long as this is true, it will be impossible to make power—economic, social or political—responsive to anything that is morally or socially motivating. Men resort to violence when they are unable or unwilling to tax their resourcefulness for methods that will inspire the confidence or the mental and moral support of other men. This is true, whether in the relationship between parents and children in the home or in great affairs of the state involving the affirmation of masses of the people. Violence rarely, if ever, gets the consent of the spirit of men upon whom it is used. It drives them underground, it makes them seek cover, if they cannot overcome it in other ways. It merely postpones the day of revenge and retaliation. To believe in some other way, that will not inspire retaliation and will curb evil and bring about social change, requires a spiritual maturity that has appeared only sporadically in the life of man on this planet. The statement *may* provide the machinery, but the functioning of it is dependent upon the climate created by the daily habits of the people.

Source

Thurman, *Deep is the Hunger*, pp. 34–35. Subtitle supplied by editor.

The Blind Man

[*This selection explores African American Christianity.*]

> Blind Man stood on the road and cried;
> Crying that he might receive his sight.[18]

Since early morning the blind man had been waiting by the roadside. Word had come to his village the night before that the Healer would pass that way in the morning. The persistent hope for sight had never left him, quite. True, he had been blind all of his life, and yet, through all the corridors of his spirit, the simple rumor of trust persisted that he would someday gain his sight. At last, with his head slightly tilted the better to reassure himself of the quiet thud of walking feet, he *knows*. All his life he had waited for that precise moment.

There is no greater tragedy than for the individual to be brought face to face with one's great moment only to find that one is unprepared. Years ago I read a poem by Sara Teasdale which pictured a woman climbing a hill. All the way up she thought how grand it would be when she reached the crest, lungs full of air, a wide, almost limitless view as far as eyes could see—but "the briars were always pulling" at her gown. Then she crossed the crest; when, she did not know, for the briars were always pulling at her gown, and now all the rest of the way would "be only going down...."[19]

But the blind man was ready. As Jesus approached, he began crying, "Jesus, thou son of David, have mercy on me."[20] Over and over he said it until the words became one with the walking rhythm of the approaching feet of Jesus and his disciples. The rest of the story depicts the healing of the blind man, who goes on his way rejoicing.

The slave singers did a strange thing with this story. They identified themselves completely with the blind man at every point but the most crucial one. In the song, the blind man does not receive his sight. The song opens with the cry; it goes through many nuances of yearning, but always it ends with the same cry with which it began. The explanation for this is not far to seek; for the people who sang this song had not received "sight." They had longed for freedom with all of their passionate endeavors, but it had not come. This brings us face to face with a primary discovery of the human spirit. Very often, the pain of life is not relieved—there is the cry of great desire, but the answer does not come, only the fading echo of one's lonely cry. Jesus, in the garden of Gethsemane, prayed that the cup might pass, but he had to drink it to the last bitter dregs. The apostle Paul prayed for the thorn to be taken from his flesh, but he had to carry the thorn to his grave. These are but two illustrations from the early history of the Church that etch in clear outline the same basic insight. For the slave, freedom was not on the horizon; there stretched ahead the long road, down which there marched in interminable lines only the rows of cotton, the sizzling heat, the riding overseer with rawhide whip, the auction block when families were torn asunder, the barking of the bloodhounds, all this, but not freedom.

Human slavery has been greatly romanticized by the illusion of distance, the mint julep, the long Southern twilight, and the lazy sweetness of blooming magnolias. But it must be intimately remembered that slavery was a dirty, sordid, inhuman business. When the slaves were taken from their homeland, the primary social unit was destroyed, and all immediate tribal and family ties were ruthlessly annihilated. This meant the severing of the link that gave to the individual African a sense of *persona*. There is no more hapless victim than one who is cut off from family, from language, from one's roots. He is completely at the mercy of his environment to be cowed, shaped, and molded by it at will. When the Negro Mission of Friendship was in India several years ago, one of the things that puzzled the students and friends there was the fact that we spoke no African language and wore no distinctive African dress. Again and again they asked, "Why do you speak only the language of the conqueror? Why do you wear only Western clothes?"[21]

Again, the slave was cut off from his religion, whatever kind it was. It is quite beside the point to say that he was given Christianity, an infinitely "better" religion than anything he had known before. When the master gave his God to the slave, for a long time it meant that it was difficult to disentangle religious experience from slavery sanction. The existence of these songs is in itself a monument to one of the most striking instances on record in which a people forged a weapon of offense and defense out of a psychological shackle. By some amazing, but vastly creative spiritual insight, the slave undertook the redemption of a religion that the master had profaned in his midst.

In instance after instance, husbands were sold from wives, children were separated from parents; a complete and withering attack was made upon the sanctity of the home and the family. Added to all of this, the slave women were constantly at the mercy of the lust and rapacity and personal affection of the master himself while the slave husband or father was powerless to intervene. Indeed the whole sorry picture is a revelation of a depth of moral degradation that even in retrospect makes forgiveness one of the greatest fruits of the spirit.

Frustration with no answer in the environment! Under such circumstances, what does one do? This is the fundamental issue raised by this song. It is quite possible to become obsessed with the idea of making everything and everybody atone for one's predicament. All of one's frustrations may be distilled into a core of bitterness and disillusionment that expresses itself in a hardness of attitude and a total mercilessness; in short, one may become mean.

You have seen people like that. They seem to have a demoniacal grudge against life; because they are unable to corner it and wreak their churning vengeance against it, they penalize everything else they touch. They show no favors, demand none. They trust no one and have no interest in doing so, but lash out in an almost maniacal fury on the slightest provocation. Sometimes they are less obvious, showing no emotions, but are deliberate and calculating in their attack and conquest. For them life is essentially evil, and they are essentially vengeful. "Cruel" is the apt word that may describe them. They are out to settle a score with life. They have nothing to lose because they have lost everything. This is one alternative for those who face a complete and overwhelming frustration.

Or such persons may withdraw into themselves completely. Very carefully they build a wall around themselves and let no one penetrate it. They carry the technique of detachment to a highly developed art. Such people are not happy; nor are they unhappy but are completely indifferent. They look out upon life through eyes that have burned out, and nothing is left but a dead, cold stare. Life has been reduced to routine, long ago learned by heart and, for them, laid aside.

There comes to mind the statue over the grave of the wife of Henry Adams in the old Rock Creek Cemetery in Washington.[22] Perhaps you have seen it. There is the seated figure of a woman whose chin is resting on her right supporting hand. The whole figure is draped in a large inclusive fold of greenish bronze. She is looking steadily ahead, the eyes are open but unseeing. The total effect is of something that is burned out—no spark is left, and yet there is a certain complete sense of being alive. This is the mood and tense of the person who embraces the second alternative. A great silence envelopes the lifelike stillness of absolute motion suddenly stopped, A proud people irretrievably beaten in battle, who must give quarters to the occupying enemy, sometimes reacts this way. It is what may be called "the silence of a great hatred." Sometimes the attitude expresses itself in terms of aggressive cynicism and a pose of bold, audacious, belligerent defiance.

The final alternative is creative, thought of in terms of a second wind. It involves the exercise of a great and dynamic will. An accurate appraisal of all circumstances is clearly seen, understood, challenged, and despite the facts revealed, hope continues even against odds and evidence. Stephen Benét depicts this very dramatically in *John Brown's Body*. There is a scene in which Lincoln is probing the universe to find the right way, the sure answer to his problem-urgency. He thinks of himself as an old hunting dog, whose energies are spent, "tail down, belly flattened to the ground"—he can't go one step further. There is complete exhaustion, but the will remains and becomes the rallying point for a new persistency that finally unlocks the door through which he moves to release and fulfillment. He goes on because he must go on.[23]

This is the discovery made by the slave that finds its expression in the song—a complete and final refusal to be stopped. The spirit broods over all the stubborn and recalcitrant aspects of experience until they begin slowly but inevitably to take the shape of one's deep desiring. There is a bottomless resourcefulness in man that ultimately enables him to transform "the spear of frustration into a shaft of light." Under such a circumstance even one's deepest distress becomes so sanctified that a vast illumination points the way to the land one seeks. This is the God in man; because of it, man stands in immediate candidacy for the power to absorb all of the pain of life without destroying his joy. He who has made that discovery knows at last that he can stand anything that can happen to him. "The Blind Man stood on the way and cried"—the answer came in the cry itself. What a panorama of the ultimate dignity of the human spirit!

SOURCE

Thurman, "The Blind Man," *Friends Journal*, Nov. 5, 1955.[24]

Eulogy for a Prophet and Peacemaker
Martin Luther King, Jr., 1929–1968

[*Thurman had befriended King when Thurman was professor and university chaplain at Boston University and when King had been a Ph.D. student there. Thurman also visited King in a Harlem hospital in 1957 after King had been stabbed and nearly killed by a demented African American woman.*]

Martin Luther King, Jr. is dead. This is the simple and utter fact. A few brief hours ago his voice could be heard in the land. From the ends of the earth, from the heart of our cities, from the firesides of the humble and the mighty, from the cells of a thousand prisons, from the deep central place in the soul of America the cry of anguish can be heard.

There are no words with which to eulogize this man. Martin Luther King was the living epitome of a way of life that rejected physical violence as the life style of a morally responsible people. His assassination reveals the cleft deep in the psyche of the American people, the profound ambivalence and ambiguity of our way of life. Something deep within us rejects nonviolent direct action as a dependable procedure for effecting social change. And yet, against this rejection something always struggles, pushing, pushing, always pushing with another imperative, another demand. It was King's fact that gave to this rejection flesh and blood, courage and vision, hope and enthusiasm. For indeed, in him the informed conscience of the country became articulate. And tonight what many of us are feeling is that we all of us must be that conscience wherever we are living, functioning, and behaving.

Perhaps his greatest contribution to our times and to the creative process of American society is not to be found in his amazing charismatic power over masses of people, nor is it to be found in his peculiar and challenging courage with its power to transform the fear-ridden black men and women with a strange new valor, nor is it to be found in the gauntlet which he threw down to challenge the inequities and brutalities of a not quite human people—but rather in something else. Always he spoke from within the context of his religious experience, giving voice to an ethical insight which sprang out of his profound brooding over the meaning of his Judeo-Christian heritage. And this indeed is his great contribution to our times. He was able to put at the center of his own personal religious experience a searching ethical awareness. Thus organized religion as we know it in our society found itself with its back against the wall. To condemn him, to reject him, was to reject the ethical insight of the faith it proclaimed. And this was new. Racial prejudice, segregation, discrimination were not regarded by him as merely un-American, undemocratic, but as mortal sin against God. For those who are religious it awakens guilt; for those who are merely superstitious it inspires fear. And it was this fear that pulled the trigger of the assassin's gun that took his life.

Tonight there is a vast temptation to strike out in pain, horror, and anger; riding just under the surface are all the pent up furies, the accumulation of generations of cruelty and brutality. A way must be found to honor our feelings without dishonoring him whose sudden and meaningless end has called them forth. May we harness the energy of our bitterness and make it available to the unfinished work which Martin has left behind. It may be, it just may be that what he was unable to bring to pass in his life can be achieved by the act of his dying. For this there is eloquent precedence in human history. He was killed in one sense because mankind is not quite human yet. May he live because all of us in America are closer to becoming human than we ever were before.

I express my deep compassion for his wife, his children, his mother, father, sister and brother. May we all remember that the time and the place of a man's life on the earth is the time and the place of his body, but the meaning of his life is as vast, as creative, and as redemptive as his gifts, his times, and the passionate commitment of all his powers can make it. Our words are ended—and for a long, waiting moment, the rest is silence.

April 4, 1968
Howard Thurman

Source

Quaker Life, January 1978. "This tribute to Martin Luther King, Jr., is reproduced from the original by special permission from Howard Thurman."

Endnotes

1 More detail on Thurman's connections with Rufus Jones and other Quakers can be found at: Stephen W. Angell, "Howard Thurman and Quakers," *Quaker Theology*, vol. 9, no. 1 (Fall-Winter 2009), pp. 28–54. Another very helpful source is Walter Fluker and Catherine Tumber, eds., *A Strange Freedom: The Best of Howard Thurman on Religious Experience and the Common Life* (Boston: Beacon Press, 1998).

2 A thoughtful comparison of the lives and writings on spirituality of these four men can be found in Leigh Schmidt, *Restless Souls: The Making of American Spirituality from Emerson to Oprah* (New York: Harper Collins, 2005), pp. 230–268.

3 Walter Fluker, ed., *The Papers of Howard Washington Thurman: Volume I: My People Need Me, June 1918–March 1936* (Columbia: University of South Carolina Press, 2009).

4 Thurman is referring here to Fox's account of his conversion experience: "Now I was come up in spirit, through the flaming sword, into the paradise of God. All things were new, and all the

creation gave another smell unto me than before, beyond what words can utter. I knew nothing but pureness, innocency, and righteousness, being renewed into the image of God by Christ Jesus." George Fox, *Journal*, in Fox, *Works of George Fox* (Philadelphia: Marcus T. C. Gould, 1831), vol. I, p. 84.

5   Thurman is quoting from George Fox's 1657 letter to Oliver Cromwell's daughter, Elizabeth Claypole. George Fox, *Journal*, in Fox, *Works of George Fox* (Philadelphia: Marcus T. C. Gould, 1831), vol. I, p. 375.

6   William Penn, "Some Fruits of Solitude," maxim 308, in *Collection of the Works of William Penn* (London, 1726), vol. I, p. 834.

7   This sentence does not appear in the eight volumes of Fox's collected *Works*, although he does use the phrase "miracles in the spirit:" Fox, "Great Mystery of the Great Whore Unfolded," *Works*, vol. III, p. 37.

8   Mary Agnes Best, *Rebel Saints* (New York: Harcourt, Brace and Company, 1925), pp. 4–6.

9   A paraphrase of Psalm 139:7–12. Psalm 139 was Thurman's favorite psalm.

10   This is a stanza of the familiar hymn, "Dear Lord and Father of Mankind," excerpted from a J. G. Whittier poem, "The Brewing of the Soma," written in 1872. See *The Complete Poetical Works of John Greenleaf Whittier* (Boston: Houghton Mifflin, 1904), pp. 571–572. This hymn is one of Thurman's favorites, and he quoted lines from it repeatedly.

11   Thurman again quotes familiar lines from Whittier's "Brewing of the Soma"; see note 10.

12   Douglas Steere, author of books on religion and spirituality and long-time professor of religion at Haverford College, was a friend of Thurman. Thurman and Steere met in 1929 when Thurman came to Haverford College to study with Rufus Jones.

13   Tobit 4:5.

14   This is another verse from the Whittier poem, "The Brewing of the Soma," cited above.

15   Thurman wrote a poem for Christmas and designed an original Christmas card each year, and this poem was originally written for that purpose.

16   Walter Fluker and Catherine Tumber supply the following reference: Kenneth E. Kirk, *The Vision of God: The Christian Doctrine of the Summum Bonum* (New York: Longmans, Green, and Co., 1931), p. 451.

17   Based on Matthew 5:9.

18   Like other African American spirituals, this is a song of unknown authorship. One version is: "The blind man stood on the road and cried (x2)/ crying, Oh, Lord, save me,/ The blind man stood on the road and cried./ Crying that he might receive his sight (x2)/ Crying, Oh, Lord, save me,/ The blind man stood on the road and cried." A You Tube version, including two additional verses as well as the melody, can be accessed at http://www.nme.com/awards/video/id/ma5nb-BvUCXc/search/609 (accessed Nov. 19, 2009).

19   Sara Teasdale, "The Long Hill," *Flame and Shadow* (Champaign, IL: Project Gutenberg, n.d.), Section X, p. 18. (Original publication, 1920.) It seems likely that Thurman was quoting from memory, because his quotations were inexact. "I must have passed the crest a while ago/ And now I am going down/ Strange to have crossed the crest and not to know/ But the brambles were always catching the hem of my gown." His general concept of the poem, however, was accurate.

20   Mark 10:47–52; Luke 18:35–43.

21   Thurman here refers to his 1936 trip to India. For more information on this, see Thurman, *With Head and Heart*, pp. 103–136.

22   An image of this monument can be found at http://commons.wikimedia.org/wiki/File:Adams-memorial-rock-creek.jpg

23   Stephen Vincent Benét, *John Brown's Body* (Garden City, NY: Doubleday, 1928), p. 220.

24 Howard Thurman, "The Blind Man," *Friends Journal*, Nov. 5, 1955. This was a chapter that would be published in his forthcoming book *Deep River* (2nd ed): Howard Thurman, *Deep River and The Negro Spiritual Speaks of Life and Death* (Richmond, IN: Friends United Press, 1975), pp. 37–43. The first edition of *Deep River* had been published in 1945, and the second in 1955. The Friends United Press 1975 edition is identical to the 1955 edition, but it differs in some small details from the version published in *Friends Journal*.

IV

Ira de Augustine Reid
(1901–1968)

edited by Harold D. Weaver, Jr.

IRA DE AUGUSTINE REID held degrees from three institutions: a B.A. from Morehouse College (1922), an M.A. from the University of Pittsburgh (1925), and a Ph.D. in sociology from Columbia University (1929).

In his role as a sociologist, Reid contributed to an understanding of race relations, adult education, Southern sharecropping, and immigration. Among his six books are *Negro Membership in American Labor Unions* (1930), *Adult Education Among Negroes* (1930), *Sharecroppers All* (coauthored with Arthur Raper, 1941), and *The Negro Immigrant*, posthumously published in 1969. He lectured and advised the United States government and such social service agencies as the American Friends Service Committee on a range of subjects, including education, human resources, youth services, and social security.

In his academic appointments as a professor of sociology, Reid was a forerunner in the desegregation of the faculties of Northern higher education by scholars from historically black colleges in the South. At Atlanta University, Reid served as a professor of sociology (1934–1946) and department chair (1944–1946). Working under his mentor, W.E.B. Du Bois, Reid was managing editor (1940–1944) and later editor of *Phylon*, the scholarly journal on race and culture published by African American scholars. He also produced adult-education radio programs for working-class listeners in Atlanta. Following a visiting professorship sponsored by the American Friends Service Committee at Haverford College (1946–1947), Reid returned to Haverford as professor and chair of the sociology department (1948–1966), becoming the college's first African American professor.

During the McCarthy era Reid was erroneously labeled a Communist by a Pennsylvania politician in 1949, leading to the seizure of his passport by the U.S. State Department. Reid joined the Society of Friends

(Quakers) in 1950. In honor of his scholarship, teaching, and contributions to peace and justice in the United States and abroad, Reid received honorary doctorates from Haverford and Morehouse. He died from cancer on August 15, 1968.

Peace and Tranquility: The Quaker Witness

[*The Young Friends Movement of Philadelphia Yearly Meeting (Religious Society of Friends) sponsored an annual William Penn Lecture "for the purpose of closer fellowship" from 1916 until 1966. The lectures were subsequently published, and the names of the William Penn lecturers constitutes a roll call of individuals still widely recognized for Quaker leadership today. In 1958, Ira Reid was their chosen speaker. Following are excerpts from his presentation.*[1]]

Peace and Tranquility

I have selected as my theme for this lecture two secrets of the Society of Friends—"Peace" and "Tranquility." I do not regard them as the same in either faith or practice. Peace I regard as a sort of harmony or concord between and among individuals and states. Tranquility is a state of being inwardly quiet, undisturbed, and calm. The former obtains for man in his collective capacities and roles. The latter is that quality which obtains for man unto himself and himself alone. The former is attained when man works for concord among his fellow men; the latter is attained only when one seeks and finds the "that" which is of God in every man. The former is made evident in the ways of men and the goals they seek; the latter in the ways and faith of the individual. Both witnesses are parts of the secrets of the religion that is called Quakerism.

For about three-quarters of a century the study of religion and religious groups has enjoyed the fruit of work done with accuracy and enlightened by a critical appreciation of religious ideas and institutions. Aided by the progress of various sciences, it has achieved a more direct and adequate understanding of religions' growth, cultural forms and social functions, as well as its bodies of belief, doctrine and ideals. The subject, as it can now be pursued, is an important contribution to any liberal study of man and society.

In the exciting volume *The Varieties of Religious Experience*, William James offered a case-book of individual religious experience, describing, to use his own words, "experiences of individual men in their solitude, so far as they apprehend themselves to stand in relation to whatever they consider the divine." That book, written from the viewpoint of individual psychology of the early 1900's and approaching a clinical description of the religious life, is of the greatest value. But James is at pains to say that he omits from discussion that great portion of the subject which involves an analysis of the social scene in which religion takes place—that is the religious tradition, institutions and arts, and what groups of men and women do in expressing and cultivating what they together hold as sacred. This corporate feeling and action—this "togetherness" of religious behavior—is the framework within which I should like to consider the two witnesses of Quaker religious life.

The "Looking-Glass Self"

The "looking-glass self" does not reveal the secrets of the Quaker religious life. These secrets include our acceptance of the principle of the "Inner Light," our recognition of the power of the listening silence, sometimes called the "hushness," our witnesses, our service, and our "concerns"—those costly inner leadings which may, in the course of their fulfillment, take over the very life of the one they engage. The secret of the witnesses for peace and tranquility rests in our knowledge that for nearly three centuries they have been reasserted and revindicated by both revealed and secular truth. We know that at times the words have become but verbal orthodoxy. We know that these witnesses have been challenged in our contemporary lives by the dreadful potency of knowledge. We know that neither faith nor practice has fully supported the import of the mighty truths espoused by early Friends.

Today, Friends find it difficult to fully support a theory that is at once scientifically tenable and spiritually propitious. Though religiously the way seems open to us, Friends are called upon to recognize the contemporary nature of peace and tranquility, both of which are being affected by the stark facts that for many people in this huge world there is a richness of life and for others little or no life. For others there is an atmosphere of apprehension in which there is no full and free ventilation of controversial issues.

For many Friends and others, life itself has become all foreground with no horizons, reducing the opportunities in which man can at once come to terms with himself on the one hand, promote the ways of affection and love, and the ways of uninhibited exchange of thoughts and actions (safe from intrusion, control, and free from the invasion of authority) on the other. There exists within the problem of peace among men a need for combining revealed with experiential truth in order that the construction of a peaceful society may be dared without apprehension.

On the other hand there seems to be a need for a restatement of the Biblical expression "Let not your heart be troubled, neither let it be afraid." In these times the Great Emptiness in our individual lives, lives so devoid of inward peace, the statement may be minuted to read "Let your heart be troubled, but be you not afraid." Faced with new challenges in a world at war with itself in deeds as well as values; sensing man's loss of privacy in modern life, his inability to be at one with himself, Friends are called upon to follow another adventuring road that would permit them to speak truth to our times, asserting new duties that attend the new occasions for world peace, and witnessing to ways in which the ancient good of spiritual certitude (which stems from tranquility) can speak truth to Friends, to man and to government where e'er they may be.

Quakerism "Set In A Larger Place"

Eighty-odd years ago John Greenleaf Whittier, in a series of letters to the Editor of the *Friend's Review* in Philadelphia, expressed his consummate faith in the Society while saying "I am not blind to the shortcomings of Friends." He expressed his concern that they had lost so much by coldness and inactivity, by the overestimate of external observances, and the neglect of their own proper work while serving as the conscience-keepers of others. Whittier suggested that Friends were too much "at ease in Zion"; that Friends in the period of reconstruction in the United States had not been active enough "in those simple duties which we owe to our suffering fellow-creatures; that there had been a decline in practical righteousness." But," said John Whittier,

> if we look at the matter closely, we shall see that the cause is not in the central truth of Quakerism, but in a failure to rightly comprehend it; in an attempt to fetter with forms and hedge about with dogmas that great law of Christian liberty.... If we did but realize it, we are "set in a large place" (for) Quakerism, in the light of its great original truth is `"exceeding broad." As interpreted by Penn and Barclay, it is the most liberal and catholic of faiths. If we are not free, generous, tolerant; if we are not up to or above the level of the age in good works, in culture and love of beauty, order and fitness; if we are not the ready recipients of the truths of science and philosophy—in a word, if we are not full-grown men and Christians, the fault is not in Quakerism, but in ourselves.[2]

Being "set in a large place" with a revealed truth which is "exceeding broad," Friends seemed called upon to rethink their revered and ancient testimony on nonviolent forms of peacemaking between states and within men. The ever-changing lot of mortal man has in it the potency of endless change. Always within it there arise disturbers and disturbances of the peace. War is one of these disturbers and disturbances. When a nation resorts to war it uses a method of settling a dispute with another state. It may be a dispute over "honor," or trade, or any of many vast concerns. Today, it is a misuse of language to call these disputes the causes of war. They are causes of war only if war is an accepted mode of settling them. War has no cause except the intention of governments, under whatever conditions, to resort to war. As has been said so often, war is an instrument of national policy and if men should decide to abandon this instrument the alleged causes could forever exist without producing the alleged consequences. War has no cause except the intention of governments to resort to it. The mode of war has changed enormously in its character and in its consequences, and it is becoming increasingly clear that the majority of men are developing an increasing dread of it.

We all know that war has become intolerable under the conditions of our civilization. We also know that mankind has the continuing power to remake its social institutions according to its needs. We know that nothing resists the will to change these institutions except the unwillingness to change them. Friends, it would seem, are called upon to re-examine their peace testimony, to see to it that the values of their ancient witness are not imprisoned within the Society's traditions. This concern becomes a heavy one when Prime Minister Nehru says to a public meeting in New Delhi (January 30, 1958) that "the peace of the world is hanging by a slender thread. It is not the big powers alone who are to decide whether to have war or not. That is bad enough. But now one man has been given responsibility which may engulf the world in war. Thousands of pilots are flying planes carrying atom bombs day and night. If any pilot lost his mind or got flurried or misunderstood orders and released the bombs, there would be a full-scale war." He added, in a plea for effective disarmament, that the path of the cold war "will not take the peoples of the world anywhere. If that is so then the world will have to follow another path. What is that path? It is clear that the path is one in which there is no dependence on armaments. *So we reach the conclusion ultimately—that the path shown by Gandhiji and Buddha is the only path that can save the world from disaster*" (italics mine).[3]

At the 300th anniversary World Conference at Oxford, 900 Quakers from 22 countries issued a message to persons everywhere which said, in part, we seek "to substitute the institutions of peace for the institutions of war." Is it possible for our witness to the peace testimony to provide such institutions for men everywhere? Is it not possible to create a politics of peace as a living substitute for the politics of war? As national politics based on war continues to seep into every fabric of our everyday lives (at present offering to the men and women of college age and intent an opportunity to secure four years of college training at government expense, providing they agree to give twelve years to the armed services in return therefore) we must realize that our ancient truth demands newer and broader implementation. One wonders if a heart-felt concern expressed in speaking truth to power is a full and sufficient method for establishing and maintaining the truth of peace abroad and at home. The peace testimony ceaselessly calls for that "and something more" which is the essence of true religion.

Inward Peace

I would speak of tranquility or inward peace honestly, wistfully, and without fear. The Quaker doctrine of inward peace, as Howard Brinton has so effectively described it, "is not a doctrine which is unique to the Society of Friends." He states:

> In its general and essential character it can be found in all the so-called higher religions. In the seventeenth and eighteenth centuries the inward and the outward were comparatively integrated. It was a time of social pioneering in such fields as equality of sexes, races and classes, simplicity of life, peace-making, prison reform, reform of mental hospitals, abolition of slavery, and education. Yet, it was also a time of intense inwardness, when the primary emphasis was placed on divine guidance and the search for inward peace. This inwardness increased men's sensitivity to moral evils, and enabled situations to be faced freshly rather than through the obscuring haze of conventional patterns.... Modern Quakerism, affected by the prevailing trends of our time, has lost much of this inwardness. Activity continues to increase. Outward peace is sought as never before but men search less intently for the inward peace which is both source and goal of outward peace.... In recent years scientific skill has been largely used for conflict, either to promote a militant nationalism or to produce a restless insatiable desire for possessions in order to increase the sale of goods. This is not the road to peace. It is clear evidence that the inner life is evaporating out of our culture, that the soul which held the culture together is vanishing, leaving outer force as a means of providing security and unity."[4]

It seems that modern day Friends are called upon to speak the truth of inward peace to the great emptiness and aloneness of modern man. The absence of any source of guidance and illumination, the absence of a spiritual or philosophical certitude, which are said again and again to typify Western man, reveal his necessity for being at one with himself. In his "Democratic Vistas" Walt Whitman wrote:

> I should say that only in the perfect uncontamination and solitariness of individuality may the spirituality of religion come forth at all. Only here, and on such terms, the meditation, the devout ecstasy, the soaring flight. Only here, communion with the mysteries, the eternal problems.... Bibles may convey, and priests expound, but it is exclusively for the noiseless operation of one's isolated self to enter the pure ether of veneration, reach the divine levels, and commune with the unutterable.

The tranquilizer of medical science may deal with the somatic aspects of this aloneness and tension which contemporary man experiences but there are no substitutes for the loss of privacy; the ways of love and affection; the uninhibited exchange of thoughts safe from intrusion and control; for freedom from the invasion of authority. There is no doubt that the dreadful potency of knowledge, cast in an atmosphere of apprehension, has made many afraid to express any kind of independent judgment (particularly on economic and political questions) lest they be suspected of being subversive. The Quaker inward peace is at once scientifically tenable and spiritually propitious. It will permit its holders to have a religion of healthy-mindedness rather than one of weary, sin-sick souls. It will permit us to deal with the uneasiness of man in society, and harrow the ground whence comes the solution for social problems. It will provide the religious enthusiasm that makes one contemptuous of danger and willing to live on chance. It will enable us to overcome the current popular fear of intelligence as one of the great dangers of our times. And since every powerful emotion and truth has its own myth-making tendency, it will enable us to bear witness to the necessity for making the attainment of peace a process that requires not only that we work on and with governments, but that we also cleanse our hearts and minds of the poisons that make military, economic, racial and religious conflicts seem reasonable: pride, fear, greed, prejudice, envy and contempt. As one of the Princeton University seniors wrote in that challenging volume *The Unsilent Generation*, the development of these qualities will enable one to have the unimpeachable integrity, the keenness of mind, and the stability and balance needed in one's approach to any problem.

The development and maintenance of an inward peace is an inescapable preliminary to the great mission Friends have set for themselves in every community throughout the world. This personal peace requires that each of us within his or her own field of action—the home, the neighborhood, the city, the region, the school, the meeting, the factory, the mine, the office, the union—must carry into his immediate day's work a changed attitude toward all his functions and obligations. The collective effort of Friends cannot rise to a higher level than his or her personal scale of values. It underlies our testimony that once this change is effected in the person, the group will record and respond to it.

Four Roads

If the mission of Friends is as George Fox expounded it; if the qualities of Friends are as William Penn described them; if the responsibility of Friends is as John Woolman lived it, then the challenge to Friends is to develop and maintain a constancy between their religious beliefs and their social practices. John Woolman in a testimony before a Meeting of English Friends suggested that if they were to attain the right true ends of peace they must travel four roads—*The Damascus Road* with its drawings, concerns the awakenings; *The Jerusalem Road*, a journey requiring conscience and a complete commitment to a rightly fashioned life; *The Jericho Road* with its action and service in the cause of one's belief; and *The Emmaus Road*, the way of true fellowship with one's fellowman. Damascus was the oldest continuously existing city in the world. It was the scene of Paul's conversion. It was also an oasis of living green between the Lebanon range and the desert. Mohammed refused to go there, saying when asked for a reason, "I shall have to go to heaven when I die; so why should I enter Damascus now." Jerusalem, then sacred to Jews, Christians, and Mohammedans alike, stood on two rocky hills. Enclosed by walls, and pierced by eight gates, it was difficult to reach. Jericho was always being sacked and rebuilt, requiring incessant activity to stay in the same place. The Emmaus Road—a not much traveled road on which the Apostles communed together, reasoned, and discovered their religious insights. It was here, Luke reports, that the Apostles discovered Jesus as one "who was a prophet mighty in deed before God and all the people."

Friends have traveled these adventuring roads with respect to many phases of human existence. They have spoken truth to ecclesiastical power and have been able to develop and maintain a religious amity that is at once peaceful and peace-promoting. They have been inventive in their ability to survive without creed and strangling theology. They have spoken truth to *political power* and have been able to maintain the dignity of a precious religion in having their views on oath-taking and military service accepted as individual and religious rights that should not be impaired. They have established, and in some instances kept open, channels of international peace when governments have failed to do so. They have spoken truth to *tribal power* which permitted the exploitation of racial and ethnic groups and have thereby promoted the causes of racial peace and human dignity. They have spoken truth to *economic power* and have taken stands on the exploitation of human labor, the manufacture of armaments, and the profits derived from each. And they have *spoken truth to their Meetings*, causing members to act within the spirit of the Society in matters of membership, marriage, education and other problems of the social order.

All of these have been great testimonies to the witnesses of peace and its abiding nature. These facts do illustrate that Friends can achieve peace once they are so minded. They further indicate that a peace witness, once projected and sustained, does not last for all time. There is ever the urgency that the cause of peace must remain under the watchful care of Friends concerns. Thus, today, the cause of peace may be observed in noting that there remains a need for demonstrating the peace testimony in the relations between church and state here in Philadelphia, in the United States, and throughout the world. The peace truth must again be demonstrated to political power as the increasing demands of the military order are superimposed on the normal activities of citizenship. Does this warrant more precise political action in a Friendly manner? Truth must be spoken to the prejudicial and discriminatory aspects of tribal power wherein racial and ethnic groups continue to experience social indignities and denials that are creating new human disunities in Africa, Asia, and the United States. The demonstration of this truth must be based on the fact that the nearer we come to making men free of the disabilities we have heaped upon them, the more closely our actions will affect our own private lives. The difficult witness lies ahead. Friends have been wary in speaking truth to economic power. Are there no problems? Or are these problems of economic peace too close for comfort? No matter what our answer we may find a leading in the historic experience of our Society.

The Dynamics of Peace

The dynamics of peace is the perpetual challenge of the Society of Friends. It is to be ever alert to the problems man faces as he tries to achieve a sane and healthy balance between the world-he-believes in and the world-he-lives-in. Failure to achieve this balance is ever a clear and present danger to humanity. The witness of Friends has provided comfort where there was despair, and hope where there was uncertainty. To the present and the future, girded with the quest for world peace and an inward tranquility, Friends seemed called upon to continue their witness and to encompass this witness with two safeguards. The one is courage which stems from their inward peace and which will give them that courage which Plato described as "Wisdom concerning dangers." The second safeguard is contained in Timothy's letter to the Christian church in Laodicea. The church was advised to be spiritually and socially keen and alert and to keep its "commission free from stain." How better can one translate into effective social action that which is of God in every man?

Source
Ira de A. Reid, "Peace and Tranquility: The Quaker Witness," William Penn Lecture. (Philadelphia: Young Friends Movement, 1958). Excerpts taken from pp. 3–27.

Negro Immigration to the United States

[*This paper was presented at the meeting of the Southern Sociological Society in Birmingham, Alabama, April 2, 1937. Ira Reid was then on the faculty of Atlanta University.*]

"Africans, Black" is the cover-all term employed by the Department of Labor's Bureau of Immigration and Naturalization to cloak with racial identification all persons of Negro extraction admitted to or departing from the United States. It is a conjure-word that metamorphoses persons who, prior to embarking for the United States, may have been known as "coloured," "mulatto," or "black," some having nationality identification without benefit of race.

Between 1899 and 1936 approximately 145,000 "Africans, Black" were legally admitted to the United States. A small number, one says. Yes, quantitatively perhaps, a very small number. But, it represents a group regarded as "utterly unassimilable" in the majority population as the native Negro population it joins. But, "Africans, Black" do come to our shores; furthermore, "Africans, Black" do assimilate. They come from the West Indies, Central America, South America, Africa, and the Azorean Islands. What type of assimilation does take place? How is it effected? And, with what significant effects upon the national social economic structure? Answers to these and other questions are to be found in the analysis of social problems this immigration presents.

Singularly, this question of Negro immigration has received only passing attention in the myriad works on immigration problems and policies in the United States. A sentence here and a paragraph there—frequently to the effect that this immigration is not extensive—represent the sum total of references in immigration literature. When, however, it is realized that the present Negro foreign-born population numbers approximately 100,000 persons; that more than 90 percent of it resides in the following cities: New York, N.Y., Boston, Mass., Cambridge, Mass., and Miami, Fla.; and that in these cities it forms from 15 to 25 per cent of the total Negro population, the subject becomes significant. Significant because these small aggregates of Negroes, with their diverse customs, traditions, institutions and ideas of homeland, are not only modifying their own culture to conform to the status accorded Negroes in the United States, but are in turn modifying the culture of the American Negro in these communities and in the country as a whole. Denied the freedom of social circulation to which many of them have been accustomed—in theory, if not in practice—they frequently refuse to let the status of the Negro become fixed at a subordinate level.

Conflict situations between the foreign-born Negro groups and the native ones, between two Negro immigrant groups, and between different generations of the same immigrant group make us aware of definite phases of social process in the phenomenon. Negro immigration being largely from the Americas does not possess the outward manifestations of the stranger that are common to European immigrants. The "standardized externals" make for less visibility. The student, therefore, must probe more deeply to find and identify the symbols and patterns of the homeland's culture. Negro immigrants are admitted in such small numbers that they find their way almost unnoticed into groups and situations that have existed for years. Here the old heritage has been so modified and the influence of the newcomer is so slight, that the differences between the "new" and the "old" immigrant are not at once evident.

However, the Negro immigrant group presents a field for the analysis of these processes of accommodation and assimilation. While it is generally accepted that individuals reared in one culture and migrating to another can never be completely absorbed in the new culture, it is noticeable that the old culture fades more and more as time goes on, and that there is always a residue of habits, ideas, points of view and ways of doing things which are never completely changed. For this reason, a great many of the adjustments that the Negro foreign-born population faces are compromises or accommodations. Sufficient changes take place to permit the newcomer to live under new conditions without coming into open conflict with them, but the resultant behavior is something new. No better example of the behavior exists than that indicated in the rise and development of Marcus Garvey's Universal Negro Improvement Association.

But the interesting factor of adjustment, the factor that distinguishes the adjustment of Negro immigrants from that of white immigrants, lies in the foreign-born Negro's dual adjustment, involving not only a reorganization of the inter-racial processes in this country. Every foreign-born Negro must readjust the concepts of "class" and "caste" to which he has been accustomed in terms of the United States' racial pattern. He has left a setting where he was one of the subjugated majority, or a hybrid status thereof, to come to one where he is one of the underprivileged racial minority, which is permitted no hybrid status.

The Negro immigrant enters the United States with benefit of official support from his native island. Moving into a few centers of Negro population in large numbers, threatening the existing order of racial things, he lays the foundation for conflict. One factor only prevents the conflict from becoming intense, the visibility of Negro immigrants is low. Except for those who are Spanish or Portuguese-speaking, and who usually move into their own language groups, the external characteristics are the same. Looking alike, they are not inherently isolated; differing in mores, they are isolated.

The first contacts of the native and foreign-born Negro groups are not of the conflict type. They are accompanied by the usual fear, uncertainty, and curiosity. There tends to be a symbiotic, categoric type of contract, which later becomes a social relation. The nature of the initial relationship determines the nature of future relationships. The first clashes between the native and foreign-born Negro involve questions of status. These are temporarily accommodated. As the immigrant is numerically weaker, he is forced to subordinate his wishes and desires to those of the majority group. But this group that comes over for economic and utilitarian purposes soon seeks status, recognition, position, and prestige within the existing political and moral order. This struggle is at the root of such conflict as exists between the native and foreign-born Negro.

The culture of the Negro immigrant is not able to survive the intensity of the resultant subtle conflict, whether it be reflected in the term "monkey-chaser," the aspersion cast upon the Garvey movement, or the effort to have foreign-born Negroes deported. As a result the culture of the immigrant tends to disintegrate. The partial isolation set up by the conflict makes necessary a greater dependence upon the native Negro group. The immigrant must reevaluate his culture in terms of his needs, and satisfy these needs in terms of the native Negro's cultural adaptation. As, and if, these various immigrant cultures break, the Negro immigrant becomes a part of the native Negro community. This process is followed more readily by the English-speaking Negro group than by those of other languages. But most importantly in the whole process of adjustment is the fact that while the Negro immigrant may rise in the economic scale by coming to the United States, he loses status as an individual and seeks to acquire a new status, which, while more profitable in facilitating economic adjustment, is wont to promote personal disorganization and additional conflict.

Early in the conflict between the two groups there tends to rise the intra-group counterpart of what Park calls the "marginal" man. This is the immigrant who first loses the traditional and externally obvious aspects of his culture and assimilates the standards of the larger and predominant group. The immigrant is not marginal if he is accepted by the native-born but he is frequently not so readily accepted. Under such conditions he is neither completely foreign-born nor native in terms of this culture. As was frequently the case during the 1920's, failure to acquire status so easily leads to the immigrant-consciousness, to the immigrant rebellion against being treated as a pariah. If he is a person who has previously enjoyed high social status, or who is capable of influencing the masses, he articulates the group's grievances. As the group experiences the same treatment he becomes a leader, and foreign-born consciousness and movements, such as the Universal Negro Improvement Association, arise. Thus, Garvey aided and abetted the process of the intra-group conflict, but he did not initiate it.

In defense, the native-born group develops and formulates stereotypes, myths and ideologies justifying its superiority over the immigrant, and designs methods to insure it. Any myth that will give credence to its ideology is employed. Prejudices arise as the immigrant menaces the partially accommodated status of the native-born. Such reactions in course produce a sentiment of nationality consciousness, which is reflected in one instance by a double-reverse method of universal black unity—Back to Africa, and in others by immigrant solidarity, pride, and national loyalties. All of these, of course, are directed toward securing status and rights. The problem becomes complicated because in the alignment of issues the status and rights of immigrants have usually been higher and greater "back home" than in the United States. Nevertheless this conflict indicates the indefiniteness of the "place" to which the Negro immigrant is assigned, not by the white population, but by the native Negro group.

The problem is further complicated by the tendency of the native group to lump all Negroes of foreign birth in one group. Virgin Islanders with American citizenship rate no higher in group evaluation than the Jamaican, a British subject. The conflict between native and foreign-born therefore becomes not one of race—but of absorption and assimilation in the common culture and the social order. In this study we have endeavored to identify some of the elements present in the problem of the Negro immigrant and his adjustment—elements that give it dimension. The statistical facts in themselves give no adequate interpretation of the problem. Equally as important are the attitudes and interests maintained by each group—what they think about themselves and what they think about the others.

The most significant differences between the native and foreign-born Negro groups are those of social backgrounds. These differences run the gamut of human experience and include the variations in the social settings of immigrant and native. Of particular moment in this connection is the immigrant's background of either a tripartite color system, or one where color was not a primary social factor.

The immigrant is brought into a relatively isolated, partially assimilated Negro group in which he becomes part and parcel of a socially restricted population. Neither the immigrant nor the native is accepted as part of the dominant white society. The former having been more accustomed to fuller participation reacts more drastically than does the more accommodated native-born. In gaining greater economic security, with restricted occupational mobility, he has sacrificed the rights of broad social participation. The immigrant moving from an area where he was the racial, if not the economic, dominant majority adjusts less easily to the fishnet-like separation of the races in the United States. Diverse cultural heritages tend to accentuate the maladjustments. As social relations and artificial values develop, the inter-racial prejudices develop, the process being no different from that obtaining in other forms of social contact between groups of diverse cultural backgrounds.

The presence of these two groups in the same area presents interesting parallels. The native-born Negro's church has been an agency of racial reform headed by his own leaders, emphasizing racial respect and programs for social reform. It was a tremendous integrating force, void of formalism, full of emotion. The formalism of the immigrant's church served as a compensation for the social disabilities he experienced. Pastored chiefly by non-Negroes it rigidly adhered to the ritualistic service, avoided championing causes of immediate import, was dignified, aloof and "respectable." The change is being experienced in the transplanted immigrant's church, for if it would survive it must meet the problems of its members.

Each group lacked social solidarity with the societal whole and developed mutual benefit societies—but their relative importance within each group is significant. Among the immigrants, at home or abroad, the mutual benefit principle is still important; at home because of the absence of insurance and the persistence of economic-social relations within the primary groups; abroad, because of the change of habitat and the need for mutual protection. The development of the insurance principle in the United States made great inroads into the native Negro's benefit societies, and was offset only by an increasing mobility after 1920. The survival rate of the native group's societies however is lower than that of the immigrant's. The "Sons and Daughters" of Virginia, Georgia, and South Carolina wane as the local interests of New York, New Jersey, and Pennsylvania increase.

Each group tends to find a vicarious comfort in the influence exerted on the affairs of the other. The development of cultural interests by the immigrant group, particularly, is pursued in part as a defense of its insecure position. There is pride in the memory of the late comedian Bert Williams as a West Indian almost equal to the appreciation of his great art. The names of Denmark Vesey who led "the most elaborate insurrectionary project ever formed by American slaves, and came the nearest to a terrible success"; John B. Russwurm, the first college graduate and the first Negro newspaper publisher; Marcus Garvey, in his hey-day; Peter Jackson, of boxing fame; Casper Holstein, the Virgin Island philanthropist; Matzeliger, the inventor; Samuel Ward, co-worker with Garrison and Lovejoy; Robert Brown Elliott, attorney general, speaker of the State assembly and twice elected representative from South Carolina in the United States Congress during Reconstruction; Peter Ogden, organizer of the first Odd Fellows Lodge for Negroes in New York City; Prince Hall, founder of Free Masonry among Negroes in the United States; Arthur A. Schomburg, foremost bibliophile; Edward W. Blyden, former Liberian Minister to London; Claude McKay, the poet-novelist; Judge James S. Watson—and others, become important to the nationality-conscious immigrant as much because they represent foreign-born Negroes who "made good," as because of their achievements. Pride in having representatives who have punctured the larger universal becomes an important constructive force not only in facilitating the participation in the general culture, but also in perpetuating the group in isolation. Their leaders, even as do the native Negro's and the white immigrant's, tend to become the Moses or the Messiah of the group's interests.

The Negro immigrant is beyond a doubt more radical than the native. He was more radical in his various home islands; the mere emigration therefrom indicated a break with certain traditional values. But protests against social and economic conditions are more pronounced among groups not so adjusted to their peculiar functioning in the new country. Furthermore, the West Indian immigrant has long fostered a movement to provide better, more representative government for the islands. The fight for federation of the British possessions; the historic importance of Hayti's rebellion and consequent status as the first republic of the Antilles; the representation in Paris of the French Islands; the Virgin Islander's fight for political freedom, representation, better government, and, now, home-rule; the chaotic uprisings in Puerto Rico—all these have engendered in the immigrant a sympathetic and aggressive attitude on matters of internal difficulty, and have led him to wonder why twelve million Negroes cannot get a mere anti-lynching bill through Congress. In the States the programs the Negro immigrants originate are seldom those with economic radicalism, but a racial radicalism to stimulate group pride and group solidarity.

The traditional background of the Negro immigrant varies from that of the native-born in other ways. The institutions of the state, religion—even public opinion—have exercised a much more rigid and uniform control over the immigrant. In the areas of greatest Negro concentration in the United States, the Negro's historical experience has been that the law and public opinion served to arrest rather than promote his complete adjustment. Here not only does the individual come more frequently into contact with the agencies of the law, but there is less respect for the institution. Thus, personal problems involving standards for children become important in the parent-child relationship of the immigrant family. "Back home," questions of morals would have been covered by the mores—here those mores are repudiated. Does not the child become non-foreign by so doing? Thus the child of foreign-born parents, or the immigrant child, is subject to a double social maladjustment because of the self-consciousness of being Negro and West Indian. These conditions affect the maladjusted adult as well. Each tends to become resentful—and not to "know his place" in inter-racial relations. But while this failure to be or to stay "put" may be a liability and cause loss of status in Negro-white relations, it makes for position and prestige within the racial minorities—foreign-born and native-born—and with the "radical" groups.

The intra-group cleavages are accentuated by the presence of an immigrant population. While all Negroes as a horizontal group may rank a wee bit lower than the whites, within the racial group these gradations are of several types.

1. Those who have achieved financial success.
2. Those who have high occupational ranking, particularly in fields where there are few Negroes.
3. Those who are in the public eye.
4. The "Race Leaders."

Many Negro immigrants must go into a mental reverse to accept such stratification, for many of the positions and occupations regarded as important in the United States would be frowned upon in the homeland—being a policeman, for example. Furthermore, unrestricted mobility in the Negro group permits the sharecropper's son to become a leading luminary in the Negro world. This would not have been so possible in a color-class structured society. One West Indian commented as followed upon the naming of a prominent man of foreign birth to an important public post—"Why the very idea! I would not even deign to speak to the fellow at home."

Even as do the white immigrants, the Negro immigrants, particularly the British West Indians, bring a zest for learning that is not typical of the native-born population; high schools and colleges in New York City have an unusually high foreign-born Negro representation. Between 1867 and 1932, Howard University had more than one thousand West Indians in its student body. It seems a justifiable opinion that Negroes, foreign and native, and Jews have developed an almost exaggerated interest in higher education, as an avenue of escape equal to the accumulation of wealth. About the West Indian Negro, particularly, there has arisen the highly exaggerated and mistaken notion that he is naturally "smarter," and more intelligent than the native Negro. And though Smith has pointed out that "the scholarship of the West Indian student in proportion to his numbers has been above average,"[5] this may mean nothing more than that the West Indian students are a more highly selected group than the native-born. The selective migration of the better educated West Indian has been a factor in the relatively high proportion of honors they have obtained in schools of the United States.

The racial amalgam represented by the native-born and the West Indian Negro is probably the heterogeneous stock in the world. Yet the learned reactions of the particular geographical and cultural settings have such deep emotional content that actions which do not conform to the prevailing norms arouse immediate and violent emotional reactions from people who live in the culture in which immigrants are prevalent. Thus, the native-born Negro's reaction to the immigrant ways is immediate and sometimes violent. One simply does not do things that way, he says. It is not in accord with the unconscious scheme of behavior he has acquired. The Negro immigrant therefore must learn to adjust himself to the new cultural environment, if he would survive. And even if he only superficially accepts the current mores, and, although his temporary isolation may bring about the creation of special cultural forms and practices within his own group, he realizes that he can only succeed as he adapts himself to the larger, the dominant, culture.

But one question, more or less academic, remains unanswered for the color-class conscious foreign-born Negro—why do native-born Negroes object to stratification on the basis of color-class when it is practiced in their everyday lives, within and without the group? So far there has been only one overt reply, the rise of "black nationalism," which has not only advocated the non-patronage of concerns not employing Negroes, but has openly and vigilantly, with fang and claw, opposed the affiliation of Negroes and various associations of the Socialist and Communist groups whose racial appeals are based upon the uniting of white and black workers. Meanwhile, the movement for naturalization continues. The barring of aliens from employment on public works, proposals frequently advanced for excluding aliens from relief rolls, are considerations which impel the Negro alien to seek naturalization. Recent European disturbances and the anomalous conditions of English affairs in India and Africa have led many to the conclusion that naturalization in the United States may be the better part.

All in all, the presence of a foreign Negro population has broadened the social vision of the native group. It has fostered and compelled unity and has certainly accelerated progress. The complexities of social process have obtained within the Negro group in more intricate variety than are even known in the predominant white group. And interestingly enough, the attitudes of that predominant white group exercise little influence upon these complexities and conditionings, except that the inter-racial prejudices and acts of suppression may increase the very qualities against which they are directed, and help to speed up the very forces of aggressiveness and self-assertion in the direction that prejudice would suppress them. For here is an activity in social process that is born of injustices and this partial accommodation to the predominant culture. And while these injustices and this partial accommodation may present tragic consequences for the individual, and temporary maladjustments for the group, they represent the race's one real and vital asset, determining the future character of social relationships between the races.

Source
Ira de A. Reid, "Negro Immigration to the United States," *Social Forces*, vol. 16, no. 3 (March 1938), pp. 411–417.

Methodological Notes for Studying the Southern City

[*This paper was read before the Southern Sociological Society in Knoxville, Tennessee, April 6, 1940.*]

The spirited and careful development of regional studies in the South during the last ten years has made increasingly evident the dearth of our knowledge about the southern city and its role in the regional economy. If the function of regional social research is to define and analyze the processes which give unity and meaning to the life of an area, and to indicate the actualities and possibilities of collective life in the regions discovered, there must be some niche in its formidable wall for including a penetrating and scientific analysis of the South's cities and towns. This point of view is expressed because: (1) There exists an apparently catholic opinion that southern cities are different from cities in other regions; (2) The data upon which such conclusions are based appear, in the main, to be based upon quantitative, categorical, and frequently stereotyped indices which do not permit a full answer to the "why" of these differences; and (3) the component parts of the suggested and implied categories of indices that might explain these differences need further examination.

It is the purpose of this paper (1) to present a profile of the southern city as seen by students and investigators, and (2) to posit some problems for research needed to fit present and future studies or urban phenomena in the larger framework of regional and subregional significance.

I

Most of the recent popular writers on the southern city seem to write to the tune of the bromide attributed to Abraham Cowley, who wrote some 250 years ago, "God the first garden made, and the first city Cain." Among the first of these analysis was George R. Leighton's impressive and realistic analysis of Birmingham.[6] Here in 1937 was a city of "perpetual promise" that was the "worst hit town in the country" in the 1935 depression; was an overseer's capital, and was dominated by absentee landlordism. It has the lowest per capita public expenditure, more illiteracy than any other city with a population between 200,000 and 300,000; next to the highest venereal disease rates. It ranked eighth from the bottom among cities of its size in the amount spent on education, and sixth from the bottom among cities of its size in appropriation for public health. It is described as a "loan shark's paradise," for wage executions in a Birmingham rolling mill averaged 651 per 1000 in 1933, and interest rates on small loans ran from 200 to 540 percent. "In that year," states the author, "it was estimated that loan sharks were taking a million dollars a year out of Birmingham. And here again, like magic in the Magic City, the absentee landlord appears: about 70 percent of the sharks represent outside companies."[7] The author observes that Birmingham's existence rests on the iron and steel industry, and therein democracy never had a chance.

Baltimore is not southern in regional reference, but the picture presented in a recent article,[8] describes it as a "gracious lady" now "grown and coarse and harsh," sitting in "smug contemplation of her navel, ignoring a thousand evils—lethargy the most vicious of them all." Baltimore is described as languid, "the smallest city in America—except for Boston," possessing "all the set conservatism of a pre-Civil War southern town, and flaunting one of the most blue-blooded aristocracies in the new world. She also tolerates a hundred thousand unblessed slum dwellers and its social structure is frozen into a rigid caste system."[9] Baltimore, says the author, has made enormous concessions to attract industrialists, has a population that has no aversion to machine government, has a labor movement that is "incredibly weak," and is a city where the emancipation of the Negro is "relatively a fiction."

Hamilton Basso was more critically analytical in his politics-centered article, "Can New Orleans Come Back?"[10] The Crescent City—Latin and Catholic, pleasure loving and easy-going, differing from the rest of the Anglo-Saxon Protestant South as does, say, Marseilles from Bristol is "the most snobbish city in the United States."

New Orleans' political background is rooted in the Reconstruction Period, maintains the author, a period which "established, in short, the theory that graft is not only legitimate but just. And New Orleans, perhaps more than any other city, responded accordingly." The present apathy of New Orleans to its political plight is summed up in three reasons, the third and most important of which "is probably contained in the fact that New Orleans, for all her cosmopolitan atmosphere, is truly a backward city. The problems now agitating many American municipalities—housing, labor reform, for example, or public ownership of utilities—seem barely to penetrate the New Orleanian, the 'man in the street' seems untouched by the politico-social tumult of the past decade."

David L. Cohn's nostalgic picture of New Orleans reflects another aspect of this southern city.[11] In "New Orleans—the City That Care Forgot," you are advised "when you tear yourself away from New York and begin to see the United States, you must see New Orleans." Later it is added that "In the store windows along Rampart [Street] you will find such exotica as pistols, brass knuckles, and dirks freely and publically displayed amid a jumble of guitars, jews' harps, accordions, hunting boots, underwear, and suitcases. And all this is the South—the South of laughter, love, music, gayety and sudden death. It is the universal law of crime everywhere on earth that violence is greatest in southern countries."[12]

Charleston, South Carolina, came in for its "Caining" in Twig's, "Charleston the Great Myth."[13] To this author, "Charleston had had its day." It is a poor man's town, not antique, just old. It has no homes—just houses. Its lethargy is due not to climate—just laziness. Its pathologies are due, not to high spirits—just crime. And Charleston survives like an old woman who has lived too long, disfigured with age, forever dying, yet always still alive. Actually, hers is a kind of life beyond the grave.[14]

II

Not all of the studies of southern cities have been picturesque. A few years ago Atlanta decided that its city government needed study. The National Municipal League's analysis of the city illustrates a purposeful investigation relating its problems to those of the wider region.[15] Here Atlanta is revealed as a city, grown through annexation, sprawled over two counties. Its political boundaries do not coincide with its broad social and economic interests. It is a city of four autonomous school systems whose *only* likeness is a term of 180 days. It is a "branch house" town with 1,500 branches of national business concerns. It is a city of office workers receiving moderate pay. It has a smaller community wealth than many cities, for the profits made here go to the home offices. The heads of these branch offices may be moved from Atlanta at any time, consequently they show little civic interest. Many never register to vote or become active in politics. The net result of this is a city poor in pocket and lacking civic interest. The city, which ranks 32nd in population, 14th in bank clearings, and 19th in postal receipts, ranks next to the lowest of eleven comparable cities in total and per capita contributions to its community chest. In commenting on this fact, the report says, "this may be partially explained by the fact that many persons in Atlanta assume heavy responsibilities in the care of Negroes connected with their families."[16]

Even more revealing is the observation that "a city like Atlanta is carrying a heavy burden because its proletarian population is so far inferior, in earning and spending capacity, to the lower classes in northern cities. The responsibilities of the white population—relic of a patriarchal era—are only another visible element of this situation. It is natural to find, then, lower property valuations in Atlanta than in comparable cities, *except other southern cities*. It is not surprising that Atlanta's building costs, rents, wages, and other elements in the cost of living for all except the elite, are low as compared with those prevailing in the East and North. "In our opinion, continues the report, "Atlantans are less able to pay taxes than the inhabitants of cities of comparable size in the North, just as they are able to pay less for food, clothing, housing, and the other necessities of life.[17]

In the investigative types of studies there have been two major investigations of American cities using selected cultural, social, and economic indices for evaluation and comparison. Ogburn's study of the *Social Characteristics of American Cities*[18] shows that the cities of the South, when compared with cities of other regions, show the lowest percentage of immigrants, the lowest percentage of men, higher birth and death rates, lowest rents, lower wages in manufacturing establishments and stores, lowest percentages of adult population paying income taxes, the smallest percentage of workers in manufacturing, and the largest in trade and transportation, smallest in the higher callings, or the professions, and the highest percentage in religion, law and medicine.

These cities have large percentages of widowed persons and domestic servants, and low percentages of homeowners. They have the largest percentage of families with lodgers, and the largest percentage of hotel keepers. They also have the lowest costs of government, low taxes, low government expenditures for health, public recreation, libraries and schools—and a high percentage of debt. But these differences are measured only by the structural indices.

Thorndike and Woodyard, in their 120-indices analysis of 117 cities, 22 of which were southern, 14 being in the Southeast, observed that in American cities "size is unimportant. Latitude is important probably chiefly by reason of other factors which have become associated with it in this country, especially in the Southeastern states. This complex matter may best be left for study with more extensive data and more refined methods. The same is true for the percentage of Negroes in the population."[19] Later the authors observe in interpretation one series of correlations, undoubtedly affected by the inclusion of southern cities, that "*nothing more is needed to explain the negative correlation than the density of the Negro element and whatever other factors are associated therewith.*"

Mauldin's study of migration to Knoxville, Tennessee[20] concludes that "there is no evidence that residence in the city raised the achievement scores of migrant children," and that "there is no evidence that the school system itself is chiefly responsible for this condition, rather it is probable that the entire urban environment acts favorably upon the migrants."[21]

In explaining the high urban crime index of the Southern States, Harry Elmer Barnes, citing Lottier, maintains that "far and away the greatest prevalence of murder and assault—crimes of violence—is to be found in the Southern States, especially those of the Southeast and Gulf area. This is the natural outgrowth, on the one hand, of a caste society given to lynching to preserve discipline, and on the other hand, of the feud traditions among families in the mountainous areas."[22]

Over and above studies of the aforementioned types there are a few studies that have endeavored to give more incisive treatment to the structure and content of the southern city. Boyd's *Story of Durham* is a social history that provides many leads and clues for the objective student.[23] Mrs. Johnson's *Social History of North Carolina*[24] has indicated developments in urban areas of that state neglected in many previous studies of the area.

These studies (and Lyle Saxon's *Fabulous New Orleans* might also be included in the group) seem to indicate that a tremendous gap has been left in our program of studying and analyzing the region in terms of the growth of its cities. Such studies as these give us comparative knowledge of our cities in time and space, and avoid the provincialism—alleged to be typical of modern urban sociology—of treating the contemporary city form as if it were in a sociological sense a final one.[25]

III

Moving toward the type of analysis which the southern city should have if its growth, character, and influence are to be made an integral part of a program for understanding the region, are the Matherly analysis of the structures and compositions of the southern city as reflected in census data[26] and Spengler's application of population theory to the South in terms of its metropolitan growth process and the influence of agricultural regions.[27] Park's analysis of "Southern Towns and Cities," in which the roles of such factors as homogeneity of population, value of tradition and family, local traits and idiosyncrasies, and the color of surrounding territory, indicate opportunities for the analysis of the city as a "way of life."[28] Hoffer's reported studies of Roanoke, Virginia, seem to indicate on a larger scale the type of research project toward which urban studies should be moving. These studies of population and culture characteristics deal with the ecology of the city, the history and functions of institutions and the institutionalized forms of social life, and the nature and trend of Roanoke's cultural life.[29]

Finally, a study made some fifteen years ago by Woofter,[30] which dealt with the migration of Negroes to northern cities, gives one of the first leads to studying the internal structure of the southern city. In this study, Woofter indicated that each city had a physical pattern of its own, determined by the percentage of Negroes in the total population, distribution of Negro employment, distribution of areas where property is within means of Negro families, the attitudes of people toward segregation and the rate of expansion of business and manufacturing sections. Furthermore, this analysis of 7 northern and 9 southern cities indicated two patterns of racial aggregation in southern cities. Richmond, Virginia, typified the larger cities, in which the Negro population was highly concentrated in several rather large parts of the city, and lightly scattered in others. Charleston, South Carolina, was cited as typical of Negro residents' concentration in the older southern cities and towns, where there is a heavy scattering of Negroes throughout the area. Woofter noted that the residential separation of Negroes even in southern cities was never complete, though all cities had some areas where the majority of Negroes lived.

The general summary of this *potpourri* of studies might be better interpreted through Parks' statement "Every possible forecast implies that the continued growth of the city, with a concomitant advance of industrialism, will tend to standardize our cities, and make them completely like all other American cities. But at present they remain a group apart, small and uncertain of their destiny, but stamped with the atmosphere of an Old South that gives to each, in varying degrees, a character and individuality all its own."[31] Assuming this conclusion to be true, what is indicated therein for the researcher on the southern city?

IV

Above all, it seems, looms the necessity for studying not only the forms and conditions of southern city life, but also its purposes and emergents—its human and cultural attributes. Such studies as have been available either have concentrated very largely upon population statistics or "color stuff" or have dealt insufficiently with matters of its institutions, social complexes, and what Munford has described as the "social esthetic structures" in terms of their function and meaning as integral parts of the urban habitat; studies that show the involved interplay between the physical environment and the conditioned functions of life on one hand and the social milieu and the released functions—in which choice, desire, fantasy, and purpose play a part—on the other."[32]

Southern cities appear to have a wide range of morphological variations; their patterns and configurations appear to have been determined, to some extent, at least, by deliberate human choices and pecuniary motivations. In these cities, the presence of a biracial population with sets of dual institutions; the unique sets of symbols and stereotypes which govern; the apparent ineffectiveness of territorial interest save in terms of the region; the role of formally organized groups in terms of the region; the personality politics; the fact that urban population accretions differ in form, quality, and quantity from those of other regions, do but further indicate the need expressed by Odum and Moore, who in regarding the city and country as one in fact, if not in feeling, observed that "the relations between the city and the country need more study than [they have] yet received, especially since it is generally agreed that the city will continue to grow for some decades at least.[33]

And standardized studies that are to be made in the near future might well be devoted to any one of several fields. There is need, of course, for the variability survey to explore social process in the southern city.

There is especial need for standardized studies in the fields of *Population* with reference to demography and ecology—the determination of social and governmental areas and their relation to rural and urban organization; and, with the development of the census tract form and technique in more southern cities, there is an increasingly great opportunity to establish the geographical approach to the study of local organizations, land occupancy, and spatial relations.

In the field of *Social Organization* there is need for studies that will indication both the general and biracial types of social forms, social structure of institutions and groups, social status and social participation. The effect new means of communication are having upon social organization seems particularly significant.

The field of *Social Psychology* seems to offer unlimited opportunities for the exploration of the psychological side of the social organization of the southern city, the folkways and mores of the people, personality, mass movements, leadership and social stratification within the community, white and black.

In the field of *Social Dynamics* standardized studies might be made of the process of social change per se in the southern city, noting changes in form and function that have occurred, changes that are likely to occur, and the factors and processes involved.

Many of our studies have been in the field of *Social Pathology*, dealing with maladjusted individuals, groups, classes and populations, but few studies have been made in the pathologies of our institutions.

All in all, there is a need for definitive studies in the field of methodology to add to our studies of phenomena. Such studies might be general or monographic ones of urban areas or problem situations therein, avoiding what has been so marked a criticism of many urban studies that they generalize results without a proper sampling knowledge. Indications that approaches to such studies have been contemplated, and that an integrated program for concerted and standardized research in this field in southern urban communities is possible, are noted in Vance's suggestion that "to study the organization of cotton marketing for the internal and export trade one would explore the question of how cities like Atlanta, New Orleans and Houston organize their hinterlands into metropolitan trade areas;[34] in Williams' suggestion that the analysis of the distribution of services of public highways and electrical power lines will give a basic approach to the interrelationships between rural and urban aggregates;[35] Speier's recommendation of an objective basis for determining social stratification—or typical behavior in relation to class alignments;[36] Warner and Davis' theory and methodology for studying the American caste principle tested in "Old Town,"[37] the Dollard and the Powdermaker approaches to the same problem in southern areas;[38] Lynd's Middletown volumes, for the participating-observing technique, though lacking in a regional point of view;[39] Guy Johnson's theory of race conflict;[40] Charles Johnson's interpretation of the role of whites and Negroes in southern communities;[41] Dollard's approach to frustration and aggression;[42] Zimmerman's thesis of centralism vs. localism in the local community and his contention that the middle classes will decline;[43] Reckless' analysis of the use of census tracts in southern cities.[44]

These studies have been cited because in several ways they have dealt with methodological approaches to what is uniformly regarded as a typical divergent chapter of southern cities when they are compared with those of other regions, namely, the presence of a large Negro population.

In addition to these sources there is a wealth of methodological suggestions to be obtained from: the basic approaches of Henry Carey, Zueblin, Turner, Geddes, J. Russell Smith, and Cooley; the specific methodological contributions of Park, Burgess, McKenzie, Ogburn, Wirth, and Carpenter; the specific analysis of the bases of urbanism in Rosenquist and Moore's analysis of Texas; the regional study; the four-dimensional approach urged by Mumford; and from the National Resources Committee's research report on urbanism. And all of these might be be shaken through the sieve provided by Gee's analysis of research barriers in the South, which, though somewhat modified by time and change, still reflects the necessity for separating intellectual and emotional sheep from goats.

The true end of the sociologist's research in the southern city should be to provide an adequate sociological analysis of the whole urban complex, studying it not only as a physical structure having a population base, a technological and ecological order, but also as a system of social organization involving a peculiarly characteristic social structure, a dual series of social institutions and a typical pattern of social relationships, as a set of attitudes and ideas differing from, yet related to, those of the surrounding rural and regional areas; and as a universe of personalities mutually affecting and engaging in typical forms of collective behavior and subject to characteristic methods of social control. Furthermore, in such studies, the present complexion of the southern city, it seems, might be regarded but as a function of its past history, and an over-all simple *a priori* hypotheses governing its growth, form, and process must be supported and tested by observation. Through such studies we might hope to bridge the gap between our knowledge of the rural and the urban forms and ways of life within the region.

Source
Ira de A. Reid, "Methodological Notes for Studying the Southern City," *Social Forces*, vol. 19, no. 2 (December 1940), pp. 228–235.

Endnotes

1 The full text of the printed lecture is available at: http://www.quaker.org/pamphlets/wpl1958a.html.

2 *The Writings of John Greenleaf Whittier* (Riverside Edition), Boston, 1889, vol. VII, "The Society of Friends," pp. 305-314.

3 "Atom Bomb in Asia Would be Dangerous," *India News*, vol. 3, no. 3 (Information Service of India, U.S. Embassy of India), February 15, 1958.

4 Brinton, Howard, "The Quaker Doctrine of Inward Peace" in Herrymon Maurer, ed., *Pendle Hill Reader*. New York: Harper, 1950, pp. 95-120.

5 Alfred Edgar Smith, "West Indians on the Campus," *Opportunity, Journal of Negro Life*, vol. 11, no. 8, pp. 238-241, August, 1933.

6 George R. Leighton, "Birmingham, Alabama—The City of Perpetual Promise," *Harpers Magazine*, 175 (August 1937), pp. 225-242.

7 *Ibid.*, p. 23.

8 Audrey Granneberg, "Indigent, Elegant Baltimore," *Forum and Century*, vol. 103, no. 2 (February 1940), pp. 54-60.

9 *Ibid.*, p. 54.

10 Hamilton Basso, "Can New Orleans Come Back?" *Forum and Century*, vol. 103, no. 2 (March 1940), pp. 124-128.

11 David I. Cohn, "New Orleans—The City That Care Forgot," *The Atlantic Monthly*, 165, no. 4 (April 1940), pp. 484-491.

12 *Ibid.*, p. 491.

13 Edward Twig, "Charleston: The Great Myth," *Forum and Century*, vol. 103, no. 1 (January 1940), pp. 1-7.

14 *Ibid.*, p. 7.

15 *The Governments of Atlanta and Fulton County, Georgia*. By the Consultant Service of the National Municipal League, New York. Published by Atlanta Chamber of Commerce, 1938.

16 *Ibid.*, p. 6.

17 *Ibid.*, pp. 6, 7.

18 W. F. Ogburn, *Social Characteristics of Cities* (Chicago: International City Managers' Association, 1937).

19 Edward L. Thorndike and Ella Woodyard, "Individual Differences in American Cities: Their Nature and Causation," *American Journal of Sociology*, XLIII, no. 2 (September 1937), pp. 191-214.

20 W. Parker Mauldin, "A Sample Study of Migration to Knoxville, Tennessee," *Social Forces*, 18, no. 3 (March 1940), pp. 360-364.

21 *Ibid.*, p.364.

22 Harry Elmer Barnes, *Society in Transition* (New York: Prentice Hall, 1939).

23 William Boyd, *The Story of Durham* (Duke University Press, 1937).

24 Guion G. Johnson, *A Social History of North Carolina* (Chapel Hill: University of North Carolina Press, 1929).

25 Vide: Lewis Mumford, *The Culture of Cities* (New York: Harcourt Brace and Company, 1938), p. 501.

26 Walter J. Matherly, "The Changing Culture of the City," *Social Forces*, 13, no. 3 (March 1935), pp. 349-357. "The Urban Development of the South," *Southern Economic Journal*, I, no. 3 (February 1935), pp. 18-26.

27 Joseph J. Spengler, "Population Problems in the South," *Southern Economic Journal*, vol. III, no. 4 (April 1937), pp. 393 ff.; vol. IV, no. 1 (July 1937), pp. 1–27; vol. IV, no. 2, pp. 131ff.

28 Edd Winfield Park, in *Culture in the South*, W.T. Couch, editor (Chapel Hill: University of North Carolina Press, 1934), pp. 501–518.

29 Noted in W.E. Cole, "Personality and Cultural Research in the Tennessee Valley," *Social Forces*, 13, no. 4 (May 1935), p. 524.

30 T.J. Woofter, *Negro Problems in Cities* (New York: Doubleday, Doran & Co., 1928).

31 Loc. Cit., p. 518.

32 Op. Cit., p. 501.

33 Howard W. Odum and Henry E. Moore, *American Regionalism* (New York: Henry Holt & Co., 1938), p. 130.

34 Rupert B. Vance, "Regional Planning with Reference to the Southeast," *Southern Economic Journal*, vol. 3, no. 1 (July 1936), p. 57.

35 B.O. Williams, "A Population Policy for the South," *Social Forces*, vol. XVI, no. 1 (October 1937), pp. 48–60.

36 Hans Speier, "Social Stratification in the Urban Community," *American Sociological Review*, vol. I, no. 1 (April 1936), pp. 193–202.

37 W. Lloyd Warner and Allison Davis, "A Comparative Study of American Caste," in *Race Relations and the Race Problem*, Edgar T. Thompson, ed. (Durham: Duke University Press, 1939).

38 John Dollard, *Caste and Class in a Southern Town* (New Haven: Yale University Press, 1937).

39 R.S. Lynd and H.M. Lynd, *Middletown* and *Middletown in Transition* (New York: Harcourt Brace and Company, 1929 and 1937).

40 Guy B. Johnson, "Patterns of Race Conflict," in *Race Relations and the Race Problem*, Edgar T. Thompson, ed. (New York: McGraw-Hill, 1934).

41 Charles S. Johnson, "Negro Personality Changes in a Southern Community," in *Race and Culture Contacts*, E. B. Reuter, ed. (New York: McGraw-Hill, 1934).

42 *Ibid.*

43 Carle C. Zimmerman, "Centralism vs. Localism in the Community," *American Sociological Review*, vol. III, no. 2 (April 1938), pp. 155–166.

44 Walter C. Reckless, "The Initial Experience with Census Tracts in a Southern City," *Social Forces*, vol. XV, no. 1 (October 1936), pp. 47–54.

V
Barrington Dunbar
(1901–1978)
edited by Paul Kriese

BARRINGTON DUNBAR was born in British Guyana and educated in the United States. He devoted his life to social work, as the director of settlement houses, camps for refugees, and other such services. He joined 57th Street Meeting in Chicago and later was active with 15th Street Meeting in New York City. Committed to both black liberation and Quakerism, he explained the Black Power movement to European Americans as a need to express rage as a step toward self-esteem. Dunbar said that it is easy for Quakers to believe in nonviolence because we are insulated from the life that poor people know, noting that we create "beautiful islands which help individuals to develop but often aren't enough concerned with the ugly world outside."

The Society of Friends and the Negro Revolution, 1964
[*This talk was presented to a meeting of the American Friends Service Committee in 1964.*]

I speak to you as a Friend. Of course, I cannot claim to be a birthright Friend. My ancestors came to America on a slave ship. But perhaps it is important for Friends to remember that George Fox was not a birthright Friend. His Quakersim was the discovery of a startling new religious insight.

What do Friends believe? It is true that Friends are not robots in the practice of their religious belief. Each one of us must respond to the light he sees. But it is equally true that unity is obtained among Friends in that we all believe that there is that of God in every man. Slavery became a matter of real concern to Friends because of this unifying belief. And through the years Friends have supported relief and social welfare programs to aid the disadvantaged, as an expression of their belief in the spiritual capacity of the human personality.

In many ways Friends have expressed concerns and lent their support to programs geared to improve race relations. Through the work camps, institutes, and projects in "industrial and community relations" of the American Friends Service Committee, young people have been brought together in new and meaningful relationships and helped to gain a perspective of urban problems that they had not had before. The American Friends Service Committee (AFSC) Merit Employment Program in urban centers of the South has helped to create jobs that heretofore were closed to Negroes, and to open channels of communication between the Negro community and the indomitable power structure of the business community. Efforts to break through the segregated patterns of suburban living have been the concern of the fair housing programs supported by regional offices of the American Friends Service Committee. Individual Friends have lent their support to the development of cooperative housing projects, such as Bryn Gweled and Tanguy, in the environs of Philadelphia.

So Friends, because of their belief and concern, have had a share in the educational and mediating process that has gradually opened up channels of communication in situations of racial distrust and misunderstanding. But the processes of "gradualism," "education," "legalism," "with all deliberate speed" have been inadequate as approaches to securing for the Negro his rights as a man and a citizen. The struggle is moving from the court rooms and conference tables to the street, and it has moved from just the South to the remainder of the country.

Friends by tradition and belief are committed to the practice of non-violence in confronting conflict situations. Through giving generously to support programs of the American Friends Service Committee, Friends have been able to express their concerns without becoming personally involved in situations of national and international turmoil. But none of us can escape involvement in the present nation-wide struggle of the Negro people. How can we escape involvement as the struggle moves to our own community? It seems to me that the individual is confronted with only two choices: to join with the Negro in upsetting the segregated pattern of his community, or join with his neighbors in resisting the intruder. Involvement in conflict and tension is so distasteful to some Friends that they may decide to remain neutral behind closed doors, but some of us can experience peace of mind even when involved in conflict because of the deep conviction that we are part of the process of change and God's creative energy in the world.

Here lies a new challenge and opportunity for service for us as individual Friends, or as supporters of the program of the American Friends Service Committee. As Friends redirect their concerns to the chaotic situation at home—to a crowded urban committee like New York City, with problems of dope addiction, youth unemployment, school drop-outs, inadequate housing, delinquency and crime—we will find additional new opportunities for service. The outstanding work of the Murrows (Hope and Dan) in converting their East Harlem project house into a haven where young people severely damaged by the defects of poverty found love, friendship, self-respect, and protection from becoming a destructive force in the community; or the program operated by Synanon House in Santa Monica, California, where drug addicts help each other to give up the "habit" and to become once again functioning members of society—these are examples of new programs that the American Friends Service Committee might like to explore further.

There is a great need for tutors to help children whose homes are inadequate to provide the resources or incentive needed to facilitate studying at home. Inter-city work camps, institutes, and other educational projects aimed at bringing people together to communicate with each other, and to be given a clearer perspective of national, international, and community problems, must continue to be included in the overall program of the American Friends Service Committee. It would seem advisable to give more emphasis to the emerging problems of American communities, even at the cost of de-emphasizing overseas relief programs.

Finally, each one of us, wherever we are, whatever our calling may be, as landlord, employer, teacher, neighbor, or citizen, must share the responsibility for removing the obstacles which stand in the way of so many of our fellow Americans from achieving the abundant life.

Source

A Quaker Speaks from the Black Experience: The Life and Selected Writings of Barrington Dunbar. James A. Fletcher and Carleton Mabee, eds. (New York Yearly Meeting of the Religious Society of Friends, 1979).

Black Power's Challenge to Quaker Power

[*In April 1968, Martin Luther King, the apostle of nonviolence, was murdered. In reaction, racial rioting erupted in cities and towns across the nation. Several months later there appeared in the* Friends Journal *what is believed to be Dunbar's first published article. It was a call for a re-examination of the implications of nonviolence for our times.*]

Vital religious experience can provide the power to overcome the world. Gandhi and his followers experienced this, as did the early Christian church and the early Quakers. Corporate worship deepens the commitment of the believers and can help them to stand firm against tyranny and oppression when they are laboring to bring about needed social reforms. For the early Quakers, such activity was the extension of worship beyond the gathered community into a world divided by hatred, fear, and exploitation.

William James described eighteenth-century Quakers as a "people among people"—a gathered sect, a religious group who saw as their mission the creation of a new society. Then and later the meeting for worship must have been a living fellowship where a social reformer like Levi Coffin, in Indiana and Ohio, could come to share his concern for the slaves and to wrestle with Friends to gain their love and understanding and their support in his work of helping slaves escape to freedom through the Underground Railroad.

This close connection between work and worship—between the gathered community of the Meeting and the wider community—seems to be a missing ingredient in the practice of the Quaker Meeting today, which often tends to serve the purpose of a social club where people meet to pursue their common interests in isolation from the rest of the community. We attend meetings to escape the agonies of an unjust society and to find personal refuge among like-minded Friends. Because our hearts are not stirred or our minds made sensitive to the injustices of the communities in which we live, we accommodate ourselves to a whole system of personal and group relationships in our neighborhoods and places of business—a system that has served to reinforce the assumption of white superiority. This way of life denies that there is that of God in every man, the vital message of Quakerism that provides the basis for the "blessed community" in which everyone can achieve freedom from want and fear and can realize his full potential as a human being.

We Friends must re-examine our nonviolent testimony in the light of today's realities. Suffering humanity sees us as another group of white Americans who are deeply implicated in the social-political-legal military system that has contributed to the violence of our times. Most Friends in America belong to the white middle class; even if we do not knowingly participate in efforts to keep nonwhites from having access to opportunity and power, we condone it by our silence. We have accepted the estrangement of nonwhites in ghetto communities as the "American Way."

To dispossessed and disadvantaged nonwhites, the nonviolence that Friends profess sounds trite and hollow; it complicates our efforts to communicate with them. Some Friends are like the Pharisee who went to the temple and prayed: "Thank God I am not like other men." "Thank God," we say, "we are not open advocates of violence like Rapp Brown or Stokely Carmichael." But these aggrieved young men would say: "For over three hundred years you have been dealing violently with us by denying us the right to participate fully as citizens of the community."

Humility is much needed among Friends, as is the acknowledgement that we share the guilt for the crucial and explosive nature of the racial situation in America. Through humility we may gain repentance and learn to respond with love to men like Brown and Carmichael, in spite of grievous wounds. To love one's enemy and to turn the other cheek are the zenith of Christian love.

Friends who have experienced love in the fellowship of the "gathered community" can demonstrate to the wider community what love can do in the following ways:

1. We need to nurture the Inner Light—the source of the phenomenal power of the eighteenth-century Quakers. "Quaker Power" can be as effective as "Black Power" in speeding up revolutionary changes.
2. We need to listen in love to the black people of America and to submit ourselves to the violence of their words and actions if we are to identify truly with their anguish and despair.
3. We need to understand, to encourage, and to support the thrust of black people to achieve self-identity and power by sharing in the control of institutions in the community that affect their welfare and destiny.
4. We must invest our resources—money and skill—to provide incentives for black people to develop and control economic, political, and social structures in the community.
5. We must support the passage of antipoverty legislation leading to programs that will remedy the deplorable economic and social conditions existing in urban ghettos.
6. We must oppose racial injustice wherever it is practiced: in the neighborhood where we live, in our places of business, and in our contacts with the wider community.

SOURCE

Barrington Dunbar, "Black Power's Challenge to Quaker Power," *Friends Journal*, September 15, 1968, p. 460.

The Revolutionary Jesus

[*Dunbar was invited to represent Friends at an interdenominational Believers Church Conference, held in Chicago. In a report on his disappointment with the conference, published in* Quaker Life, *October 1970, Dunbar sees God working through both Martin Luther King and Malcom X.*]

Perhaps my expectations were too high. I expected the Believers Church to be ecumenical in character. Ecumenical both in its membership and its contents. I expected to discern in the composition of the participants and in their theology, a life style that is uniquely Christian.

Among the sixty-five or more attendees, there were two blacks, three women, and two Catholics. Representatives from the Mennonites, Southern Baptist, Methodist, Brethren, Church of God, and the Society of Friends participated. The participants were made up almost exclusively of men aged thirty-five and older, representing the leadership of their respective religious groups—pastors, professors of religion and sociology, and religious editors. Many of them were PhDs and authors. Youths and laymen were conspicuously absent.

Throughout the three days of my intense involvement in listening to daily biblical presentations by John Howard Yoder, scholarly addresses by Rosemary Reuther, Howard University, Carl Bangs, St. Paul School of Theology, Arthur Foster, Chicago Theological Seminary, and Dale Brown, Bethany Theological Seminary, and of my participation in the seminar discussions which followed, I felt something was lacking. The stirring of new life within the church was not evident. The marks of the Believers Church were fuzzy and not clearly defined, and the response of the religious leaders to conflict within their congregations or in a split society lacked commitment and resolve.

I do not know if an unsophisticated layman like me can claim membership in the Believers Church, but I can identify with Jesus the revolutionary personage who, perhaps with a measure of indignation, exclaimed, "Woe unto you Scribes and Pharisees." Perhaps there are those of us who might accuse Jesus of advancing the demonic-angelic theory, but I see it as his way of saying an emphatic NO to the Establishment of his day. His mission was not to provide a neutral platform for the reconciliation of opposing forces, but to point men to a new fellowship which is grounded on the revolutionary concept of God's Fatherhood and the brotherhood of man. The opening words of the Lord's Prayer are, "Our Father." And he abbreviated the Ten Commandments to two: "Thou shalt love the Lord thy God with all thy heart and thy neighbor as thyself."

I can identify with Jesus, a man of deep commitment and with a revolutionary strategy who gathered together a disciplined people in his effort to share with them his vision of the beloved community, of the Kingdom of God, freed of the barriers of race, class, clan, or creed.

I can identify with Jesus the revolutionary who was put to death on a cross because he proved to be a threat to the existing social order, as he sought to remove the barriers which separated Jews from Gentiles, the taxpayer from the fisherman.

As I identify with Jesus—the revolutionary—and with the historical circumstances of his human life, I see an example of a personal encounter, through which God makes himself known to men. And my experience leads me to a fuller understanding of the power of contemporary men like Malcolm X and Martin Luther King, men who have demonstrated by their lives "the mighty works of God" and whose life styles have supported the Quaker idea of "continuing revelation." We see in the lives of these men new and creative power for the renewal of society entering into the stream of history.

It was Malcolm X who referred to white men living in Christian America as "Devils"—even white people who profess to be righteous like the Scribes and Pharisees. That was a guilt reaction growing out of the experience of alienation and exploitation that he had known in relating to whites in America. But Malcolm X's opinions of white people underwent radical change during his visit to the Muslim communities of North Africa. There he experienced a brotherhood that had no racial overtones, and there he had an opportunity to discover the humanity of other men. The mighty acts of God are indeed acts of redemption. "If Christ be lifted up he would draw all men unto him."[1]

Non-violence was a way of life for Martin Luther King. He understood that the violence of poverty and racial oppression is as real and tragic as the physical violence of war, and he consistently identified with the struggles of the poor and oppressed to throw off their yoke of oppression. Nonviolence took him beyond conscientious objection to war. His goal was the establishment of God's Kingdom on earth—the Kingdom of righteousness and justice for all mankind.

Both Malcom X and Martin Luther King shared the penalty of the cross for having dared to turn the Establishment from its evil ways and point to a social order based on justice and freedom.

What greater core principle is laid upon the Believers Church than to have a radical apprehension of how unchristian the present social order is and how urgently it needs to be revolutionized?

SOURCE
Barrington Dunbar, "A Reaction to the Believers Church Conference," *Quaker Life*, October, 1970, p. 16/324–17/325.

Friends and the White Backlash

[*The Earlham School of Religion, at Earlham College, Indiana, invited Dunbar to speak at its Tenth Anniversary dinner, October 30, 1970. Dunbar did not speak in the congratulatory manner which might be expected on such an occasion. Instead he played the role of a "thorn in the flesh," and he knew he was doing so.*]

Friends have difficulty empathizing with the new mood of Black people—their clamor for self-identity, separation, black power, reparations, and their turning away from non-violence as a revolutionary strategy advocated by Martin Luther King. I have heard some Friends say: "They don't need our help anymore, why bother?" This attitude expresses the backlash that is so prevalent among White Americans and indicates a lack of understanding of the frustrations, needs and aspirations of Black people.

As a Black member of the Society of Friends, I have become a "thorn in the flesh" having constantly to remind Friends that the violence of racial discrimination which has prevented a whole race of people in America from achieving self-respect and self-fulfillment—stamping out the image of God from their personality—cannot escape reaping the penalty of sin. And the wages of sin is death. Death in this sense is the moral and spiritual decay which results when hate replaces love in the world and man experiences separation from God and his fellowmen.

An example of how generously Friends have responded to the urgent pleas of Blacks for social justice is the result of the action taken by New York Yearly Meeting to establish the Black Development Fund.

Approved in 1969, an amount of $50,000 was set as the annual goal of the Fund to stimulate programs in housing, education, job training, community organization, and legal services in the Black community in the area of the Yearly Meeting. The Race Relations Committee of the Yearly Meeting assumed responsibility to implement the action by seeking contributions from members of the Yearly Meeting. The Minute encourages Friends to commit one per cent of their annual income to the Black Development Fund. Conservatively estimated, if each member of the Yearly Meeting had contributed one per cent, a total amount of $120,000 would have been collected. The fact is, however, that only $19,000 of the goal of $50,000 was collected from only two hundred families of the Yearly Meeting in the first year.

How feeble is our response to support the preventative programs that might restore hope and forestall violence in the Black communities.

The Black members of the Society of Friends do not amount to more than a handful of convinced Friends, not large enough to form a viable coalition within the organization. Maintaining our identity among Quakers who preach non-violence, but yet by their complicity and silence support the violence of the status quo, poses a problem. The Black members of the Society of Friends must not be expected to embrace a cultish pacifism. Perhaps their presence in the Society might contribute toward making pacifism a radical and revolutionary social goal having as its ultimate end not only the end of war, but the regeneration of a sick society.

At a recent meeting with the Panthers held at the 15th Street Meeting, New York City, I introduced myself as a Quaker, but "Black and beautiful."

The reference to my Blackness struck a discordant note among some Friends. I received a note a few days later from a trusted friend quoting Buber's *I and Thou* and saying: "We are all human before we are of one race or another, and it is on this common ground of being human that we live truly, and on which we meet." Frantz Fanon says: "Man is human only to the extent to which he tries to impose his existence on another in order to be recognized by him, and he who is reluctant to recognize me opposes me." The "I and thou" relationship between Blacks and Whites in America has been reduced to the "I and it" for over three hundred years. In affirming my Blackness I am responding to a world that has defined me as a non-person, as a chattel and slave with no rights that a White man was bound to respect. The affirmation is an act of rebellion to achieve my identity as a man, and solidarity with the human race.

The history of Black-White relations in America reveals that Blacks who manage to win their way into White-dominated organizations are expected to behave in ways acceptable to the dominant group. We are called upon to sell our birthright to adjust to the requirements of the group. As Catholics, Blacks repeat "Hail Mary" with more fervor and devotion than other Catholics. Even among Friends, disfranchised Blacks are expected to profess a class-limited pacifism in a time of revolution. My well-meaning friend quotes the philosophy of Buber rather than that of Malcolm X, James H. Cone, Vincent Harding or any of the other Black social and religious thinkers with whom I can identify.

Perhaps no White man can adequately comprehend the meaning of the Black experience in America. Because Friends cannot fathom the violence of racial discrimination, they are prone to condemn the riots and the violence of the Panthers, and bless by their silence the conditions which produce rebellion. Fearful of supporting violent confrontations, Friends have not gone where the action is, in support of the just demands of the oppressed. These are critical times when Black people, having seen the light, are demanding equality and social justice *now* and are prepared to stand as men even against the terrors of White power.

Militants like the Black Panthers believe that achieving Black dignity and Black liberation is not possible in the United States without profound changes—revolutionary changes in the system. They believe that racism is built so deeply in the social structure of America that it is going to take a deep and painful incision to remove it. But reconciliation is the way advocated by some well meaning Friends. These Friends who argue that if progress is to be made it will be through a rational, reasonable and peaceful approach to conflict situations are deeply offended when Blacks refuse to listen, advocating instead "Black Power"—the full participation in the decision making process affecting the lives of Black people. This may not always be achieved by an orderly process. Black Power conveys the utter determination of Blacks to be free. Depending on the response of Whites, it may have to take the form of outright rebellion to achieve the goal of freedom.

Like the average White American, Friends react negatively to the stance of Black Power. They see it as an expression of a power struggle with Blacks trying to wrestle power from Whites. But power is freedom. It is what happens to a man inside so that he is ready to say no to slavery and oppression. Freedom is not a gift from Whites. It is as essential to human existence as the air one breathes, and with this discovery Blacks are ready to affirm their existence at any price. Confrontation and conflict may result from the failure of the White society to understand that freedom is not a gift but a right worth dying for.

Whitney Young indicates that the Black man is powerless because he is unable to make and enforce decisions for his own community or to have a significant influence in the public and private institutions that control his life. This is the kind of power that Black people now seek.

Do Friends have a role to play in the struggle of Black people for power? Training non-violent technicians to avoid the use of violence in revolutionary confrontations is not the best that we can do.

A recent *New York Times* article commenting on the Newark election says: "In Newark mayoral elections significant numbers of Whites ignoring appeals to their fears and prejudices joined Blacks in naming as the head of their municipal government the best qualified candidate, Kenneth A. Gibson."

This is a striking example of the kind of action that Friends may take to support Black people in their struggle for power and equality and to put an end to racism in America.

Source

Barrington Dunbar, "Friends Response to Racism in the United States," in *Three M's of Quakerism: Meeting, Message, Mission: Tenth Anniversary Lectures* (Richmond, IN: Institute of Quaker Studies, Earlham School of Religion, 1971), pp. 57–70.

Sharing My Experience in Friends Schools

[*After he had visited at least eight Friends schools, Dunbar summarized his impressions about his visits in* Quaker Life *in 1975. Altogether his experience seemed to renew his faith in the possibilities of integration.*]

It was my happy privilege to be invited by Friends Council on Education to serve as "Friend in Residence" during the past school year in a cluster of Friends schools in the Philadelphia area. I visited the following schools: Friends Select, George School, Abington Friends School, William Penn Charter, and

Germantown Friends School, spending a month at each school. In addition, I spent two weeks at Wilmington Friends School in Delaware, one week at Carolina Friends School in North Carolina, and three days at Oakwood School in Poughkeepsie, New York.

In recognition that the "Light" within needs nurture in order to glow and reflect the spirit of God—the spirit of love—Friends who settled in Pennsylvania in the early seventeenth century established schools within their religious communities to provide for the moral and spiritual nurture of their children. Because the public schools in Pennsylvania were not established until 1840 many children whose parents were non-Quaker enrolled in the Quaker schools—a trend that is still prevalent today, although perhaps for different reasons.

Some Friends are concerned about the paucity of Friends children attending Friends schools. Friends schools, they say, are for the education of Friends children—to preserve the sense of community where the growth and nurture of the moral and spiritual roots of Quakerism can be fostered. But we face a real dilemma because of the dearth of teachers who are members of the Society of Friends and who can help in the process of preserving the religious ideal and practices of the Quaker community. Yet in the absence of the religious ingredient I have experienced a quality of life—an openness, a sense of freedom and a deep respect for persons in all of the schools that I have visited that is unique in its Quaker implications. I have felt in every situation the warmth of a loving, caring community, and at the end of my stay have experienced a tinge of regret from having to part from friends. Children of the lower schools were more open and receptive. Here are some comments made by a group of fourth grade students following my visit to their class: "I think you are a nice man. The talk you had with us was great. Before you came I thought Martin Luther King was a king in the Middle Ages." "Thanks so much for telling me about Martin Luther King, because I am Black and wanted to find out about more people like me." "We enjoyed having you and liked the poems you read. You taught me a lot I did not know." "Thanks for sitting at our table. My father is chief of X-ray, my mother is a nurse, and I am a Black school boy. I thank you for the poems. I did not know about Martin Luther King until you told me."

Quaker schools have become one of the most viable forms of outreach of the Society in the community. The schools continue to attract students from the wider community and students of diverse religious backgrounds. But the schools that I have visited are isolated from the real community where the stress and strain of life tend to develop concerns. Germantown Friends School is perhaps the only exception. The school still operates in a community that shows obvious symptoms of blight and decay. When I visited Abington Friends

School, the fleet of buses which I was told transported children from a surrounding environment of approximately 100 square miles, revealed the extent of voluntary busing that goes on—a luxury that only privileged children can enjoy.

The diversity of Friends schools now includes a growing number of Black students for affluent black families are enrolling their children in Friends schools. In 1697 when Abington School was started Blacks were considered nonpersons without the capacity to learn. Even Friends until recent years have excluded Blacks from their schools—denying them the opportunity to grow in the nurture of the Quaker community. No doubt, this is one of the reasons for the scarcity of Blacks in the Society of Friends in the U.S.A.

While progress is indicated by the increasing number of Blacks attending Friends schools, there is the tendency to admit Blacks who have become a part of America's middle class. Only at Germantown Friends School has there been any real effort to attract students from the ghetto who would otherwise not know of the school. The Germantown Friends School Community Scholarship program, which started in 1963, emerged out of a concern to reach out to under-privileged students. Its purpose, as stated by Elizabeth Kalkstein, vice-principal, "was to include in the student body students who would otherwise not be aware of us, nor we of them. In the belief that there is something unique in Quaker education, we hoped that some of our principles would be transmitted through these students to the community in which we are located." The school invested $637,000 in the program over the ten years of operation, and so far, says Elizabeth Kalkstein, "it has been a splendid investment."

Helpful relationships are beginning to develop as Black and White students encounter each other in the Friends school setting. A Black student who lived in a ghetto community near a Friends school confided how he felt about White people before enrolling. Said he, "I regarded them as enemies. We lived in different worlds and there was no chance for communication, but here at Friends Select I am beginning to talk to Whites, to enjoy their friendship. And I have discovered that White people can be real people capable of love and affection. But my friends on the block won't believe me. How can I share my experience with them?"

How can Friends help to mitigate the violence inherent in the inequity of our social relationships? Preaching nonviolence to those victimized by violent situations is a palliative that will not heal hate, fear, and distrust. It is only as we are able to help people to live nonviolently by bringing them into nonviolent relationships that healing and transformation will take place.

As Friends schools lose their isolation and begin to reach out to the community social concerns begin to emerge. During the meeting for worship at

Germantown Friends School, a sixth-grade student broke the silence and queried: "If there is that of God in every one of us, why is the world in such danger? Why do people get mugged? Why do people kill their enemies? Does killing get a point across? Why are people sent to jail if they steal something? People need help—I wonder why God doesn't help them?"

The timely and significant program observing the birthday of Martin Luther King held at George School and the impressive exhibit of Afro-American art displayed at Germantown School during the Afro-American Week have enriched their educational programs and suggest ways to enhance the relevance of education for Blacks in Friends schools.

Source

Barrington Dunbar, "Sharing My Experience in Friends Schools," *Quaker Life*, November 1975, pp. 12–13. Reprinted with permission of *Quaker Life* © 1975.

Endnotes

1 John 12:32.

VI
Helen Morgan Brooks
(1904–1989)

edited by Anne Steere Nash

[*The section on Helen Morgan Brooks is guest edited by Anne Steere Nash, whose selections of poems are guided by her personal memories of the author.*]

Helen Morgan Brooks, a warm, caring, generous, poetic soul, was born March 4, 1904, in Reading, Pennsylvania. After her death of cancer at age 85 at Kendal at Longwood in Pennsylvania, her sister Doris Baxter recalled Helen saying months before her passing: "I simply want to sit out on the beach and watch the wonder of the rain, smell its fragrance and marvel at the miracle of God's works."[1] She had a deep feeling for the beauty of nature, for family, for language, and for children. She was so treasured by her friends and colleagues that three memorial services were held for her: one at a Friends meetinghouse in Philadelphia, one at Kendal at Longwood, and one at Friends Hospital.

After earning a B.A. in home economics at St. Augustine College, Raleigh, North Carolina, in 1924 at the age of 20, she later studied education at Temple University. She worked for many years as a home economist and dietitian, and in the later part of her life she taught restaurant practices at the O.V. Cato School for Boys in the Philadelphia school system. Throughout her working years she wrote poetry. Several collections of her work were published, and she won awards for her poetry. She was editor of the poetry magazine *Approach*. So important was her writing that it was also included in *New Negro Poets, U.S.A.* (1964), edited by Langston Hughes, and in *The Poetry of the Negro 1749–1970*, edited by Langston Hughes and Arna Wendell Bontemps. Helen Morgan Brooks wrote with emotion and from her own experience.

Helen Morgan Brooks showed another side of her sensibility in a 1955 publication, *A Practical Guide: One Person, One Meal, One Burner*, for needy people trying to eat on a weekly budget of $5. She experienced the effects of poverty herself when, as an adolescent, she was sent to live in an orphanage for six years when her family experienced hard times after a move to Philadelphia. She was the oldest of six children. Her father was a barber and her mother a homemaker.

Helen Morgan Brooks became a member of the Monthly Meeting of Friends of Philadelphia (Arch Street) in 1956 when she was 52 years old. She served that meeting as an overseer and was an active member of the Peace and Race Relations Committee of Philadelphia Yearly Meeting. She was a member of the Friends Hospital Board of Managers, a trustee at Friends Select School, a member of the Friends Journal Board of Managers, and received a fellowship to Pendle Hill in the 1940s where she wrote, taught, and cooked. Later she served on Pendle Hill's board.

In 1930, when she was 26, she married William T. Brooks, from whom she later separated. She had no children of her own but was devoted to her nieces and a nephew. She taught poetry to children in the summers for many years at Virginia Beach, Virginia.[2]

The poems that have been chosen for this anthology reflect the depth of her concern with the spirit and with human rights. As a ten year old in 1945, I recall loving to be in her presence in the kitchen or on the path at Pendle Hill, where she always had a warm greeting and time to talk. The following poems express what I remember fondly of who she was.

— *Anne Steere Nash, July 2008*

Revelation

[*Unpublished manuscript from The Log Book at Pendle Hill.*]

I too bear record and testify to the things that I saw. Praying all Saints and our Father in Heaven to have mercy on all little people, all hopeless ones, all hired hands, all share croppers, all tired washer women, all scrub women, the carriers of the hod, the laborers with pick and shovel, all menials, all who are rejected, all derelicts, all the abandoned.

The worn prostitutes, the whoremongers, the parasitical, the slaves of uncertainty, the nervous, the mentally deficient, the failing, the unwanted, the lonely, the degraded, the fallible, the delusioned, the dejected, the injured, the maligned, the sick, the weak.

All Pharisees, all pretentious ones, all sinners and transgressors and lastly the Judas Iscariots, the betrayers and the betrayed.

O my people, my people, if I could gather you together as a hen gathereth her brood under her wing and save you from sedition, false doctrine, heresy, schism and contempt of God's Word and Commandment.

The things we hear with our ears we can refuse to believe but the things we see with our eyes we are bound to believe.

Therefore those who have ears to hear let them hear. Those endowed with reason, let them reason, those who know how to pray let them pray and those who have tears to shed let them shed them now for my People's sake.

Meeting For Worship

After awhile,
after the settling down.
waiting,
in the deep quiet time.
We are embraced
by the silence
that was there,
expecting us,
when we entered.[3]

Faith

Tears I've known and pain and sorrow past all trying,
this way I've come so sharp, so cruel each turn.
My faith I've flown as some small kite aflying,
atop the wind and sometimes far below,
but always through the weariness of trying.
This much I feel and find it ever odd,
my faith in spite of everything
keeps straining up to God.[4]

Slum House

Grass does not grow
before the slum house,
nor in the back yard.

Grass does not grow—
only the brown earth shows,
bare, hard, smooth—trampled
from too many feet
in too great a hurry
to leave the tired, sagging, hull
where rats scream and roaches crawl,
and the smell of urine is on the floor;
where the odor of hog meat permeates
the walls, and liquor fumes stalk
the stairs like demented ghosts:

No grass grows before such a house.
Grass is for sowing and mowing,
for weeding out, and being proud of.
Grass responds to the sun and the rain—
it must be loved and admired:
grass will not grow where no love is.[5]

Black Child

This child is called Black—
    Once her folks were called Africans,
Then Negro, then Colored,
    Now they are all called Black.

She is not the black—a black of one's true
    Love's hair,
Nor the all black of the famous painting
    In the museum, simply titled, "Black,"
Or the black hole, black of far off stars dying.

Her Black can be the color of honey,
    Or sunsets lowering,
The color of Autumn leaves, mingled
    With brown branches bending;
There's the color of new earth turned,
    Joyfully feeling great oaks,
Russet violets, or wheat fields waving;
    Black can be the color of sand—
Seashore sand, washed by the movement of

Rhythmic waves crisscrossing.

All these colors strangely evident
　　As you look at the child;
All the tans, the browns,
　　All the colors of mankind,
All neutral, all blended
　　into the color of her people
In this one child called, Black.[6]

Double Chain

Portray her as you will.
If you see a black queen's grace,
a slattern or a wench
beneath the pale yellow of her face,
try to conjure from your mind
the will and soul to learn
this strange alchemy of her race.
If you of one continuous strain
of tranquil thought and blood
back through a hundred years or more,
would call once to that strange
god-made protoplasm,
that lithe body that walks with measured tread;
those eyes that see, the ears that hear,
the tongue that speaks your language
or some other God-like nation's;
who reads and learns, who lives and loves;
who sickens as you do and dies;
she never will be free,
but bound fast with iron bands,
or, stranger still,
with chains of heritage
to the songs of her soul,
the soul of an ancestral slave,
that makes her in the dead of night
mourn softly to herself;
　　I am bound I am bound can't be free
　　soul save yourself and then save me

> *I am bound and can't be free.*

How often have you called back down to her,
when deep, the soul still cries aloud:
> *I am climbing Jacob's Ladder Ladder Ladder*
> *I am climbing Jacob's Ladder,*
> *Soldier of the Cross?*

You read, that in some tyrant's state,
blood brothers have been lynched.
She would not be so far concerned
if tried, they went to death—
but the injustice of it all! —
or was it injustice too
when her grandmamma first reasoned thus:
> *Were you there were you there*
> *when they crucified my Lord?*

But trouble trouble
swinging down a narrow lane
cannot pass her by
or, just enough to hear her cry:
> *Nobody knows de trouble I see,*
> *Nobody knows but Jesus.*

O then for freedom in your soul, to know,
to recognize the courage and the hope
it takes to sing aloud at last:
> *Hush Hush Somebody callin' yo name*
> *Hush Hush Somebody callin' yo name*
> *Come up my chile on my right hand*
> *and look and see de Promised Land*
> *Hush Hush O yes Somebody callin' yo name!*[7]

Ancient Message

Between full daylight and this thronging
twilight hour
the inner part of me is stilled;
by work, by rushing here and there
my hours are crowded with emotion,
and gayety short lived;
until at even-time
when all men find their home

and having nothing else,
I come to solitude.

Lone hours, I raise to you
this cup of tears,
not if self-pity—
sooner would I beg for bread—
but,
deep in the city
youth calls, of lights, of music, laughter, love;
unheard.

Then like drums
relaying the ancient message to my soul
All's done ... All's done ...
now what to do ... what to do ...
to do, to do??
Lone hours, I raise to you
this cup of tears.[8]

The Bus Comes

There must be love remaining.
I believe in love
In spite of things said
And deeds done or hate.
There must be love
In the space of things—
Worlds turning and fixed
Stars burning.

Love does remain.
It is deep in a child's eye
in wonder at a pink ribbon,
water falling,
a china cup, a gold ring,
a healing kiss on the forehead.

Children know love
and flowers.

Love keeps the Michaelmas Daisies

blooming beside the gas station door,
in spite of dust
and the oil splashed sidewalk.

Love is in the fragrance
that lingers around the altar rail,
After the lilies and the carnations
have been taken out
to lie beside the new coffin.

Love lives and is vital
in the mien of those
who sit on facing benches
in quiet meeting houses,
Praying in silence,
in strong silence,
that reaches out and embraces
all gypsying thoughts
and gathers them in
to be blessed.

Love is the promise,
"I will not leave you comfortless."
Comfortless in a deep shadowed crevice,
deprived of the newness of morning,
The arch of noon,
The purple royal,
Surrounding the pin oaks at evening.

I must believe in love
As a testimony against madness
and war and broken promises.
I choose love.

The Bus comes,
The train leaves on schedule
And love, arriving or departing,
remembers me.[9]

The City

You may not find
On the streets of this city,
One barren fig tree in full leaf,
That you will curse into forever withering.

Nor will you be so sure
Of a furnished room,
That you can single just one out,
Prepared and waiting
For you and your friends,
To take over for a quiet supper.
People require references.

You may never find
Two brothers mending nets
Beside our river's edge,
Or a Publican free to follow you,
To leave the business of our custom house,
It's against the law.

Do not be discouraged,
Walk on among us
Through littered streets,
Past graffiti-covered walls,
Call out to us,
Whenever, wherever you see us,
In the suburbs, on the beaches.
Be careful of large gatherings,
Parades need permits.
Palms will not be tolerated
Strewn upon our macadam roads.

You keep walking,
Call out to us,
Some of us, perhaps some of us
Will hear and follow you.[10]

Against Whatever Sky

So you would have me choose?
Tell you what my preference is,
among these three.
A plum tree, radiant in full blossom.
The willow rustling in an evening dress of green.
A copper beech against a tawny, autumn sky.

My choice is not the plum tree.
Reminding me of promise time,
those flowering days—
all white and pink and scented.
I cannot bear the aching grief
of April rain in tantrum,
stamping petals on the ground.

I will not take the willow,
keepsake of one brief, gay summer—
with whispering branches, trailing music
of one loved melody
through morning mists, flushed days,
and the witchery of long nights
while the moon changed.

My preference is the beech tree
coppered by that subtle alchemy
of spring's new hope
and summer's ripe experience.
I claim the beech
against whatever sky
for needed winter treasuring.[11]

SOURCE

The above poems have all been transcribed from *I Choose Love* (Wallingford, PA: Pendle Hill Publications, 1990). Previous publications are identified in endnotes.

ENDNOTES

1 From "Introductory Remembrances" in *I Choose Love* published in 1990 by Friends of Helen Morgan Brooks to fulfill her desire at the end of her life to assemble and collect her poems. "Over a hundred friends have contributed time, special skills, and money to make this collection a living memorial to Helen Morgan Brooks" ("Introduction"). Her published poems included here have all been transcribed from *I Choose Love.*

2 Information for this biography was gleaned from: "Milestones," *Friends Journal*, May 1990, p. 42; her obituary in the *Philadelphia Inquirer*, October 19, 1989; and Kenneth Ives et al., *Black Quakers: Brief Biographies* (Chicago, IL: Progresiv Publishr, 1991), pp. 131-134.

3 Helen Morgan Brooks, *I Choose Love* (Wallingford, PA: Pendle Hill Publications, 1990), p. 3; Brooks, *A Slat of Wood and Other Poems* (Otego, NY: The Whimsie Press, 1976), p. 26.

4 *I Choose Love*, p. 29; Brooks, *From These My Years* (Wilmington, DE: Hambleton Printing and Publishing, 1945), p. 19.

5 *I Choose Love*, p. 36; *A Slat of Wood*, p. 34.

6 *I Choose Love*, p. 40.

7 *I Choose Love*, pp. 44-45; Brooks, *Against Whatever Sky* (Wilmington, DE: Wilmington Poetry Society and Delaware Writers, 1955), pp. 16-17.

8 *I Choose Love*, p. 70; *From These My Years*, p. 15.

9 *I Choose Love*, pp. 30-31; *A Slat of Wood*, pp. 24-25.

10 *I Choose Love*, p. 10; *A Slat of Wood*, pp. 29-30.

11 *I Choose Love*, p. 52; *Against Whatever Sky*, p. 9.

VII

Bayard Rustin
(1912–1987)

edited by Harold D. Weaver, Jr.

B AYARD RUSTIN was born in West Chester, Pennsylvania, on March 17, 1912, to Florence Rustin and Archie Hopkins. He was raised in a Quaker community by his grandparents, Julia and Janifer Rustin, as their youngest child. Only as an adult did Rustin learn that he was their grandchild and that one "sister" was actually his mother. Julia, his grandmother, was a charismatic Quaker and a founding member of the NAACP. Rustin was drawn to the unprogrammed tradition of Quakerism by its "intellectual openness, broad range of doctrinal acceptability, disciplined spirituality and the peace witness."[1] His grandfather, Janifer, belonged to the African Methodist Episcopal Church, and this exposure to African American spirituals and gospel music was important in developing Rustin's exceptional tenor singing voice.

Rustin attended the public schools in West Chester where he was a gifted student and athlete, and where a new high school now carries his name. He continued his education at Wilberforce University, Cheney State Teachers College, and City College of New York, where he began to organize for the Young Communist League in 1936. Though he never got a degree, he was the recipient of more than a dozen honorary doctorates in his lifetime.[2]

As a member of Fifteenth Street Meeting in New York City, Rustin was entitled to alternative service, but when he was drafted, he chose instead to go to jail. In 1944 he was sent to federal penitentiaries until 1947. In prison he resisted the pervasive segregation as he would later resist North Carolina's Jim Crow law against integration in transportation. This show of resistance earned him a beating and twenty-eight days of hard labor on a chain gang and set the model for the Freedom Rides of the 1960s.

Rustin was drawn to the Young Communist League because of its progressive stance on the issue of racial injustice but broke with the Party in 1941 when it reversed its stance on segregation in the American military. This early, brief connection was to be used against him, especially during the McCarthy era.

Though he was a brilliant organizer, working for the Fellowship of Reconciliation, the American Friends Service Committee, the Democratic Socialist Party, and the War Resisters League, Rustin was often forced to work behind the scenes, not only because of his communist past, but because he was openly gay and was arrested in 1953 on a highly publicized morals charge in California.

As a close advisor, Rustin gave Martin Luther King, Jr., practical advice on how to apply the Gandhian principles of nonviolence to the 1955 boycott of public transportation in Montgomery, Alabama. In his association with A. Philip Randolph, head of the Brotherhood of Sleeping Car Porters, he organized the youth wing of the March on Washington that Randolph envisioned (later called off). He organized the Prayer Pilgrimage for Freedom in 1957 and the National Youth Marches for Integrated Schools in 1958 and 1959. These experiences gave him the background to become the chief organizer and logistics person for the August 28, 1963, March on Washington for Jobs and Freedom. In 1964 Rustin organized a school boycott in New York City to protest the slow pace of integration and organized civil rights demonstrations at the Democratic and Republican conventions.

Bayard Rustin played a large role in the birth of the Southern Christian Leadership Conference, was a part of the Congress of Racial Equality (CORE), and worked tirelessly for the War Resisters League as well as leading campaigns for the American Friends Service Committee. In 1964 he helped to found the A. Philip Randolph Institute that came to have 200 affiliates. It provided voter registration drives and programs to strengthen relations between the black community and the labor movement. He remained its CEO until his death in 1987.

Letter to His Draft Board (1943)

Local Board No. 63
2050 Amsterdam Avenue
New York, N.Y.

Gentlemen:

For eight years I have believed war to be impractical and a denial of our Hebrew-Christian tradition. The social teachings of Jesus are: (1) Respect for personality; (2) Service the "summum bonum"; (3) Overcoming evil with good; and (4) The brotherhood of man. These principles as I see it are violated by participation in war.

Believing this, and having before me Jesus' continued resistance to that which he considered evil, I was compelled to resist war by registering as a Conscientious Objector in October 1940.

However, a year later, September 1941, I became convinced that conscription as well as war equally is inconsistent with the teachings of Jesus. I must resist conscription also.

On Saturday, November 13, 1943, I received from you an order to report for a physical examination to be taken Tuesday, November 16, at eight o'clock in the evening. I wish to inform you that I cannot voluntarily submit to an order springing from the Selective Service and Training Act for War.

There are several reasons for this decision, all stemming from the basic spiritual truth that men are brothers in the sight of God:

1. War is wrong. Conscription is a concomitant of modern war. Thus conscription for so vast an evil as war is wrong.

2. Conscription for war is inconsistent with freedom of conscience, which is not merely the right to believe, but to act on the degree of truth that one receives, to follow a vocation which is God-inspired and God-directed.

Today I feel that God motivates me to use my whole being to combat by nonviolent means the ever-growing racial tension in the United States; at the same time the State directs that I shall do its will; which of these dictates can I follow—that of God or that of the State? Surely, I must at all times attempt to obey the law of the State. But when the will of God and the will of the State conflict, I am compelled to follow the will of God. If I cannot continue in my present vocation, I must resist.

3. The Conscription Act denies brotherhood—the most basic New Testament teaching. Its design and purpose is to set men apart—German against American, American against Japanese. Its aim springs from a moral

impossibility—that ends justify means, that from unfriendly acts a new and friendly world can emerge.

In practice further, it separates black from white—those supposedly struggling for a common freedom. Such a separation also is based on the moral error that racism can overcome racism, that evil can produce good, that men virtually in slavery can struggle for a freedom they are denied. This means that I must protest racial discrimination in the armed forces, which is not only morally indefensible but also in clear violation of the Act. This does not, however, imply that I could have a part in conforming to the Act if discrimination were eliminated.

Segregation, separation, according to Jesus, is the basis of continuous violence. It was such an observation which encouraged him to teach, "It has been said to you in olden times that thou shalt not kill, but I say unto you, do not call a man a fool—and he might have added: "for if you call him such, you automatically separate yourself from him and violence begins." That which separates man from his brother is evil and must be resisted.

I admit my share of guilt for having participated in the institutions and ways of life which helped bring fascism and war. Nonetheless, guilty as I am, I now see as did the Prodigal Son that it is never too late to refuse longer to remain in a non-creative situation. It is always timely and virtuous to change—to take in all humility a new path.

Though joyfully following the will of God, I regret that I must break the law of the State. I am prepared for whatever may follow. I herewith return the material you have sent me, for conscientiously I cannot hold a card in connection with an Act I no longer feel able to accept and abide by. Today I am notifying the Federal District Attorney of my decision and am forwarding him a copy of this letter.

I appreciate now as in the past your advice and consideration, and trust that I shall cause you no anxiety in the future. I want you to know I deeply respect you for executing your duty to God and country in these difficult times in the way you feel you must. I remain

Sincerely yours,
Bayard Rustin

P.S. I am enclosing samples of the material which from time to time I have sent out to hundreds of persons, Negro and white, throughout our nation. This indicates one type of the creative work to which God has called me.

Source

Bayard Rustin, "Letter to the Draft Board (1943)," in Devon W. Carbado and Donald Weise, eds., *Time on Two Crosses: The Collected Writings of Bayard Rustin* (San Francisco: Cleis Press, Inc., 2003), pp. 11–13.

Non-Violence in Action

[*This account appeared in* Fellowship, *the newsletter of the Fellowship of Reconciliation, June 2, 1942. It was introduced by the following paragraph:*

A striking example of the power of non-violence in meeting a racial conflict situation was recently given on a bus in Tennessee by Bayard Rustin, a Negro Youth worker for the F.O.R. Getting on the bus at Louisville, Ky., he took a seat in the middle of the bus; the driver asked him to move to the very back, which he refused to do, and after a consultation with company officials, the driver dropped the point and the bus started out. Negroes continuously went to the rear of the bus. Here is the story of what happened in Bayard's words.]

About thirteen miles north of Nashville, I heard the racket of approaching police cars.

In a few seconds the bus came to a sudden stop. A police car and two motorcycles drew up to us. Four police came thundering into the bus. They consulted shortly with the driver and then came back to me.

"Get up! You God-damned Nigger."

"Why?" I asked.

"Get up; You black son-of-a-bitch."

"What have I done that I should move?" Is it . . ."

That was the last word I could say. Three of these policemen began to beat me about the head and shoulders. Suddenly I found myself on the floor. They were dragging me out and kicking me. (Even yet I have a dark spot on my hip. Lucky it was not a few inches away). They threw me on the ground and continued (all four of them) to kick and beat me.

I jumped to my feet, held out my arms parallel to the ground and said, "There is no need to beat me. I am not resisting you." At this point three white men, obviously southerners from their speech, came out of the bus. They said, "Why do that to him? He has done nothing. Why not treat him like a human being? He is not resisting you." One little fellow grabbed the policeman's club as he was about to strike me, saying, "Don't you do that!"

The police was about to strike him when I said to him, "Please don't do that. There is no need, for I am protected well. There is no need to fight. I thank you just the same."

These three white friends began to collect my clothes and luggage which the bus driver had thrown out of the bus to the side of the road.

One elderly man asked the police where they were taking me. They said, "Nashville." He promised me that he would be there to see that I got justice.

During the thirteen-mile hectic ride to town they continuously called me every kind of name and said anything which might incite me to violence. I sat absolutely still, looking them straight in the eye whenever they dared to face me. The fact that they could not look at me gave me courage and hope, for I knew they were aware of injustice. This made them quite open for development.

When I reached Nashville, they went through my luggage and papers. They were most interested in the *Christian Century* and *Fellowship*.

Finally, the captain said, "Come here, Nigger."

I walked directly to him.

"What can I do for you?" I said.

"Nigger," he said, "you're supposed to be scared when you come in here."

"I am fortified by truth, justice and Christ," I said, "there is no need for me to fear."

He was flabbergasted. For a time he said nothing, Then he walked to another officer and said, in his frustration, "I believe the Nigger's crazy."

I waited there an hour and a half.

The next thing I knew [I] was taken for a long ride across town. At the Courthouse I was taken into the office of the Assistant District Attorney, a Mr. Ben West. As I entered the door I heard someone in the hallway say, "Say, you colored fellow, hey." I looked about and there was the white gentleman who said he would see that I got justice.

The District Attorney questioned me about my life, the *Christian Century*, the F.O.R., pacifism and the war for one half hour. He then asked the police to tell their side of the story. They told several lies. He then asked me to tell my side. This I did, calling upon the policemen to substantiate me at each point.

The District Attorney dismissed me. I waited an hour longer in a dark room all alone. Then he came in and said very kindly, "You may go, Mr. Rustin."

In amazement, I left the courthouse, being all the stronger a believer in the non-violent approach, for I am certain that I was called Mr., that I was assisted by the elderly gentleman, and assisted by the three men in the bus because I had, without fear, faced four policemen, saying, "There is no need to beat me. I offer you no resistance."

SOURCE

Bayard Rustin, "Non-Violence in Action," *Fellowship*, June 2, 1942.

You Don't Have To Ride Jim Crow

[*Composed by Johnny Carr, Donald Coan, Coreen Curtis, A.C. Thompson and Bayard Rustin at the Interfaith Workshop, July 7, 1947, to be sung to the familiar Negro tune, "There's No Hidin' Place Down Here."*]

1. (chorus)
You don't have to ride Jim Crow
You don't have to ride Jim Crow
On June the third, the high court said
If you ride, Jim Crow is dead
You don't have to ride Jim Crow.

2. And when you get on the bus
And when you get on the bus
Get on the bus, set any place,
'Cause Irene Morgan won her case
You don't have to ride Jim Crow.

3. Now you can set anywhere
Now you can set anywhere
Set anywhere, don' raise no fuss,
Keep cool, but firm, your cause is just
You don't have to ride Jim Crow.

4. And if the driver man says "move"
And if the driver man says "move"
If he says "move," speak up polite,
But set there tight, you're in the right
You don't have to ride Jim Crow.

5. You don't have to ride Jim Crow
You don't have to ride Jim Crow
Go quiet-like, if you face arrest;
NAACP will make a test
You don't have to ride Jim Crow.

6. But someday we'll all be free
But someday we'll all be free
When good will action turns the tide
And black and white sit side by side
Yes someday we'll all be free.

Repeat verse 1 (chorus)

"In Apprehension How Like a God!"

[*The Young Friends Movement of Philadelphia Yearly Meeting (Religious Society of Friends)* sponsored an annual William Penn Lecture *"for the purpose of closer fellowship" from 1916 until 1966. The lectures were subsequently published, and the names of the William Penn lecturers constitutes a roll call of individuals still widely recognized today for their Quaker leadership. In 1948, Bayard Rustin was their chosen speaker. Following is a short excerpt from his presentation.[3]]*

> What a piece of work is a man! how noble in reason! how infinite in faculty! in form and moving how express and admirable! in action how like an angel! in apprehension how like a god!
>
> — W. Shakespeare, *Hamlet*, Act II, Sc. 2

On August 6, 1945, a bomb fell on Hiroshima. At that same moment a bomb fell upon America, and its impact was felt around the world.... The atomic bomb has forced us to raise a question: Will not those who rely on violence end not only in utilizing any degree of violence, but in justifying it? If the answer to this question is Yes, then the use of violent force becomes the greatest problem of our time. In his book, *Thieves in the Night*, Arthur Koestler recognizes this fact when he says, "We are entering a political ice-age in which violence is the universal language and in which the machine gun is the Esperanto to be understood from Madrid to Shanghai."

The world over, suspicion is so intense, apathy so wide-spread and reliance on old methods so established, that man has become cynical and frustrated.

We thus observe the eternal truth proclaimed by Laotse, Buddha, Jesus, St. Francis, George Fox and Gandhi: the use of violence will destroy moral integrity—the very fundamental of community on which peace rests. We cannot remain honest unless we are opposed to injustice wherever it occurs, first of all in ourselves.

Individual responsibility is the alternative to violence; individual responsibility is capable of overcoming fear; it is capable of converting nation-worship back to the Judaeo-Christian tradition and ethic; it is capable of re-establishing moral integrity. How can we begin? We can begin by opposing injustice wherever it appears in our daily lives. As free men we can refuse to follow or to submit to unjust laws which separate us from other men no matter where they live, nor under what government they exist. As the now-famous editorial in Life Magazine pointed out, in our time it is "the individual conscience against the atomic bomb." In the parochial states of the world today, it is the responsible man, the man against all injustice, who can save us, and this in a very real sense means man against the state.

Justice Jackson of the United States Supreme Court, in his opening statement at the Nuremberg trials, addressed to the people of the civilized world, castigated the German people for refusing to recognize this principle. Mr. Jackson said over and again that German citizens had been irresponsible in following the cruel and antisocial directives of the Hitler government. He reiterated that responsible people would have resolved to end the Nazi regime and its wide-spread injustice, even though they were aware that to have done so would have meant severe punishment or even death for many of them and their families. There is some question in my mind that Mr. Jackson understood the total implication of his words, since he had issued no such statement in defense of the conscientious objectors in this country, who refused to register under what they considered the antisocial Selective Service and Training Act. I agree with him, however, that the failure of the German citizens to resist unjust laws from the beginning of Hitler's regime logically ended in their placing Jews in gas furnaces and lye pits, although many who did these things, no doubt, worked with "heavy hearts and without enthusiasm."

It would, however, be a mistake to make simple the matter of resistance to the state. Several of the greatest teachers of the past, and such practicers of civil disobedience as Mahatma Gandhi, have never taken lightly their inability to follow the directives of governmental officials, and have with intense study and grave concern for all persons involved, weighed many aspects of the question under consideration before appearing to set themselves off from the will of an organized social group. Although there has not been complete agreement among those who have practiced civil disobedience, most leaders have generally adhered to certain very basic principles. Chief of these is that no individual has the right to rebel against the state. One has not the right to resist the social group of which he is a part. This is particularly true where decisions made have been reached after extensive democratic discussion. One has, on the other hand, a duty to resist, and one resists because the state is poorly organized and one's everlasting aim is to improve the nature of the state, to disobey in the interest of a higher law. Hence, one has the duty but not the right to rebel. But before rebelling, one must clearly examine the questions outlined by the British scholar, T. H. Green, in his Lectures on the Principles of Political Obligation:

I must ask:

(a) Have I exhausted all possible constitutional methods of bringing desired change?
(b) Are the people I ask to rebel keenly conscious of a flagrant wrong to them? Or do I excite their passions?

(c) What is likely to be the effect of the resistance? Will the new state be worse than the first?
(d) What of my own motives? Have I removed all EGO?

To these one must add another: Can I accept punishment, prison, or even death, in that spirit which is without contention? It is most important to examine one's own motives, for even if a given resistance fails, this does not disprove its validity; repeated attempts and repeated failures may be necessary to success. But, since it is not possible to see completely what the results of any given resistance will be, one must therefore be careful that one's character and motives are clear. Henry Thoreau, sitting in prison, was visited by Ralph Waldo Emerson, who urged him to forego his useless efforts to stop slavery and an unjust war. But Thoreau, whose aim was clear, held to his belief and action. Little did Emerson realize that Thoreau's action was to be one of the chief factors in the development of the life and spirit of Mahatma Gandhi, and that Thoreau's resistance was to move through history and help bring freedom to four hundred million people, far exceeding the number Thoreau attempted to free in the middle of the 19th century.

We cannot convert nation-worship back to Christianity again unless we care enough, unless we can believe that man is in apprehension like a god, unless we are able so to revolutionize and to discipline ourselves that those who behold us exclaim of us, "In action how like an angel!" unless like Jesus and Gandhi we attain that spirit which makes it possible for us to stand with arms outstretched, even unto death, saying, "You can strike me, you may destroy my home, you may destroy me, but I will not submit to what I consider wrong; neither will I strike back." Many will question the practicality of such a course, but has not the life, the work, the death of Gandhi demonstrated in our time that one man holding fast to truth and to non-violence is more powerful than ten thousand men armed? Yet even though failure should seem certain, the faith we profess demands allegiance. But how are we different from the heathen if we strike back or submit to unjust demands and laws; or what have we left to protect if in the process of defending our freedom we give up both democracy and principle? How can we love God, whom we have not seen, if we cannot, in time of crisis, find the way to love our brothers whom we have seen?

Source
Bayard Rustin, *"In Apprehension How Like a God!"* (Philadelphia: The Young Friends Movement of Philadelphia Yearly Meeting, 1948).

Speak Truth to Power
A Quaker Search for an Alternative to Violence
[*This publication of the American Friends Service Committee, which first appeared in 1955 and saw several reprintings, was widely influential among Friends, and is credited with making the phrase "speak truth to power" common in Quaker speech and beyond. We have taken the liberty of restoring Bayard Rustin's name to the list of authors at the end of this introductory section. Although Rustin was active on the committee that drafted this paper, and in fact was credited by the committee's chair, Stephen Cary, as being, with A. J. Muste, one of the two major intellectual powers in their thinking, upon completion of the work, the AFSC initiated action to remove Rustin's name. The Board feared that recent unfavorable publicity stemming from a morals charge in California (Rustin was gay) would create controversy that could detract from the importance of the publication's message. At first, Rustin contested this decision, feeling it unfair, and then agreed, taking full responsibility for the removal of his name. We are including it in anticipation that the AFSC will have restored it by the time of the publication of this book.*[4]]

A Note to the Reader

For more than thirty-five years the American Friends Service Committee has worked among those who suffer, recognizing no enemies, and seeking only to give expression to the love of God in service. Out of this experience, gained under all kinds of governments and amidst all kinds of people, has come some appreciation of the problems of peacemaking in the modern world. This has led the Committee to issue over the past five years a series of studies on possible ways to ease tension and move toward international peace. The series began in 1949 with the publication of *The United States and the Soviet Union*. It was continued in 1951 with *Steps to Peace* and in 1952 with *Toward Security through Disarmament*. This is the fourth of the series, while a fifth, dealing with the future of the United Nations, is now in preparation.

All of these reports have been prepared for the American Friends Service Committee by study groups convened especially for the purpose. They have been approved for publication by the Committee's Executive Board—not as official pronouncements, but in the interest of stimulating public discussion of the issues raised, and in the hope that such discussion will contribute to the formation of policies that will bring peace.

The other studies have been developed on the assumption that reliance on military power is so integral in the policy of every major nation, that the most practical approach to peacemaking is to suggest specific next steps to reduce tension and thereby move gradually away from the reliance on force. Many other individuals and organizations have made similar suggestions, so that discussion of such alternatives to present policy has been fairly widespread. A large area of agreement has indeed been reached, and many Americans both in and out of government concur on the kind of constructive measures needed.

Yet American policy has continued to develop in the opposite direction. This study attempts to discover why this should be so. It finds its answer not in the inadequacy of statesmanship or in the machinations of evil men, but in what seem to the drafters of this report to be the unsound premises upon which policy is based. Most Americans accept without question the assumption that winning the peace depends upon a simultaneous reliance upon military strength and long-range programs of a positive and constructive character. They accept also the assumption that totalitarian communism is the greatest evil that now threatens men and that this evil can be met only by violence, or at least by the threat of violence. We believe these assumptions cannot be sustained, and therefore that the policies based on them are built upon sand. We have here attempted to analyze our reasons, and without denying the value of proposals that might ease present tensions, to suggest another and less widely considered alternative built on a different assumption, namely, that military power in today's world is incompatible with freedom, incapable of providing security, and ineffective in dealing with evil.

Our title, *Speak Truth to Power*, taken from a charge[5] given to Eighteenth Century Friends, suggests the effort that is made to speak from the deepest insight of the Quaker faith, as this faith is understood by those who prepared this study. We speak to *power* in three senses:

> To those who hold high places in our national life and bear the terrible responsibility of making decisions for war or peace.

> To the American people who are the final reservoir of power in this country and whose values and expectations set the limits for those who exercise authority.

> To the idea of Power itself, and its impact on Twentieth Century life.

Our *truth* is an ancient one: that love endures and overcomes; that hatred destroys; that what is obtained by love is retained, but what is obtained by hatred proves a burden. This truth, fundamental to the position which rejects reliance on the method of war, is ultimately a religious perception, a belief that stands outside of history. Because of this we could not end this study without discussing the relationship between the politics of time with which men are daily concerned and the politics of eternity which they too easily ignore.

But our main purpose is not to restate the many prophetic expositions of the pacifist position. Beginning with The Sermon on the Mount, the Christian tradition alone has produced a library of enduring religious statements, and the same can be said for the literature of other great faiths. The urgent need is not to preach religious truth, but to show how it is possible and why it is reasonable to give practical expression to it in the great conflict that now divides the world.

In recent years, outside of theological circles, and infrequently there, there has been little able discussion of the pacifist point of view. Pacifism has been cataloged as the private witness of a small but useful minority, or as the irresponsible action of men who are so overwhelmed with the horror of war that they fail to see that greater evil sometimes exists and that the sacrifices of war may be necessary to turn it back. Whether condemned or in a sense valued, pacifism has been considered irrelevant to the concrete problems of international relations.

This study attempts to show its relevance. It is focused on the current international crisis. It begins with a survey of the same concrete problems with which any discussion of world affairs must deal. It is concerned with problems of security, the growth of Russian and American power, the challenge to American interests presented by Soviet Communism. It recognizes the existence of evil and the need to resist it actively. It does not see peacemaking as the attempt to reconcile evil with good. It speaks to the problem of inevitable conflict.

We believe it is time for thoughtful men to look behind the label "pacifist," to deal fairly with the ideas and beliefs which sustain those whose approach to foreign policy begins with the rejection of reliance upon military power. We speak to the great majority of Americans who still stand opposed to war, who expect no good of armies and H-bombs. Their reluctant acceptance of a dominantly military policy has been based on the belief that military power provides the necessary security without which the constructive work that builds peace cannot be undertaken. They are for a military program because they feel they must be. "There is no alternative."

We have tried to present an alternative and to set forth our reasons for believing that it offers far greater hope and involves no greater risk than our present military policy. Our effort is incomplete, but we believe it is a step toward the serious examination of a nonviolent approach to world problems. Is there a method for dealing with conflict which does not involve us in the betrayal of our own beliefs, either through acquiescence to our opponent's will or through resorting to evil means to resist him? Is there a way to meet that which threatens us, without relying on our ability to cause pain to the human being who embodies the threat?

We believe there is a way, and that it lies in the attempt to give practical demonstration to the effectiveness of love in human relations. We believe able men, pacifist and non-pacifist alike, have taken this initial insight, developed it, demonstrated it, and built understanding and support for it in field after field of human relations. In view of this, it is strange that almost no one has made a serious attempt to explore its implications in international affairs. There is now almost no place in our great universities, few lines in the budgets of our great foundations, and little space in scholarly journals, for thought and experimentation that begin with the unconditional rejection of organized mass violence and seek to think through the concrete problems of present international relations in new terms. It is time there was.

New conditions demand new responses. We have tried here to suggest a new response. We hope the reader will bring to it an open mind, and if in any way challenged, will join in a serious effort to explore farther the lines of thought we have suggested.

Submitted to the Executive Board [American Friends Service Committee] and approved for publication March 2, 1955.

> Stephen G. Cary, *Chairman*
> James E. Bristol
> Amiya Chakravarty
> A. Burns Chalmers
> William B. Edgerton
> Harrop A. Freeman
> Robert Gilmore
> Cecil E. Hinshaw
> Milton Mayer
> A. J. Muste
> Clarence E. Pickett
> Robert Pickus
> Bayard Rustin
> Norman J. Whitney

From Protest to Politics:
The Future of the Civil Rights Movement

[*This 1964 essay was introduced with the following note: Bayard Rustin, who organized the March on Washington and has been a close associate of Martin Luther King, is widely recognized as the leading tactician of the civil rights movement. This is his first appearance in* Commentary.]

The decade spanned by the 1954 Supreme Court decision on school desegregation and the Civil Rights Act of 1964 will undoubtedly be recorded as the period in which the legal foundations of racism in America were destroyed. To be sure, pockets of resistance remain; but it would be hard to quarrel with the assertion that the elaborate legal structure of segregation and discrimination, particularly in relation to public accommodations, has virtually collapsed. On the other hand, without making light of the human sacrifices involved in the direct-action tactics (sit-ins, freedom rides, and the rest) that were so instrumental to this achievement, we must recognize that in desegregating public accommodations, we affected institutions which are relatively peripheral both to the American socio-economic order and to the fundamental conditions of life of the Negro people. In a highly industrialized, 20th-century civilization, we hit Jim Crow precisely where it was most anachronistic, dispensable, and vulnerable—in hotels, lunch counters, terminals, libraries, swimming pools, and the like. For in these forms, Jim Crow does impede the flow of commerce in the broadest sense: it is a nuisance in a society on the move (and on the make). Not surprisingly, therefore, it was the most mobility-conscious and relatively liberated groups in the Negro community—lower-middle-class college students—who launched the attack that brought down this imposing but hollow structure.

The term "classical" appears especially apt for this phase of the civil rights movement. But in the few years that have passed since the first flush of sit-ins, several developments have taken place that have complicated matters enormously. One is the shifting focus of the movement in the South, symbolized by Birmingham; another is the spread of the revolution to the North; and the third, common to the other two, is the expansion of the movement's base in the Negro community. To attempt to disentangle these three strands is to do violence to reality. David Danzig's perceptive article, "The Meaning of Negro Strategy,"[6] correctly saw in the Birmingham events the victory of the concept of collective struggle over individual achievement as the road to Negro freedom. And Birmingham remains the unmatched symbol of grass-roots protest involving all strata of the black community. It was also in this most industrialized of Southern cities that the single-issue demands of the movement's classical stage gave way to the "package deal." No longer were Negroes satisfied with integrating lunch counters. They now sought advances in employment, housing, school integration, police protection, and so forth.

Thus, the movement in the South began to attack areas of discrimination which were not so remote from the Northern experience as were Jim Crow lunch counters. At the same time, the interrelationship of these apparently distinct areas became increasingly evident. What is the value of winning access to public accommodations for those who lack money to use them? The minute the movement faced this question, it was compelled to expand its vision beyond race relations to economic relations, including the role of education in modern society. And what also became clear is that all these interrelated problems, by their very nature, are not soluble by private, voluntary efforts but require government action—or politics. Already Southern demonstrators had recognized that the most effective way to strike at the police brutality they suffered from was by getting rid of the local sheriff—and that meant political action, which in turn meant, and still means, political action within the Democratic party where the only meaningful primary contests in the South are fought.

And so, in Mississippi, thanks largely to the leadership of Bob Moses, a turn toward political action has been taken. More than voter registration is involved here. A conscious bid for *political power* is being made, and in the course of that effort a tactical shift is being effected: direct-action techniques are being subordinated to a strategy calling for the building of community institutions or power bases. Clearly, the implications of this shift reach far beyond Mississippi. What began as a protest movement is being challenged to translate itself into a political movement. Is this the right course? And if it is, can the transformation be accomplished?

The very decade which has witnessed the decline of legal Jim Crow has also seen the rise of *de facto* segregation in our most fundamental socio-economic institutions. More Negroes are unemployed today than in 1954, and the unemployment gap between the races is wider. The median income of Negroes has dropped from 57 percent to 54 percent of that of whites. A higher percentage of Negro workers is now concentrated in jobs vulnerable to automation than was the case ten years ago. More Negroes attend *de facto* segregated schools today than when the Supreme Court handed down its famous decision; while school integration proceeds at a snail's pace in the South, the number of Northern schools with an excessive proportion of minority youth proliferates. And behind this is the continuing growth of racial slums, spreading over our central cities and trapping Negro youth in a milieu which, whatever its legal definition, sows an unimaginable demoralization. Again, legal niceties aside, a resident of a racial ghetto lives in segregated housing, and more Negroes fall into this category than ever before.

These are the facts of life which generate frustration in the Negro community and challenge the civil rights movement. At issue, after all, is not *civil rights*, strictly speaking, but social and economic conditions. Last summer's riots were not race riots; they were outbursts of class aggression in a society where class and color definitions are converging disastrously. How can the (perhaps misnamed) civil rights movement deal with this problem?

Before trying to answer, let me first insist that the task of the movement is vastly complicated by the failure of many whites of good will to understand the nature of our problem. There is a widespread assumption that the removal of artificial racial barriers should result in the automatic integration of the Negro into all aspects of American life. This myth is fostered by facile analogies with the experience of various ethnic immigrant groups, particularly the Jews. But the analogies with the Jews do not hold for three simple but profound reasons. First, Jews have a long history as a literate people, a resource which has afforded them opportunities to advance in the academic and professional worlds, to achieve intellectual status even in the midst of economic hardship, and to evolve sustaining value systems in the context of ghetto life. Negroes, for the greater part of their presence in this country, were forbidden by law to read or write. Second, Jews have a long history of family stability, the importance of which in terms of aspiration and self-image is obvious. The Negro family structure was totally destroyed by slavery and with it the possibility of cultural transmission (the right of Negroes to marry and rear children is barely a century old). Third, Jews are white and have the option of relinquishing their cultural-religious identity, intermarrying, passing, etc. Negroes, or at least the overwhelming majority of them, do not have this option. There is also a fourth, vulgar reason. If the Jewish and Negro communities are not comparable in terms of education, family structure, and color, it is also true that their respective economic roles bear little resemblance.

This matter of economic role brings us to the greater problem—the fact that we are moving into an era in which the natural functioning of the market does not by itself ensure every man with will and ambition a place in the productive process. The immigrant who came to this country during the late 19th and early 20th centuries entered a society which was expanding territorially and/or economically. It was then possible to start at the bottom, as an unskilled or semi-skilled worker, and move up the ladder, acquiring new skills along the way. Especially was this true when industrial unionism was burgeoning, giving new dignity and higher wages to organized workers. Today the situation has changed. We are not expanding territorially, the western frontier is settled, labor organizing has leveled off, our rate of economic growth has been stagnant for a decade. And we are in the midst of a technological revolution which is altering the fundamental structure of the labor force, destroying unskilled and semi-skilled jobs—jobs in which Negroes are disproportionately concentrated.

Whatever the pace of this technological revolution may be, the *direction* is clear: the lower rungs of the economic ladder are being lopped off. This means that an individual will no longer be able to start at the bottom and work his way up; he will have to start in the middle or on top, and hold on tight. It will not even be enough to have certain specific skills, for many skilled jobs are also vulnerable to automation. A broad educational background, permitting vocational adaptability and flexibility, seems more imperative than ever. We live in a society where, as Secretary of Labor Willard Wirtz puts it, machines have the equivalent of a high school diploma. Yet the average educational attainment of American Negroes is 8.2 years.

Negroes, of course, are not the only people being affected by these developments. It is reported that there are now 50 percent fewer unskilled and semi-skilled jobs than there are high school dropouts. Almost one-third of the 26 million young people entering the labor market in the 1960's will be dropouts. But the percentage of Negro dropouts nationally is 57 per cent, and in New York City, among Negroes 25 years of age or over, it is 68 per cent. They are without a future.

To what extent can the kind of self-help campaign recently prescribed by Eric Hoffer in the *New York Times Magazine* cope with such a situation? I would advise those who think that self-help is the answer to familiarize themselves with the long history of such efforts in the Negro community, and to consider why so many foundered on the shoals of ghetto life. It goes without saying that any effort to combat demoralization and apathy is desirable, but we must understand that demoralization in the Negro community is largely a common-sense response to an objective reality. Negro youths have no need of statistics to perceive, fairly accurately, what their odds are in American society. Indeed, from the point of view of motivation, some of the healthiest Negro youngsters I know are juvenile delinquents: vigorously pursuing the American Dream of material acquisition and status, yet finding the conventional means of attaining it blocked off, they do not yield to defeatism but resort to illegal (and often ingenious) methods. They are not alien to American culture. They are, in Gunnar Myrdal's phrase, "exaggerated Americans." To want a Cadillac is not un-American; to push a cart in the garment center is. If Negroes are to be persuaded that the conventional path (school, work, etc.) is superior, we had better provide evidence which is now sorely lacking. It is a double cruelty to harangue Negro youth about education and training when we do not know what jobs will be available for them. When a Negro youth can reasonably foresee a future free of slums, when the prospect of gainful employment is realistic, we will see motivation and self-help in abundant enough quantities.

Meanwhile, there is an ironic similarity between the self-help advocated by many liberals and the doctrines of the Black Muslims. Professional sociologists, psychiatrists, and social workers have expressed amazement at the Muslims' success in transforming prostitutes and dope addicts into respectable citizens. But every prostitute the Muslims convert to a model of Calvinist virtue is replaced by the ghetto with two more. Dedicated as they are to maintenance of the ghetto, the Muslims are powerless to affect substantial moral reform. So too with every other group or program which is not aimed at the destruction of slums, their causes and effects. Self-help efforts, directly or indirectly, must be geared to mobilizing people into power units capable of effecting social change. That is, their goal must be genuine self-help, not merely self-improvement. Obviously, where self-improvement activities succeed in imparting to their participants a feeling of some control over their environment, those involved may find their appetites for change whetted; they may move into the political arena.

Let me sum up what I have thus far been trying to say: the civil rights movement is evolving from a protest movement into a full-fledged *social movement*—an evolution calling its very name into question. It is now concerned not merely with removing the barriers to full *opportunity* but with achieving the fact of *equality*. From sit ins and freedom rides we have gone into rent strikes, boycotts, community organization, and political action. As a consequence of this natural evolution, the Negro today finds himself stymied by obstacles of far greater magnitude than the legal barriers he was attacking before: automation, urban decay, *de facto* school segregation. These are problems which, while conditioned by Jim Crow, do not vanish upon its demise. They are more deeply rooted in our socio-economic order; they are the result of the total society's failure to meet not only the Negro's needs, but human needs generally.

These propositions have won increasing recognition and acceptance, but with a curious twist. They have formed the common premise of two apparently contradictory lines of thought which simultaneously nourish and antagonize each other. On the one hand, there is the reasoning of the *New York Times* moderate who says that the problems are so enormous and complicated that Negro militancy is a futile irritation, and that the need is for "intelligent moderation." Thus, during the first New York school boycott, the *Times* editorialized that Negro demands, while abstractly just, would necessitate massive reforms, the funds for which could not realistically be anticipated; therefore the just demands were also foolish demands and would only antagonize white people. Moderates of this stripe are often correct in perceiving the difficulty or impossibility of racial progress in the context of present social and economic policies. But they accept the context as fixed. They ignore (or perhaps see all too well) the potentialities inherent in linking

Negro demands to broader pressures for radical revision of existing policies. They apparently see nothing strange in the fact that in the last twenty-five years we have spent nearly a trillion dollars fighting or preparing for wars, yet throw up our hands before the need for overhauling our schools, clearing the slums, and really abolishing poverty. My quarrel with these moderates is that they do not even envision radical changes; their admonitions of moderation are, for all practical purposes, admonitions to the Negro to adjust to the status quo, and are therefore immoral.

The more effectively the moderates argue their case, the more they convince Negroes that American society will not or cannot be reorganized for full racial equality. Michael Harrington has said that a successful war on poverty might well require the expenditure of a $100 billion. Where, the Negro wonders, are the forces now in motion to compel such a commitment? If the voices of the moderates were raised in an insistence upon a reallocation of national resources at levels that could not be confused with tokenism (that is, if the moderates stopped being moderates), Negroes would have greater grounds for hope. Meanwhile, the Negro movement cannot escape a sense of isolation.

It is precisely this sense of isolation that gives rise to the second line of thought I want to examine—the tendency within the civil rights movement which, despite its militancy, pursues what I call a "no-win" policy. Sharing with many moderates a recognition of the magnitude of the obstacles to freedom, spokesmen for this tendency survey the American scene and find no forces prepared to move toward radical solutions. From this they conclude that the only viable strategy is shock; above all, the hypocrisy of white liberals must be exposed. These spokesmen are often described as the radicals of the movement, but they are really its moralists. They seek to change white hearts— by traumatizing them. Frequently abetted by white self-flagellants, they may gleefully applaud (though not really agreeing with) Malcolm X because, while they admit he has no program, they think he can frighten white people into doing the right thing. To believe this, of course, you must be convinced, even if unconsciously, that at the core of the white man's heart lies a buried affection for Negroes—a proposition one may be permitted to doubt. But in any case, hearts are not relevant to the issue; neither racial affinities nor racial hostilities are rooted there. It is institutions—social, political, and economic institutions—which are the ultimate molders of collective sentiments. Let these institutions be reconstructed *today*, and let the ineluctable gradualism of history govern the formation of a new psychology.

My quarrel with the "no-win" tendency in the civil rights movement (and the reason I have so designated it) parallels my quarrel with the moderates outside the movement. As the latter lack the vision or will for fundamental change, the former lack a realistic strategy for achieving it. For such a strategy they substitute militancy. But militancy is a matter of posture and volume and not of effect.

I believe that the Negro's struggle for equality in America is essentially revolutionary. While most Negroes—in their hearts—unquestionably seek only to enjoy the fruits of American society as it now exists, their quest cannot *objectively* be satisfied within the framework of existing political and economic relations. The young Negro who would demonstrate his way into the labor market may be motivated by a thoroughly bourgeois ambition and thoroughly "capitalist" considerations, but he will end up having to favor a great expansion of the public sector of the economy. At any rate, that is the position the movement will be forced to take as it looks at the number of jobs being generated by the private economy, and if it is to remain true to the masses of Negroes.

The revolutionary character of the Negro's struggle is manifest in the fact that this struggle may have done more to democratize life for whites than for Negroes. Clearly, it was the sit-in movement of young Southern Negroes which, as it galvanized white students, banished the ugliest features of McCarthyism from the American campus and resurrected political debate. It was not until Negroes assaulted *de facto* school segregation in the urban centers that the issue of quality education for *all* children stirred into motion. Finally, it seems reasonably clear that the civil rights movement, directly and through the resurgence of social conscience it kindled, did more to initiate the war on poverty than any other single force.

It will be—it has been—argued that these by-products of the Negro struggle are not revolutionary. But the term revolutionary, as I am using it, does not connote violence; it refers to the qualitative transformation of fundamental institutions, more or less rapidly, to the point where the social and economic structure which they comprised can no longer be said to be the same. The Negro struggle has hardly run its course; and it will not stop moving until it has been utterly defeated or won substantial equality. But I fail to see how the movement can be victorious in the absence of radical programs for full employment, abolition of slums, the reconstruction of our educational system, new definitions of work and leisure. Adding up the cost of such programs, we can only conclude that we are talking about a refashioning of our political economy. It has been estimated, for example, that the price of replacing New York City's slums with public housing would be $17 billion. Again, a multi-billion dollar federal public-works program, dwarfing the currently proposed $2 billion program, is required to reabsorb unskilled and semi-skilled workers into the labor market—and this must be done if Negro workers in these categories are to be employed. "Preferential treatment" cannot help them.

I am not trying here to delineate a total program, only to suggest the scope of economic reforms which are most immediately related to the plight of the Negro community. One could speculate on their political implications—whether, for example, they do not indicate the obsolescence of state government and the superiority of regional structures as viable units of planning. Such speculations aside, it is clear that Negro needs cannot be satisfied unless we go beyond what has so far been placed on the agenda. How are these radical objectives to be achieved? The answer is simple, deceptively so: *through political power.*

There is a strong moralistic strain in the civil rights movement which would remind us that power corrupts, forgetting that the absence of power also corrupts. But this is not the view I want to debate here, for it is waning. Our problem is posed by those who accept the need for political power but do not understand the nature of the object and therefore lack sound strategies for achieving it; they tend to confuse political institutions with lunch counters.

A handful of Negroes, acting alone, could integrate a lunch counter by strategically locating their bodies so as *directly* to interrupt the operation of the proprietor's will; their numbers were relatively unimportant. In politics, however, such a confrontation is difficult because the interests involved are merely *represented*. In the execution of a political decision a direct confrontation may ensue (as when federal marshals escorted James Meredith into the University of Mississippi—to turn from an example of non-violent coercion to one of force backed up with the threat of violence). But in arriving at a political decision, numbers and organizations are crucial, especially for the economically disenfranchised. (Needless to say, I am assuming that the forms of political democracy exist in America, however imperfectly, that they are valued, and that elitist or putschist conceptions of exercising power are beyond the pale of discussion for the civil rights movement.)

Neither that movement nor the country's twenty million black people can win political power alone. We need allies. The future of the Negro struggle depends on whether the contradictions of this society can be resolved by a coalition of progressive forces which becomes the *effective* political majority in the United States. I speak of the coalition which staged the March on Washington, passed the Civil Rights Act, and laid the basis for the Johnson landslide—Negroes, trade unionists, liberals, and religious groups.

There are those who argue that a coalition strategy would force the Negro to surrender his political independence to white liberals, that he would be neutralized, deprived of his cutting edge, absorbed into the Establishment. Some who take this position urged last year that votes be withheld from the Johnson-Humphrey ticket as a demonstration of the Negro's political power. Curiously enough, these people who sought to demonstrate power through the non-exercise of it, also point to the Negro "swing vote" in crucial urban areas as the source of the Negro's independent political power. But here they are closer to being right: the urban Negro vote will grow in importance in the coming years. If there is anything positive in the spread of the ghetto, it is the potential political power base thus created, and to realize this potential is one of the most challenging and urgent tasks before the civil rights movement. If the movement can wrest leadership of the ghetto vote from the machines, it will have acquired an organized constituency such as other major groups in our society now have.

But we must also remember that the effectiveness of a swing vote depends solely on "other" votes. It derives its power from them. In that sense, it can never be "Independent," but must opt for one candidate or the other, even if by default. Thus coalitions are inescapable, however tentative they may be. And this is the case in all but those few situations in which Negroes running on an independent ticket might conceivably win. "Independence," in other words, is not a value in itself. The issue is which coalition to join and how to make it responsive to your program. Necessarily there will be compromise. But the difference between expediency and morality in politics is the difference between selling out a principle and making smaller concessions to win larger ones. The leader who shrinks from this task reveals not his purity but his lack of political sense.

The task of molding a political movement out of the March on Washington coalition is not simple, but no alternatives have been advanced. We need to choose our allies on the basis of common political objectives. It has become fashionable in some no-win Negro circles to decry the white liberal as the main enemy (his hypocrisy is what sustains racism); by virtue of this reverse recitation of the reactionary's litany (liberalism leads to socialism, which leads to Communism) the Negro is left in majestic isolation, except for a tiny band of fervent white initiates. But the objective fact is that *Eastland* and *Goldwater* are the main enemies—they and the opponents of civil rights, of the war on poverty, of medicare, of social security, of federal aid to education, of unions, and so forth. The labor movement, despite its obvious faults, has been the largest single organized force in this country pushing for progressive social legislation. And where the Negro-labor-liberal axis is weak, as in the farm belt, it was the religious groups that were most influential in rallying support for the Civil Rights Bill.

The durability of the coalition was interestingly tested during the election. I do not believe that the Johnson landslide proved the "white backlash" to be a myth. It proved, rather, that economic interests are more fundamental than prejudice: the backlashers decided that loss of social security was, after all, too high a price to pay for a slap at the Negro. This lesson was a valuable first step in re-educating such people, and it must be kept alive, for the civil rights movement will be advanced only to the degree that social and economic welfare gets to be inextricably entangled with civil rights.

The 1964 elections marked a turning point in American politics. The Democratic landslide was not merely the result of a negative reaction to Goldwaterism; it was also the expression of a majority liberal consensus. The near unanimity with which Negro voters joined in that expression was, I am convinced, a vindication of the July 25th statement by Negro leaders calling for a strategic turn toward political action and a temporary curtailment of mass demonstrations. Despite the controversy surrounding the statement, the instinctive response it met with in the community is suggested by the fact that demonstrations were down 75 percent as compared with the same period in 1963. But should so high a percentage of Negro voters have gone to Johnson, or should they have held back to narrow his margin of victory and thus give greater visibility to our swing vote? How has our loyalty changed things? Certainly the Negro vote had higher visibility in 1960, when a switch of only 7 per cent from the Republican column of 1956 elected President Kennedy. But the slimness of Kennedy's victory—of his "mandate"—dictated a go-slow approach on civil rights, at least until the Birmingham upheaval.

Although Johnson's popular majority was so large that he could have won without such overwhelming Negro support, that support was important from several angles. Beyond adding to Johnson's total national margin, it was specifically responsible for his victories in Virginia, Florida, Tennessee, and Arkansas. Goldwater took only those states where fewer than 45 percent of eligible Negroes were registered. That Johnson would have won those states had Negro voting rights been enforced is a lesson not likely to be lost on a man who would have been happy with a unanimous electoral college. In any case, the 1.6 million Southern Negroes who voted have had a shattering impact on the Southern political party structure, as illustrated in the changed composition of the Southern congressional delegation. The "backlash" gave the Republicans five House seats in Alabama, one in Georgia, and one in Mississippi. But on the Democratic side, seven segregationists were defeated while all nine Southerners who voted for the Civil Rights Act were re-elected. It may be premature to predict a Southern Democratic party of Negroes and white moderates and a Republican Party of refugee racists and economic conservatives, but there certainly is a strong tendency toward such a realignment; and an additional 3.6 million Negroes of voting age in the eleven Southern states are still to be heard from. Even the *tendency* toward disintegration of the Democratic party's racist wing defines a new context for Presidential and liberal strategy in the congressional battles ahead. Thus the Negro vote (North as well as South), while not *decisive* in the Presidential race, was enormously effective. It was a dramatic element of a historic mandate which contains vast possibilities and dangers that will fundamentally affect the future course of the civil rights movement.

The liberal congressional sweep raises hope for an assault on the seniority system, Rule Twenty-Two, and other citadels of Dixiecrat-Republican power. The overwhelming of this conservative coalition should also mean progress on much bottlenecked legislation of profound interest to the movement (e.g., bills by Senators Clark and Nelson on planning, manpower, and employment). Moreover, the irrelevance of the South to Johnson's victory gives the President more freedom to act than his predecessor had and more leverage to the movement to pressure for executive action in Mississippi and other racist strongholds.

None of this *guarantees* vigorous executive or legislative action, for the other side of the Johnson landslide is that it has a Gaullist quality. Goldwater's capture of the Republican party forced into the Democratic camp many disparate elements which do not belong there, Big Business being the major example. Johnson, who wants to be President "of all people," may try to keep his new coalition together by sticking close to the political center. But if he decides to do this, it is unlikely that even his political genius will be able to hold together a coalition so inherently unstable and rife with contradictions. It must come apart. Should it do so while Johnson is pursuing a centrist course, then the mandate will have been wastefully dissipated. However, if the mandate is seized upon to set fundamental changes in motion, then the basis can be laid for a new mandate, a new coalition including hitherto inert and dispossessed strata of the population.

Here is where the cutting edge of the civil rights movement can be applied. We must see to it that the reorganization of the "consensus party" proceeds along lines which will make it an effective vehicle for social reconstruction, a role it cannot play so long as it furnishes Southern racism with its national political power. (One of Barry Goldwater's few attractive ideas was that the

Dixiecrats belong with him in the same party.) And nowhere has the civil rights movement's political cutting edge been more magnificently demonstrated than at Atlantic City, where the Mississippi Freedom Democratic Party not only secured recognition as a bona fide component of the national party, but in the process routed the representatives of the most rabid racists—the white Mississippi and Alabama delegations. While I still believe that the FDP made a tactical error in spurning the compromise, there is no question that they launched a political revolution whose logic is the displacement of Dixiecrat power. They launched that revolution within a major political institution and as part of a coalitional effort.

The role of the civil rights movement in the reorganization of American political life is programmatic as well as strategic. We are challenged now to broaden our social vision, to develop functional programs with concrete objectives. We need to propose alternatives to technological unemployment, urban decay, and the rest. We need to be calling for public works and training, for national economic planning, for federal aid to education, for attractive public housing—all this on a sufficiently massive scale to make a difference. We need to protest the notion that our integration into American life, so long delayed, must now proceed in an atmosphere of competitive scarcity instead of in the security of abundance which technology makes possible. We cannot claim to have answers to all the complex problems of modern society. That is too much to ask of a movement still battling barbarism in Mississippi. But we can agitate the right questions by probing at the contradictions which still stand in the way of the "Great Society." The questions having been asked, motion must begin in the larger society, for there is a limit to what Negroes can do alone.

Source

Bayard Rustin, "From Protest to Politics: The Future of the Civil Rights Movement," in *Commentary*, February 1964, reprinted in Devon W. Carbado and Donald Weise, eds., *Time on the Cross: The Collected Works of Bayard Rustin* (San Francisco: Cleis Press, Inc., 2003), pp. 116–129.

Endnotes

1 Profile of Bayard Rustin by Michael Westmoreland-White, August 4, 2003.

2 *Ibid.*, p. 5.

3 The full text of the published lecture may be read at: http://www.quaker.org/pamphlets/wpl1948a.html.

4 AFSC has restored Bayard Rustin's name to this publication by an act of its board. Stephen Cary's account of this episode is included in Jervis Anderson, *Bayard Rustin: Troubles I've Seen, A Biography* (New York: HarperCollins, 1998). Another biography is John D'Emilio, *Lost Prophet: The Life and Times of Bayard Rustin* (New York: Simon and Shuster, 2003).

A recent, unpublished document, using the AFSC archives, is Wendy Chmielewski, "Speak Truth To Power: Religion, Race, and Sexuality, and Politics during the Cold War," prepared for an international conference in 2008 at Oxford University, UK. Chmielewski is curator of the Swarthmore College Peace Collection.

5 Numerous scholars have searched for a record of such a "charge" without success. Most historians now assume that the authors of this publication were mistaken, although the search continues.

6 *Commentary*, February 1964.

VIII
Mahala Ashley Dickerson
(1912–2007)

edited by Harold D. Weaver, Jr.

MAHALA ASHLEY DICKERSON was a lawyer and a human rights activist in the states of Alabama and Alaska. She was also a philanthropist for Quaker causes, donating property to the Alaska Friends Conference. She held a law degree, cum laude, from Howard University and graduated from Fisk University cum laude in 1935. Raised a Baptist, Dickerson became a pacifist and a Quaker after World War II. She was the first African American woman to be admitted to the Alabama Bar in 1948. She went to Alaska with her young, triplet sons in 1958. Her impact on Alaskan law, civil rights, and women's rights was strong. She was the first African American woman to practice law in Alaska. Dickerson had faced discrimination in Alabama and she faced it again in Alaska. When she went to file a homestead claim on her first day in Anchorage, the clerk would not take her application. The next day she went back after studying the homesteading regulations all night, prepared to argue for her right to make a claim, but a new clerk filed her claim right away, and six years later the homestead on Knik Road was hers. Throughout her fifty-year career, Dickerson fought in court as she did in life and won landmark cases for civil rights and against discrimination and prejudice. She ran for state representative in 1968.[1] Her personal story is told in her memoir, *Delayed Justice for Sale: An Autobiography*, first published in 1991 and amended in 1998, and in a two-part series in *Friends Intelligencer* (a predecessor of *Friends Journal*) in 1950.

Negro Lawyer in the South—Part I

[*While she was Alabama's only woman African American lawyer, Mahala Ashley Dickerson was a member of the Pendle Hill staff in the summer of 1950. Following are her experiences in the South, as shared with the summer school.*]

Greetings from Montgomery, Alabama! Alabama, the first state to secede from the Union! Montgomery, its capital and the "Cradle of the Confedcracy"! This city and this state, holding the positions which only they could hold in our country's history and present struggle for maturity, offer an enviable point from which to observe many struggles.

One year and three months ago I opened offices for the general practice of law about six blocks from the First White House of the Confederacy. Outwardly, it appeared that the stage was well set for another Alabama lawyer of the Negro race, even though that lawyer was a woman. The major battles were won. The philosophy of Dred Scott v. Sanford was inconceivable. Negroes by Constitution enactments and judicial interpretations were no longer thought of as mere chattels, so I thought. The opening of my office was without incident, although it was the first ever opened by a Negro in the capital city. The members of the bar were generally kind and helpful; a few sent congratulations.

Despite the United States Supreme Court's famous Gaines decision, Alabama had not and still has not recognized its duty to all of its citizens to provide within its own borders equal facilities for legal training. As yet no Negro has been admitted to the University of Alabama. I was trained in a law school of colored students; we did have two Jewish professors. There are no truer words spoken on the disadvantage of such training than those of the United States Supreme Court's Chief Justice Vinson when he says:

> Although the law is a highly learned profession, ... it is an intensely practical one. The law school, the proving ground for legal learning and practice, cannot be effective in isolation from the individuals and institution with which the law interacts. Few students and no one who has practiced law would choose to study in an academic vacuum, removed from the interplay of ideas and the exchange of views with which the law is concerned. The law school to which Texas is willing to admit petitioner excludes from its student body members of the racial groups which number 85 per cent of the population of the state and include most of the lawyers, witnesses, jurors, judges, and other officials with whom petitioner will inevitably be dealing when he becomes a member of the Texas Bar.

Despite Alabama's inaction in providing for legal education for its Negro citizens, I believe that the judges and lawyers of our state realize the truth of these words and because of that show genuine aid and courtesy to a new Negro member of the bar.

Although I knew there was much to be done, I really felt that the hardest work on racial issues and Constitutional law had already been done. I was to learn that much of this was and is in name only, yes, even to the extent of the prohibition against slavery.

The Texas Primary cases had presumably cleared the polls of obstacles between the former rejected citizen and the exercise of his franchise. As a step further, a local Federal Court had declared invalid a statute which had served to disenfranchise arbitrarily many Negroes and poor whites. Yet there are still those here who time and again have presented themselves for certification as voters but who have never been registered, despite the fact that they have all qualifications which could legitimately be asked for.

The cases of Morgan v. State of Virginia and Mitchell v. United States had to a certain extent made for a possibility of comfortable interstate travel for Negroes. It was my experience when travelling to Pendle Hill on the first of July 1950 to eat in the middle of the diner just outside Atlanta, Georgia. The spot formerly covered by the ugly "iron curtain" hiding the Negro diners was now occupied by a clear glass panel, skillfully decorated with flowers. People of all races were free to use that table, and it seemed a favorite table, now that its odium was removed and its curtain.

The Supreme Court of the United States had decided Henderson v. United States on June 5, 1950. Yet on my way back to Alabama on the first of August 1950 my children and I, though interstate passengers, were given the choice of standing for a few hundred miles after crossing the Mason and Dixon line or getting off the train at Louisville, Kentucky. We got off at Louisville, and it seems that the responsibility of getting a clarification of the status of the interstate passenger traveling by day coach will fall on me.

The remainder of this article will not deal with what has happened to me personally but to the men and women who have entered my office or sent their agents there. Perhaps if my experiences before beginning the practice of law had been more diverse, many of the things which I have seen would not have made me so depressed and unhappy. The life of a schoolteacher is not too full of exposure to human woes, however. The only Court I had ever visited was the United States Supreme Court, where I had spent days upon days and had learned to love the law more and more, to glorify the legal profession, and to expect nothing but fairness from the men entrusted with the interpretation of our laws and Constitution.

After my short period of practice, I wonder if an appropriate addition to the symbol for law should not be the addition of another set of scales, one set marked "white only" and the other marked "colored." To make the symbol more in keeping with reality, the bandage should be removed from the eyes of

Justice. Before I began practice, I had never seen a jail or a prison, but since practice I have frequently entered and had descriptions of events in Alabama's famous Kilby Prison. I know that every word of *Scottsboro Boy*[2] is true.

My practice moved steadily on from my opening day with run-of-the-mill cases of man maltreating wife, or vice versa, borrower in clutches of usurious lender, and smart real estate dealers dispossessing the poor unschooled purchaser, but by the end of my third month I got my first real shock.

My First Shock

A woman in her early thirties entered my office one Saturday afternoon. Two things about her impressed me as she told her story—one, her calmness in the face of such disaster, and the other, her cleanliness. Tears rolled down her round brown face as she spoke with no facial contortions at all, saying: "And he can have my cows, he can have my furniture, if he'll just give me my children."

It took no second glance to see that she was about seven months pregnant. Her husband was mysteriously missing, and her eight children were being held as slaves by her former landlord.

Relations first became bad between the couple and the landlord one morning around 5 o'clock, when the landlord came by to pick them up for a day's labor in the field. The husband had suggested that since the wife felt ill, she be allowed to remain in that day. In the ensuing argument over this request the landlord shot at the husband, barely missing him.

On the other hand, by plantation regulations the share croppers were not allowed to visit anyone, not even to leave the plantation; nor were persons from the outside allowed to visit them. Despite this ruling, husband and wife had dared to go over into a nearby county to the home of the wife's mother and father, leaving the children with relatives and neighbors. Upon learning of this secret departure, the landlord confiscated all livestock (including three Jersey cows, the separate property of the wife, given her by her father), nailed up the house, and gave wide publicity to his intentions of killing both husband and wife if they ever returned to the plantation. The children he placed in homes of certain well disciplined share croppers, with strict orders that they were to be released to no one.

It is still rumored that the father first returned for the children. What transpired on this alleged trip and his present whereabouts are still mysteries.

After the failure of the father to return, the mother, despite her illness and pregnant state, returned to the county for her eight children. The landlord cursed her and threatened to kill her, but finally agreed that if she would leave the county never to come back, he would spare her life. However, he was never going to give up the children. They were going to stay there and work for him to make up for the money he had lost on their "lazy parents." He also assured her that he would permanently keep all livestock, household goods, and personal property which they had brought to his plantation when they moved there almost a year ago.

She appealed to the sheriff, but he laughed at her when she requested a warrant for the landlord's arrest. She appealed to the department of child welfare, but after an "investigation," the "welfare lady," told her that she was sorry, but Mr. X refused to give up the children. The mother then went to a local law firm, asking assistance in regaining her children. Although I can find no legal basis for such advice, these lawyers assured her that unless she would get a divorce (despite the fact that her husband's whereabouts were unknown), she could have no grounds upon which to claim her children. I would not have believed this, but I saw the letter myself, setting forth this advice. The divorce would have cost $50.00, and the day she showed me the letter I had to lend her fifty cents.

Obstacles Everywhere:

Not until she had exhausted most white firms in the city did she come to me. To relieve suspense, I will say at once that after the woman and I annoyed the officials of the United States District Attorney's Office for about a week, the woman (who was later arrested) and her eight children were freed. Due to the fact that these offices are filled by local men who do not wish to antagonize the local people, it is my sincere opinion that they help very little. It appears that the best results are achieved when special investigators are sent from other places for the investigation of each incident.

Before leaving this story, however, I must say that even when upon the advice of the United States District Attorney's Office the woman returned to her county for her children, the same sheriff who had refused to arrest her landlord for wrongfully holding her children arrested her on a vagrancy charge from him. She was forced to stay in jail for three days until her sister, who happened to accompany her on the trip, got a bond for her for which the sister paid $5.00. It took the sister three days to borrow the money from other relatives and friends.

The Alabama law under which she was arrested makes persons not gainfully employed who do not own a certain amount of personal or real property subject to fine and imprisonment. Its administration makes for a type of perpetuation of peonage since the landlord can arrest the tenant the moment he quits his job. Since only the landlord will know about the arrest or be immediately prepared to pay the fine, the tenant falls right into the situation from which he had attempted to escape. While this woman was in jail, she ran into people whose whereabouts had been unknown for months but who chose to remain in jail rather than go back to the plantations from which they had escaped.

When this family was brought into Montgomery, it presented a deplorable sight. The children, ranging from 19 months to 13 years, all were wearing the same outfits, unlaundered, in which their mother had left them seven weeks ago. The two older boys who worked in the fields, appeared to be less starved than the others, for they had slept at the landlord's house on the kitchen floor and had been given remains from his table. The diet of the other children had consisted exclusively of a piece of cold corn bread at the close of each day. The stomachs of the smaller children were enlarged, and the legs of all of the children emaciated.

But for the total disappearance of the father, the whole incident was beneficial to the family, now consisting of nine children, for the general standard of living of the family was soon raised to a higher one than that of the attorney for the family who, of course, receives no fee for cases like this one. It was not long before kind citizens of Montgomery of both races had supplied the children with food, clothing, and shelter. So many of these items of clothing were brought to them that the Federation of Colored Women's Clubs, which was officially receiving them, was in a position to pass many of them on to other needy families. The children were now permitted to enter school. No one on the plantation they had left went to school, not even after cotton was picked for the year.

The significant thing about the aforementioned case was the woman's indomitable courage. The trait is not common among persons so situated. Evidently her love for her children overpowered that deep-rooted fear which I believe to be the Negro's greatest handicap in the South.

SOURCE

Mahala Ashley Dickerson, "Negro Lawyer in the South—Part I," *Friends Intelligencer*, vol. 107, no. 47 (November 25, 1950), pp. 687–689.

Negro Lawyer in the South—Part II

On another occasion a Negro woman brought into my office two teenage boys about 17 years old, one her own son and the other the son of a friend. These boys had worked for a landlord who had refused to pay them and who had upon their refusal to work for him the following week taken them by force to the woods one night, and along with a companion, between drinks, beaten them all night long. There were knots on their heads, and their features were barely distinguishable.

The mother of one, who brought them to my office, told of her futile efforts to get redress for the wrong in her county. Thinking that since Montgomery was the capital, she had come here as a more likely place to get redress. Of course, she had been to most of the white law firms first. I explained to her the remedies open to us through the office of State Attorney General and failing there, the office of the U. S. District Attorney. I promised that I would take them both places the next day. (It was around 6 p.m. when they reached my office.) Their first request, however, was that I somehow initiate the action without disclosing the fact that they had told me of the incident, because they had been told before leaving their county that if they took it any further they would all be killed. I explained that their method was impossible, first, because under Alabama law an attorney representing without the client's authority would be subject to disbarment, and second, there would have to be affidavits drawn as to facts which only they could swear to. I could see despair in their faces upon being so informed, and they never came back. Strangely, no matter how hopeless his plight, the Negro's love for life itself seems usually to overcome all other loves.

It would appear that it is the Negro who is poor and obscure who is usually the victim of the more unchristian and uncivilized conduct in the South. He is the man who will not have an attorney's fee. He is the man who would not have his fine or enough real and personal property to be protected from a vagrancy charge. He is the man who is always accused of rape, and strangely enough, the prosecuting witness in the rape cases is always poor, ignorant, and obscure. There seems to be eternal war between white and black of this class, whereas clashes of other segments of the two races are intermittent.

In a rape case in which I was retained after the defendant had been sentenced to the electric chair and had lost his appeal to the Alabama Supreme Court, I saw a striking example of the clash of the first type referred to above. The defendant was a poor, ignorant country lumberjack. He was arrested for the first time in his life one night while he held his five-month-old baby and his wife was cooking supper. He was asked if he owned a black hat and a brown leather jacket. These questions he answered in the affirmative. When ordered to do so, he produced the items, which any lumberjack might own. He was carried to the police station, where he was first accused of operating a still with another "very black _____." Then he was taken out and placed in a line-up of seven other Negroes. In due course a white woman entered the room and pointed to him. He later swore that he never knew what he was charged with until after being rushed to Kilby (home of *Scottsboro Boy*) for "safe keeping," he saw a newspaper item saying that he had raped a white woman. He was rushed back in a few days for an arraignment, at which time he swears that his court-appointed lawyer refused even to listen to him when he protested his innocence.

Strangely, this case arose less than two months after two white men had been given short sentences (two or three years) for raping two Negro girls at the point of guns. This meting out of sentences to whites for such conduct was unprecedented, it seems.

It is to be observed from the record of the trial of my client that no witnesses as to character or alibis were called for the defendant and that there was no cross-examination of the prosecutrix herself. There were no Negroes on the jury, but it would have been improbable that any jury would have brought in any verdict except "guilty," since there was no impeachrnent of the State's case. Significantly, since the Scottsboro case, our state now provides counsel in capital cases, but the guarantee of counsel cannot amount to guarantee of competent counsel, and no one can expect a lawyer who has no personal interest in a case to spend the hours and days necessary for the preparation for trial of an unpopular cause for the small fee allowed. Another point against the defendant in this case was that at one point he agreed to plead guilty after being told that a plea of guilty would mean the electric chair. It developed that he did not know what an electric chair was. He told me that he thought it was a chair with an electric light over it in which he would have to be confined for awhile, and that he thought this would be the best way out of a situation which he could not understand. It was upon being told by other inmates at Kilby what an electric chair was that he became more persistent that his lawyer plead him innocent.

His trial was conducted in an atmosphere of mob violence, and the patrolmen present had to attempt to draw their guns at several points. This can be accounted for by the fact that wide newspaper publicity had been given to his plea of guilty. After attempts for almost two years to save this man from death in the electric chair through the courts, executive clemency was resorted to. His Excellency James E. Folsom commuted the death sentence to life imprisonment on September 28, 1950. At the clemency hearing I tried to show the Governor how many uncontrollable elements stand between a defendant and a fair trial under the present state of the law and the present state of civilization, especially if that defendant is a Negro. Being a Negro, he stands little chance of being able to find an attorney who will take his case at all, or one who will take it if he is without funds, or of getting a fair trial even with an attorney. But despite these disadvantages, the courts have been kinder to him than the mobs.

The instances cited are not atypical; there are many others of similar nature which I discussed with the Pendle Hill family last summer but which would make this article entirely too long.

The Negro's problem does not limit itself to civil rights. His property rights are also in need of protection.

Regarding these rights, the ignorant Negro is not the only victim, for apparently "the separate but equal" school system carefully trains Negroes to be dreamers, artists, dilettantes, etc. In matters of business and law the educated Negro is so often the most gullible.

Generally, the oppressive "loan shark" and the discriminating keeper of various businesses, assisted by the police force, exercise the same control over the Negro in the cities that the rural landlord and the sheriff exercise over him in the country. Instances of unpunished murder of Negro citizens by policemen are more frequent in Alabama than ever. But these instances are too complicated for discussion in an article such as this one. Yet it is the consensus "that things are generally getting better." Perhaps this optimism is based on statistics showing larger funds for Southern Negro education and larger numbers entering certain professions, but unfortunately figures are not publicized on police brutality, peonage, slavery, short school terms, inadequate teachers and facilities, lack of preparation for practical living in the Negro educational system, and the lack of due process. The instances which I have cited in this article would not have been known to me had I not been practicing law. So completely have the extenuating features of the South's growth been emphasized that many organizations which in the past have offered help in education have withdrawn their assistance. Actually help is needed more than ever.

We are now in a crisis wherein the liberal white Southerner is trying to assist that element of the Negro population which is on its way up. However, this liberal white element is almost unconscious of the element below the one it is assisting. Another element of white Southerners is struggling to keep both elements of the Negro population down. Having its foot on the neck of the lower element, it can do an effective job there easily, but it does not lose sight of the element with education and money. Therefore, occasionally, these people become targets of police brutality, price discrimination, and general[ly] unfair business deals. But generally these people are so pleased with the material goods bestowed upon them and the fact that they enjoy a modicum of freedom, that they ignore these thrusts and seldom attempt to in any way become concerned over the status of their less fortunate brothers and sisters. They seldom assert any of the rights of true citizenship. Only in very small numbers do they attempt to exercise the franchise, and never do they aspire to active participation in the government of their towns and states.

The South offers a challenge to anyone with a true missionary spirit. We are suffering for leadership of white and black. Despite a large number of churches cluttering our streets and highways, Christianity gets little hearing in our plantation system regulations, in the operation of our cities, and in our courts. Judge or jury will believe the statement of one white witness to that of ten black witnesses making an opposite statement.

"Our way of life" in this area has become a Southern tradition, with no place for equality even under the law, for white and black. Perhaps sincere missionaries could start a new philosophy based on the Christian doctrine and the Christian way of life instead of ours, thus saving our crumbling backward areas.

It is not so much the law on record that makes for unchristian relations as its administration. Religion, education, and money, in the order named, are sorely needed. Religion of a different type is necessary for both races. Education is needed for both races. The Negro needs training in matters of business, property, and earning a living. His present educational system leaves him prepared for so few jobs, usually no job at all. Every school or phase of training in the South that was discontinued should be reopened.

As much as we lawyers would like to feel that under our present system of government there is no wrong without a remedy, as men and women we must admit that the judicial, legislative, and administrative bodies of our country are composed of mere men and woman. We must admit that no greater justice can come from a court than that which the majority of its judges metes out. We know that no fairer decision can come from a jury than that to which its most partial juror agrees. It is therefore submitted that the law *per se* can do little to help our backward areas. The law must be assisted by religion, for there must be in the hearts of the beings administering the law a fundamental quality which only a religion can place there.

SOURCE

Mahala Ashley Dickerson, "Negro Lawyer in the South—Part II," *Friends Intelligencer*, vol. 107, no. 48 (December 2, 1950), pp. 707–708.

The World of Religion

Perhaps I have always been interested in human equality or perhaps, even more, I am a bit of a feminist. There is a type of Puritanism that comes from living in the conservative rural south similar to that depicted in Hawthorne's *Scarlet Letter*. I can, for example, recall as a small child hearing whispers about whether a certain young lady would be "begging back" into church. On certain Sunday nights it appeared that if an unmarried female had become pregnant, there would be a motion made to strike her name from the church roles. The motion would be carried, and the young lady would be officially "turned out of church." After the birth of her baby, certain times were set aside for the young lady to "beg back." She would stand in tears before the whole congregation and in tears say, "Brothers and sisters, I know I did wrong. Won't you please forgive me? I promise not to do it anymore."

There would be a motion made to take the sister back into the fold, to forgive her and give her the right hand of fellowship. The whole church membership would then line up and shake hands with her. All was forgiven. As I grew older and learned more about the "birds and the bees," I wondered why the father of the baby was never required to "beg back." I do not know when this antiquated custom was abandoned but I am sure it no longer exists.

I never thought I would see a time when the mother and the child would be provided for by the state. Stranger yet, a time when an unwanted pregnancy could be legally terminated. Equally forceful today is the right-to-life movement. Despite the antithesis of these movements somehow the realization has evolved (thankfully) that the old scarlet "A" no longer exists.

The solution of offering a meaningful life both to these wanted and planned, *and* unwanted and unplanned children has not evolved. We wonder why so many who have everything, as well as those who have nothing, find a way to keep interested in living only through the use of drugs.

I once asked my dear friend of forty-two years, Juanita Kidd Stout, then a Justice of the Supreme Court of the State of Pennsylvania, what our careers would have been like had we been born in the present era, with its temptations of drugs, crime, et cetera. Her reply was, "Our careers would have been the same if we had had the same parents which we had."

I had to agree. We exchanged with laughter the spankings we got as children. I recalled our conversations about our strict parents—landowners, schoolteachers, idealists. It makes a striking contrast with what so many children of today have for role models.

Despite my great love for Alaska, I still have fond memories of Indiana. My visit there in 1986 brought back fond memories. Life in Indiana was delightful in so many ways. I was able to renew contact with the Quakers, from whom I had received so much inspiration. I attended an unprogrammed silent meeting which met on week nights. Most of the meeting members also belonged to a regularly organized Quaker Church, with a minister, which was generally referred to as Programmed Friends. They had a very fine minister and an excellent choir. However, the periods of silence were so short that, by the time you were just beginning to get deep into your contemplation, the sermon would begin or the choir would start. It was enjoyable, but more like attending another denomination than what I had always thought of as Quaker.

An embarrassing situation arose when the minister visited our home and invited us to join. He brought applications and we signed them. We had no intention of splitting the congregation, but learned that the old expression "Sunday morning is the most segregated time in America" definitely applied to my newly found Indiana home. The minister, whom I had the opportunity to see on a visit to Indiana in 1986, and who was then in his nineties, remembered me and gave me an autographed copy of his memoirs. He called my attention to the place in his book where he mentions this incident. A minority of members objected to a black family joining their church. It seems the fact that they had built a beautiful new church in a high-priced neighborhood was a major factor, as membership for black persons might cause a depreciation in property values.

I wanted to withdraw our applications immediately, but our friends urged us not to. Some of them stated that this was the first real test of their Quakerism and what it really meant to them, and they wanted to see how everything would turn out. Quakers are never supposed to do anything without first obtaining full consent from all members. In his book the former minister describes it as a minority of the members who objected, but somehow we never knew how many and exactly which ones.

My three sons, who were registered as conscientious objectors, had attended a private Quaker school. In Indianapolis they attended the partially unsegregated schools for two years. They did not bear the full brunt of what it was like. After two years at a private Quaker school, one of them had gone to a very exclusive prep school in New England, while the other had gone to a very exclusive black prep school in North Carolina. I never discussed it too much with them. I had become so hardened by my many experiences of living in a segregated world that at this point my skin was as thick as a crocodile's hide, and I never knew how deep the impact of rejection might hit them.

They had never known much rejection. As triplets they had been the spoiled darlings of their hometown, and had continued as spoiled darlings wherever they went. If for no other reason than for the novelty of being triplets.

A small group of Quakers left this particular Quaker church after discovering what some of the others were like. One very staunch Friend, a very good friend of my family, explained why she had to stay. She stated that when she married her husband, she took his letter to that particular church, and he had died a member. She considered him still a member, although he was dead, and since he could not withdraw his membership, she was forced to remain there—despite her staunch disapproval of the prejudice shown by some of the other Friends. It was not until the summer of 1986 that I had a chance to see the meetinghouse and cemetery. It had been revived by a small minority of members, who had left the other fashionable church. Because of dwindling membership and the travel involved, that meeting had dwindled in numbers to the extent that its few remaining members were more frequently attending a closer Friends group, a less fashionable and silent group.

One of my greatest sources of happiness in Alaska has been attending the very small silent meetings held at various places in Anchorage, Wasilla, Fairbanks, and Palmer. To watch a meetinghouse being humbly built from the ground up, with no fanfare and with everyone putting in at least one nail, was an inspiring sight. It stands unfinished, but love built it, and somehow I feel love will finish it. It is not what George Fox, founder of Quakerism, would call a "steeple house" to which I had been denied membership. Several years later, however, I was to be rendered a blow by two white male members indicating racism lurking even in this little haven.

I often wonder how much harm religion has done the world. My attraction to Quakerism was largely on its simplicity and what I have perceived as its sincerity, although years of worship in various Quaker settings taught me that it too has blind spots. There are those who are drawn to it because of the fact that it attracts relatively few, which gives it a certain snob value. Of course, this was never the intent of the original movement.

The peace and quiet of it had a special appeal for me in view of my early childhood years, when I sat for hours and hours in the Baptist church listening to much noise. Although all Baptist churches did not emit these loud noises, mine did. Visiting churches throughout my years, speaking at them, made me realize I needed quiet contemplation when I tried to worship. To be able to listen also attracted me.

I have always had a deep abiding belief in God and cannot remember how it first came to me. I joined the Baptist church, and had been immersed in a creek at the age of seven, after the Baptist custom. I suppose, in a way, I am still a Baptist. There is a popular saying: "Baptist birth and Baptist born, and when I'm dead it's a Baptist gone." My father, a staunch Baptist Sunday-School teacher and Baptist deacon, never knew I had abandoned his faith.

I am reminded of a joke I heard the great Douglas Steer[e], one of my Quaker Friends, now deceased, tell. One of his friends, who had been a Baptist, became a Quaker but still remained Baptist in many of his ways, so they dubbed him a "Quaptist." The contact with the various religions through the years has probably left me a Quaptimethocat, Quaker, Baptist, Methodist, Catholic.

Throughout the last fifty years of my life, I have had very pleasant contacts with the Baha'is. I never officially became one but found we had much in common and developed long-lasting friendships among them. One of the greatest thrills of my life occurred when I was awarded the Honor Kempton Award by the Baha'i Assembly of Alaska. It was the most impressive ceremony I ever attended. I could not believe it was all being done in my honor.

My Quaker paradise was destined for trouble. In the same year that the American Bar Association was giving [me] one of its Margaret Brent Awards, I was destined to overhear racist remarks concerning me being made [by] Robert Sullivan and James Schiable, ranking Quakers, in my own home where they had been welcome to swim in my indoor heated pool. After that, Quakers were no longer welcome in my home but restricted to the meeting house area. I never felt quite the same as the lack of sensitivity was obvious to me by this racist interchange though it did not matter to the other members. Obviously, I am destined to worship alone and I feel that God understands.

SOURCE

M. Ashley Dickerson, *Delayed Justice For Sale: An Autobiography* (Anchorage: Al-Acres, Inc., 1998), chapter 25, "The World of Religion," pp. 144–147.

Negative Action Destroying Affirmative Action in a Country For Sale

Epilogue no. 7-1997

When first beginning this book ten years ago I called it *Delayed Justice for Sale*. In watching the way in which elections have come and gone, I fear that a more appropriate name would have been *A Country for Sale*. It is tragic to think that only money can buy a political seat. Until such time as truth prevails and there is actually a reformation of our system of government, actual campaign reformation, our country will continue to be for sale. Now that at least there is the vote, even though every attempt has been made and the United States Supreme Court has gone along with almost destroying districts which gave the black minorities an opportunity to block the continued sale. By its action, which could be called the deciding death vote to Affirmative Action, it could have destroyed the concept. The ballot box remains free but is there a chance at true democracy in our country if only money can purchase the seats of government? Although slavery has been legally abolished we must ask ourselves to what extent is our population still being enslaved by a system which is determined to keep a certain number of its people, the actual majority which if properly linked together would be the true majority, at the bottom.

ENDNOTES

1 Source: M. Ashley Dickerson, *Delayed Justice for Sale: An Autobiography* (Anchorage: Al-Acres, Inc., 1998), pp. 247–248) first published in 1991 and amended in 1998. This book is her privately published memoir.

2. *Scottsboro Boy*, by Haywood Patterson, refers to a book that details the charges leveled against one of the young African American boys, falsely accused of raping a European American woman in Alabama. This case brought worldwide attention to the injustices of the U.S. legal system. To learn about further injustice in Alabama in the broader context of the peonage system, read *Slavery by Another Name: The Re-Enslavement of Black Americans from the Civil War to World War II* by Douglas A. Blackmon, a Wall Street Journal bureau chief (New York: Doubleday, 2008). This recent, chilling, detailed account tells of the vicious, post-Emancipation system of peonage that kept thousands of formerly legally enslaved African Americans in actual, illegal slavery of imprisonment and exploitation in Alabama by some of the United States' leading, respected companies.

IX

Bill Sutherland

(1918–2010)

edited by Harold D. Weaver, Jr.

BILL SUTHERLAND was born and educated in the United States, but lived for almost thirty years in Africa. He moved to Ghana prior to its 1957 independence from the United Kingdom. His three children were born there and they think of Ghana as home. In the early 1960s he moved to Tanzania, which at the time was the center of Pan-African liberation forces. He was often in dialogue with Julius K. Nyerere and Kenneth Kaunda of Zambia, who shared his commitment to nonviolence.

As a youth, Sutherland's was the only African American family to live in his white neighborhood, which failed to welcome them, and he learned early the need to build bridges. His early exposure to Gandhi and the independence movement in India as well as his active involvement with the NAACP and youth groups that dealt with international relations and socialism laid the groundwork for his later life focus.

As a student at Bates College Sutherland continued his work for racial justice and pacifism through the North East Student Christian Movement. Here he met Dave Dellinger. Dellinger, who later was a leader in the anti-war movement and one of the Chicago Seven, founded an ashram as a community center in Newark based on the Gandhian approach. After graduation from Bates in 1940, Sutherland volunteered for the student peace service of the American Friends Service Committee in Chicago and joined the Newark Ashram. The connection with AFSC was to continue throughout his lifetime.

The military draft, instituted at this time, led Sutherland to become a conscientious objector. He was imprisoned from 1942 to 1945 at the Lewisburg Federal Penitentiary. Dellinger and other war resisters later joined him there where they protested prison segregation and mail censorship. On release from prison, Sutherland helped to found the Congress of Racial Equality along with Bayard Rustin and others.

He traveled through Europe with the Peace Makers Project and met Russians and Africans on his journeys.

Bill Sutherland was later to follow Bayard Rustin to Africa and worked with Kwame Nkrumah in Ghana from 1953 until 1961. Growing out of the Fellowship of Reconciliation, he had earlier founded Americans for South African Resistance to support the efforts against unjust laws. This later became the American Committee on Africa with which the AFSC worked closely in the 1970s and 1980s.

In Africa, including Ghana and, later, Tanzania, Sutherland advocated the importance of nonviolence. He was active in the World Peace Brigades and was special assistant to the 6th Pan African Congress in Tanzania in 1974. He also sustained his work with AFSC through its Third World Coalition and its Community Relations Division. He developed the practice of board dialogue throughout AFSC linking African liberation with peace and justice movements in the United States. He brought an international perspective to community based work.

In 2000, Bill Sutherland and Matt Meyer published *Guns And Gandhi in Africa*. This book details the many persons and movements that Sutherland touched and influenced in his travels around the world. His commitment to world revolutionary nonviolence over many years has brought him attacks from intelligence organizations, right wing, and violent revolutionary movements. Still, he has held fast and has earned the title "Nonviolent Warrior for Peace."

Why Examine Violence and Nonviolence in Africa?

The themes of this book are multi-faceted and interconnected, and grow primarily out of our political principles and perspectives. While advocates of the power of nonviolence, we have never been among those who equate nonviolence with non-action, or who see nonviolence as the opposite of revolution. Just as pacifism has been confused by some with a form of passivity or pacification, we are uncomfortable with the negativism in the word "non-violence" itself, preferring the more positive approach of Gandhi's Satyagraha.[1] A nonviolence that ultimately upholds or excuses the status quo is fundamentally false; it helps perpetuate violence. Our main concerns have been the overwhelming structural and institutional roots of conflict—such as racism, sexism, and capitalism—which in themselves constitute the greatest violence of our times.

As commonly defined, nonviolence is no more than a momentary tactic which can therefore be used for both revolutionary or reformist efforts. But as far as we are concerned, the creation of a truly nonviolent world would call for total global revolution. In this light, we have often identified with Che Guevara's assessment that one cannot be a true revolutionary without great feelings of love. Our own perspective is not that far off from Mao Tse Tung's assessment that weapons are not the decisive factor in determining victory or defeat: "it is people, not things, that are decisive."[2] We agree with the Chinese and Indian notions that no revolution, whatever the methods used, can take place without the spiritual transformation of the people.

We strongly believe that the institutionalized violence of society cannot be eradicated without revolutionary social upheaval, and we are also well aware of examples of narrow-minded reformists among both the pacifist and armed-struggle camps. If we are to achieve our goals, we believe that dialogue is essential, especially among all those searching for truly revolutionary alternatives.

Defining our terms—the true meaning of nonviolence, armed struggle, or revolution—must be taken more seriously. Looking at the reality rather than the rhetoric of what has been done and of the relationship between cause and effect is an ongoing task. We have tried to be careful and objective in our use of language, recognizing the cultural, linguistic, and political complexity of the issues involved.

"OBI NKA BI"—a stylized image of two fishes or centipedes attempting to bite each other's tails, one of the symbols used in the Adinkra cloths of the Akan peoples of West Africa—is the closest phrase Amowi Sutherland Phillips could come up with on short notice. During a brief stay on the Caribbean island of Jamaica, where Bill's daughter and son-in-law live and work, dinner conversation turned to the meaning of nonviolence, and to the words that one might use to express this concept in Amowi and Allen's native Ghanaian language of Fanti. "One Love"—the unity of peoples, especially Africa peoples—is more easily heard in this land of Bob Marley, where the rhythms of reggae sway with the trees and most people still remember Marley's ability to join the hands of the political leaders in fierce opposition—Manley and Seaga—on stage in concert for a momentary display of togetherness. But nonviolence in any language is a tougher concept to express or demonstrate or define.

In English, nonviolence has always been an inadequate expression of the Gandhian term Satyagraha, roughly translated from Hindi as "soul force." For Gandhi, spiritual power is the strongest force in the universe and the basis of all transformation, social and personal. His struggle to keep his deeply held beliefs from becoming dogma is reflected in the title of his autobiography, *The Story of My Experiments with Truth*. But his experiments, like all others worthy of the name, were carried out as though the premise were absolutely true. The best known examples of Satyagraha have been the strikes, boycotts, fasts, and mass demonstrations associated with civil disobedience campaigns to free India from British domination. Gandhi, however, made the foundation of his movement human relations and development at the local level. For him, real and lasting social change would come about through the establishment of what he called "village republics." At this level, it was not necessary to achieve independence from Britain for the people to institute fundamental changes.[3] We have difficulty in relating to a number of his experiments in the areas of health and personal morality, but we fully identify with his basic premise that real and lasting change can come about only through struggle rooted in the positive aspects of the values and cultures of the people involved.

Some aspects of the present movements that we can identify with, apparently coming from the North and West (pro-democracy, environmentalism, women's liberation, human rights), can actually be found in the history of Africa. This aspect of their history, all too often, is being rejected by Africans in their rush to "catch up" with the more industrialized nations, and has long been ignored and denied in Europe and the U.S. But what of these roots of democratic and peaceful structures and processes in Africa and the so-called Third World? As far as nonviolence is concerned, Allen Phillips' answer is quick but common: "There is no such equivalent concept to be found in Fanti."

"obi nka bi," the creatures locked in connection with one another's tails, translates roughly as: "Bite not one another." It has been used for centuries as a warning against backbiting and to advocate harmony, peace, unity, forgiveness and fair play.[4]

The Future of Nonviolence, Armed Struggle, and Revolution in Africa

A summary of other themes of our dialogues, and of the methods used to bring about peace and justice in modern-day Africa, shows that, in several countries, there was a conscious use of Gandhian nonviolence as the principal means of struggle. In Ghana, Nkrumah changed the name to positive action, but credited Gandhi in his writings and speeches. In Zambia, Kaunda was the most explicit in his use of principled nonviolent action. The first experiments by Gandhi, and the influence in South Africa, had some consideration beyond simple pragmatism. In these cases, as well as Tanzania and Namibia, where Nyerere and Nujoma engaged in nonviolence on a pragmatic basis, the example of India's struggle was an inspiration. This was also because there had been a connection between the Pan-African movement leaders, such as George Padmore, and the leaders of the Free India movement in London.

Most countries that turned to armed struggle, earlier had engaged in some form of nonviolent action. This was true of Algeria, South Africa, Namibia, Mozambique, Zimbabwe, and in Kenya's Mau Mau experiences. Even after being committed to armed struggle, nonviolent actions proved to be quite effective. We recall the FLN in Algeria was losing militarily when its nonviolent response to Red Hand action kept world pressure on France. It was Black Consciousness action and the United Democratic Front in 1980 that gave focus to the external support afforded the anti-apartheid freedom fighters. External support—the pressure of worldwide public opinion—has always been an essential element in successful nonviolent action, and certainly played a major role as Northern powers used newly independent African nations as pawns in the Cold War game. People-to-people solidarity, against political and economic domination, is the foundation for a positive globalization.

So often, in societies which have undergone dramatic change, the structures which brought about the changes were disbanded because people felt that they had achieve their goal, whether political independence or socialist revolution. History indicates that once leaders take state power, divisions often develop between the ruling party and the people. This has been true in countries that have followed Western capitalist, Eastern socialist, and non-aligned political models. Nyerere's Ujumaa, Kaunda's humanism, South Africa's freedom charter—all attempted innovative changes and faced with difficulty the traps set by the neocolonial and neoliberal Northern powers. There has, throughout the world, been a gulf between radical theory and practice; the question now is how to work the system between a rock and a hard place.

In looking at strategies for the future, several points stand out. First, the most effective forms of struggle have always involved mass participation. This is true whether the struggles are nonviolent or armed, whether based on mass action (as in Ghana or South Africa) or on people's armies (as in Algeria or Zimbabwe). Secondly, no struggle has ever been entirely nonviolent or military in nature, and support for revolutionary movements must not be contingent on these elements. Finally, it must be understood that, in one sense, the matrix for revolution is never peace; it is static violence. Colonialism in Africa and segregated society in the U.S. constituted classic examples of static violence, of basic social injustice where peace could not be possible. It should be no surprise, then, that the primary agents for change were fundamentally inter-related, with Malcolm X and Martin Luther King having their effects on one another as they did on African society, even while Lumumba, Nkrumah, Haile Selassie, and Nyerere were having their effect upon movements in the United States and the rest of the Diaspora.

In the world of globalization, the Pan-African movement must also be global. As it continues to work for the unity of people of African descent throughout the world, it must also unite with other movements seeking peace and justice. Connections between Pan-Africanists must be made with environmentalists, feminists, human rights advocates, and those seeking economic justice. No struggle is won without allies. Our movements must learn not simply to unite or merge, but to build cooperation through parallel action.

In a world of institutionalized militarism as well as war, where there is an inextricable mix of physical, psychological, and spiritual violence, one may well find more love and creativity in people engaged in armed struggle than in those who refuse to risk violence yet remain inactive in the face of injustice. But while nonviolent resisters must not be rigid in promoting their method of struggle, we do not accept that the tragedy of taking life—even in the struggle for a just cause—is somehow cathartic or without negative social consequences. The connectedness between the means and the ends, like the links between the personal and the political, suggests that nonviolence must be the leading part of any constructive social movement.

Source
Bill Sutherland and Matt Meyer, *Guns And Gandhi in Africa: Pan-African Insights On Nonviolence, Armed Struggle And Liberation in Africa* (Trenton: Africa World Press, Inc., 2000), pp. 15-20.

Endnotes

1 M.K. Gandhi, *An Autobiography or The Story of My Experiments with Truth*, Ahmedabad: Navajivan Publishing House, 1927. Gandhi attributed the birth of the term Satyagraha to struggles in South Africa, around 1906. He noted that Europeans interpreted the term "passive resistance" too narrowly, and stated that "it was clear that a new word must be coined by the Indians to designate their struggle" (p. 239). Later, his developing thoughts were compiled in *The Science of Satyagraha* (edited and published by Anand T. Hingorani), Bharatiya Vidya Bravan, Bombay, 1970. (Note in original.)

2 Mao Tse Tung, *On People's War*, Peking: Foreign Language Press, 1967. The full quote, "every Communist must grasp the truth, 'Political power grows out of the barrel of a gun,'" comes from Mao's essay "Problems of War and Strategy," November 6, 1938, *Selected Works*, vol. II. Earlier that year, Mao had written: "Weapons are an important factor in war, but not the decisive factor; it is people, not things, that are decisive. The contest of strength is not only a contest of military and economic power, but also a contest of human power and morale" (from "On Protracted War," May 1938, *Selected Works*, vol. II). An interesting review of the strategic implications of these quotes took place as A.J. Muste replied to the writings of Chinese Communist Minister of Defense Marshall

Lion Piao in his famous essay, "Who Has The Spiritual Atom Bomb," *Liberation*, November 1965. As Muste noted. the phrase "spiritual atom bomb" was actually coined by Lin Piao. This essay was recently reprinted and is available in pamphlet form from the A.J. Muste Memorial Institute, http://www.ajmuste.org/index.html. (Note in original.)

3   Bharatan Kumarappa, *Capitalism, Socialism or Villagism?* Rajghat: Sarva Seva Sangh Prakashan, 1945. This volume, with a forward by Gandhi, details the Indian movement's views on the village republics. These ideas were adapted for post-independence issues in Jayaprakash Narayan's *Towards Total Revolution: India and Her Problems*, Bombay: Popular Prakashan, 1978. (Note in original.)

4   Bruce Willis, *The Adinkra Dictionary*, Washington: The Pyramid Complex, 1998; Alfred Kofi Quarcoo, *The Language of Adinkra Symbols*, Legon: Sebewie Ventures (Publications), 1972. (Note in original.)

X
Charles H. Nichols
(1919-2007)
edited by Harold D. Weaver, Jr.

CHARLES H. NICHOLS was born on July 6, 1919, in the Bedford Stuyvesant neighborhood of Brooklyn, New York. He was the last of seven children born to Charles F. and Julia Nichols, Plymouth Church of the Brethren missionary immigrants from Barbados. His gift for study became obvious during childhood, and he was admitted to the prestigious Boys High School in Brooklyn. Thereafter, he attended Brooklyn College on a Regents scholarship and graduated with honors in 1942. After two years as a teaching assistant at Hampton University, he applied and was admitted to the graduate program in American Literature at Brown University in Providence, Rhode Island, as a Rosenwald Fellow. The abolitionist record, the World War II era conscientious objection to war and violence, and the witness for peace of the Quakers attracted him to the Quaker meeting in Providence, where he became a member.

His dissertation at Brown focused on the first person accounts of Africans enslaved in America—the slave narratives—for which Brown awarded him a Ph.D. in English in 1948. Academic appointments soon followed at Morgan State University in Baltimore and later at Hampton University in Hampton, Virginia. It was at Hampton that he met Mildred Thompson, then a student in one of his English classes, who became his wife for 56 years.

The site of his academic career shifted to Europe in 1954 with the award of a Fulbright professorship at Aarhus University, Denmark. While in Denmark, Professor Nichols lectured throughout Europe, including at the Free University in Berlin. After returning to Hampton for four years, he accepted the position of professor of English and director of the department of North American Literature at the Free University. In 1969 he returned to Brown as professor and chairman of the newly founded department of Afro-American (now Africana) Studies.

Nichols was a prolific writer, lecturer, mentor, and teacher. His books include *Many Thousand Gone: The Ex-Slaves' Account of their Bondage and Freedom*; *Black Men in Chains*; and *Arna Bontemps-Langston Hughes Letters 1925–1967*.

He served on several boards including the Moses Brown School Board of Overseers, the Woolman Hill Board of Directors, and the advisory editorial boards of *African American Review*, *Black Literature Forum*, and the *Lexikon der Philosophie*. Among his many honors were the Distinguished Contribution Award of the Society for the Study of Multi-Ethnic Literature of the United States and the Education Award of the Providence Branch of the NAACP, as well as grants from the National Endowment for the Humanities, the Danforth Foundation, and the Fulbright Commission. Brown University has named the Charles H. Nichols National Scholarship and the Charles H. Nichols Award for Africana Studies in his honor.

Source
Mildred Nichols, Obituary, January 2007.

Many Thousand Gone
Introduction

> If any of them will tell me that to make a man into a sausage would be much worse—would be any worse, than to make him into a slave... I will accuse him of foolishness, of intellectual incapacity, of making a distinction without a difference. The one is just as reasonable a proposition as the other.
> — *Thoreau*

Nearly everyone concerned with American slavery has had his say, but in our time we have forgotten the testimony of its victims. This is a history of slavery told, essentially, from the point of view of those whose unpaid labor maintained the plantation system of the Old South. The sources used are selected from among the hundreds of slave biographies and autobiographies published between 1760 and 1865. These "slave narratives" present valuable information on the slave trade, the master class, the plantation system, the reactions of the enslaved Negro and the lives of the fugitives in the North and in Canada.

What does it mean to be another man's property? How does it feel to work without wages, or, as a field hand, coerced into producing another's cotton, corn or sugar, to be forced in all society's arrangements to accept the blight of inferiority? What emotions inflamed their murderous and abortive revolts? What compelled them into submission and disingenuous cooperation, what was the nature of their tenuous "adjustment" to slavery? Or having fled the plantation, what had slavery done to their personality and behavior? These are questions which only the slave himself can directly answer. They are answered in the narratives. Although a few histories of slavery have employed some of these autobiographies as sources, there is no overall account of them in print. Nor is there any work presenting the plantation system from the slaves' point of view.[1] Above all, there is no intimate study of the psychology of the enslaved. At least a beginning is made here in examining the meaning of the slaves' experiences.

Slave narratives appeared in America in colonial times and in our early national period. The genre began with John Saffin's *Adam Negro's Tryall* written in 1703 in answer to Samuel Sewall's well known antislavery tract, *The Selling of Joseph*. Other eighteenth century works include *The Address of Abraham Johnstone* who was hanged at Woodbury, New Jersey for the murder of another Negro; *A Narrative of the Uncommon Sufferings and Surprising Deliverance of Briton Hammon, a Negro Man* (Boston, 1760); the broadside entitled *The Life and Dying Speech of Arthur*, published in Boston in 1768; *A Narrative of the Lord's Wonderful Dealings with John Marrant, a Black* (London, 1785); *The Interesting Narrative of Olaudah Equiano* or *Gustavus Vassa, the African* (London, 1789); and *A Narrative of the Life and Adventures of Venture, a Native of Africa* (New London, 1798). When the antislavery crusade entered its major phase after 1831, however, thousands of slave biographies and autobiographies appeared. Some were published in abolition periodicals; others were separately printed. There is no doubt that most of the narratives were produced with the aid of the antislavery men of Boston and New York, and contain literary, ethical and sentimental elements added by the white ghost writers and editors. Indeed it has often been charged that most of the narratives were, in effect, written by abolitionists to whom they were sometimes dictated. Ulrich Phillips felt that this made their authenticity doubtful.[2] Like all autobiographies they must be critically evaluated by the accepted standards for historical evidence, but the genuineness of the great majority of the works employed in this study is unquestioned. Moreover abolitionist editorship does not necessarily impugn their reliability, for only superficial aspects of narratives have been challenged and even fictionalized accounts are striking in their essential truth. As the victim's personal account of bondage, these autobiographies provide a unique and essential perspective of American slavery.

Works of doubtful authenticity include such fictitious accounts as Hildreth's *Archy Moore*, Mattie Griffith's *Autobiography of a Female Slave*, Mrs. Pierson's *Fugitive*, and the Reverend Mr. Hawkins' biography of Lunsford Lane[3] which read like novels, replete with reconstructed dialog and false sentiment. There are also fictionalized elements in Kate Pickard's *Kidnapped and the Ransomed* and the narratives of Charles Ball and James Williams. No doubt some of the fugitives, though essentially trustworthy, used fictitious names and places because they feared recapture.

In the battle for men's minds, the slaveholding interests could be expected to challenge the sweeping denunciations of abolitionists. *The Narrative of James Williams, an American Slave Who Was for Several Years a Driver on a Cotton Plantation in Alabama* was dictated to John Greenleaf Whittier and published by the American Antislavery Society in 1838. A short time after the narrative appeared, the editor of *The Alabama Beacon* asserted that no such plantation or planter as Williams mentioned was to be found anywhere in Alabama. It was then rumored that Whittier had been hoodwinked by a free Negro pretending to be a fugitive slave. By the time of the exposé, James Williams had gone to England, and the Antislavery Society suppressed the book. Wrote Whittier: "Our cause needs no support of a doubtful character, and if the narrative in any essential particular is untrue, the slaveholders of Virginia and Alabama would confer a favor on us by immediately pronouncing testimony to that effect."[4] Yet James Birney, a former Alabama slaveholder converted to abolitionism, assured Whittier that statements made by Williams accorded well with his own knowledge of slavery in that state. The slaves' amanuenses—Lydia Maria Child, John G. Whittier, Edmund Quincy, Samuel Eliot—were persons of proved integrity. They were well aware that their propaganda effort against slavery could not be advanced by fraud. They present in the books documents which establish their trustworthiness. For example letters secured from his former owners are printed in the preface to Henry Bibb's narrative together with the report of a committee which substantiates the truth of his experiences. The editors were at great pains to state carefully the extent of their tampering. Moreover, any reasonably well informed reader can separate the facts from the sentimental moralizing of an editor whose meddling tended to mitigate the stark realities narrated rather than to exaggerate them. Lydia Maria Child, who revised Harriet Jacobs' narrative, *Incidents in the Life of a Slave Girl*, insisted, "Such changes as I have made have been mainly for purposes of condensations and orderly arrangement."[5]

Thus many more of these autobiographies are the work of the ex-slaves themselves than is commonly supposed. Moses Roper, William Grimes, William Hayden, John Thompson, Frederick Douglass, William Wells Brown,

James Pennington, Austin Steward, Henry Bib and others wrote the accounts of their lives. These men told their experiences dozens of times on the antislavery platform before they came to write them. At the time he dictated his narrative, Lewis Clarke had been telling his story to abolition audiences in eight states for three years. Furthermore, the narratives do not, by and large, exhibit any stylistic excellences which are beyond the reach of fairly intelligent, if poorly educated, men. Then too, the abolitionists were eager to have the fugitives write their own books since such works were, they felt, arguments against the notion of Negro inferiority. Men like Gustavus Vassa, William Grimes, Noah Davis and John Thompson not only wrote their autobiographies but published their books themselves.

Another common objection to the slave narratives is the claim that the writers were not representative of the masses of slaves. Some commentators insist that only the more discontented and abused Negros fled slavery, and only the more enterprising would ever write their experiences. Although this argument seems plausible enough, the body of writings used here runs the whole gamut from the relatively contented, well treated and cooperative slaves like Josiah Henson to the bitterly rebellious ones like Henry Bibb. Even the casual reader will see that men like Henry Watson and William Grimes were, after all, ordinary men. And it is reasonable to suppose that the great majority of bondmen had similar trials and reactions. In fact, the narrators had so many ordeals in common (work loads, living conditions, punishments, feelings of fear and guilt) that it seemed intelligent to give this work a topical organization rather than reproduce a series of capsule biographies tedious in their repetition of details.

Although they are now largely out of print, the narratives were widely read in the nineteenth century. Indeed they were so popular that almost any victim of slavery could get published. Among these were manumitted slaves, like Sojourner Truth, those who had bought themselves, like Moses Grandy, and many fugitives, like Frederick Douglass. A large number of narratives were issued as paper bound pamphlets and sold for twenty-five cents. The longer and better bound ones could be had for a dollar and a half. *The Interesting Narrative of the Life of Olaudah Equiano or Gustavus Vassa, The African* went into at least ten editions by 1837; a Dutch and a German edition are extant. At least six editions of Charles Ball's *Slavery in the United States* were issued between 1836 and 1859. By 1856 the *Narrative of Moses Roper's Adventures and Escape from American Slavery*, first published in 1837, had reached ten editions and had been translated into Celtic. Josiah Henson's narrative had sold six thousand in 1852, having been published in England as well as in America. By 1858 advanced orders for the "Stowe edition" of Henson's book totaled 5,000 copies. In the 1878 edition it is claimed that 100,000 copies of the earlier book had been sold.

Henson's life story was translated into Dutch and into French. Within two years after its publication in 1853, *The Narrative of Solomon Northup* had sold 27,000 copies. *The Narrative of William Wells Brown* sold 8,000 copies by 1849, and Douglass' narrative had, by the same year, gone through seven editions. So widespread was the circulation of these autobiographies that Olmsted remarked[6] that northern views of the peculiar institution were largely derived from the narratives of fugitive slaves.

How accurate are the narrators' impressions of the slaveholding system? The reports of Frederick Douglass, Henry Bibb, Solomon Bayley or William Grimes can be checked against other historical evidence. Sources used here for purposes of verification include the accounts of travelers (Thomas Hamilton, Philo Tower, Harriet Martineau, Frederick Law Olmsted, Charles Dickens, Fanny Kemble, Charles Lyell and James Redpath), newspaper advertisements, contemporary documents and letters gathered by Ulrich Phillips, the *Documentary History of American Industrial Society* (vols. 1 and 2), Elizabeth Donnan's *Documents Illustrative of the History of the Slave Trade to America* and John Spencer Bassett's *The Southern Plantation Overseer as Revealed in His Letters*. Valuable data was taken, too, from DeBow's *Industrial Resources for the Southern and Western States* and *Judicial Cases concerning American Slavery and the Negro* as well as other sources.

The African slave trade began like a small errant cloud on the horizon. Soon it had blotted out the humane influence of the Enlightenment, and as the plantation system took root, substituted the rationale of a "Greek democracy," and enriched the empires of the Old World. Eventually, it put American democracy to its severest test, and the rumblings of the storm it brought shook the republic to its foundations. Yet the enslavement of the Negro is still not wholly ended. And all of us who have had to preserve our hard-won liberties against the totalitarianisms of the Left and the Right know that freedom is always in jeopardy.

This is an account of oppression and wrong, but it is also a history of the struggle to establish human rights, carried on by any Americans—black and white. Perhaps with their splendid example, the men and women of our time can bring America's promise of liberty closer to fulfillment.

Source

Charles Nichols, *Many Thousand Gone: The Ex-Slaves' Account Of Their Bondage And Freedom* (Leiden, Netherlands: E. J. Brill, 1963), pp. ix–xiv.

Prologue: A Roll Call of The Narrators

They stretch in unending line across a hundred years from Colonial plantation to Appomattox: black men, brown men, sons and daughters of the Gold

Coast or Senegal, bastard sons of Virginia planters. Dragged from homeland, auctioned, mortgaged, bequeathed, driven. With stripes on their naked backs and a price on their heads, seeking by the North Star a name and an identity in some far-off land of Canaan. Who were they? Venture—exchanged for four gallons of rum on the Guinea coast, brought to Rhode Island, a man-mountain of legendary strength, living out his days in Connecticut. Gustavus Vassa—snatched from Benin, sold to a captain in the Royal Navy, a chattel in Barbados and Georgia, joining with Granville Sharp in petitioning parliament for an end to the slave trade. Solomon Northup—free New Yorker, kidnapped and sold into bondage on a Louisiana plantation. And those born in chains, the half-white sons of planters—William Grimes, Lewis And Milton Clarke, Henry Bibb, Moses Roper—Moses Roper, chained to his master's chaise, trotting fifteen miles back to the bondage he sought to escape. Item: Henry "Box" Brown, shipped by freight to freedom from Richmond to Philadelphia. John Brown of Georgia, intrepid as his namesake at Harper's Ferry, the Guinea pig of a sadistic doctor. Harriet Jacobs—a latter-day Pamela, prey to the master's lust. And the bold ones: Nat Turner—stoic, fanatic, visionary, a firebrand in the calm summer night of Tidewater Virginia, in desperate rebellion slaying fifty odd whites in their beds. William Grafy—disguising his near-white wife as his master, travelling, a thousand miles to free land. Harriet Tubman—"Moses" who could "tote a flour barrel" in one hand, returning to the South nineteen times to lead away over three hundred fugitives with $40,000 on her head. In 1862 a scout for Union forces, leading a raid in South Carolina, freeing 750 slaves. Frederick Douglass—breaker of slavebreakers, escaping in a borrowed navy uniform with forged papers. A great brown man with a lion's mane of white hair, roaring against slavery and, after Emancipation, advising presidents. William Parker—fugitive, boldly frustrating attempts to recapture slaves in Pennsylvania. And the energetic ones: William Wells Brown—assistant to a slave trader, refugee, abolition orator, author. James Pennington—fugitive blacksmith, scholar, physician, abolitionist—invested with an honorary degree by the University of Heidelberg. Austin Steward—sold to pay horse racing debts, leader of the Wilberforce Colony of fugitives in Canada. Moses Grandy—shrewd worker and ferryman, paying his purchase price three times over. Elizabeth Keckley—popular modiste and friend of Mary Todd Lincoln, revealing what lay behind the scenes at the White House. John Thompson—eluding Maryland patrols to ship, Melville-like, on a whaling vessel from New Bedford.

And the God-intoxicated ones: Solomon Bayley—schooled in the Bible, a nineteenth century John Bunyan, prostrate before the Almighty. Ralph Roberts—a pathetic penitent, confessing his ornery ways and dictating his life story to his master. Sojourner Truth—a wizened black Sybil, seeking in every

Tabernacle the heavenly city, chiding skeptic Douglass into hope of freedom with: "Frederick, is God dead?" Last of all, the cunning compromisers: William Hayden—informer, trusted slave, tricking his dishonest master into signing papers. And Josiah Henson—a specialist at charlatanry, his owner's overseer, refusing a life of freedom to protect the slaveholder's interest, embezzling funds of the refugee's Canadian community, celebrated as Mrs. Stowe's "original Uncle Tom," presented to Queen Victoria.... And a host of others. The fearful, the aggressive, the guilty, the bold, the strong, the weak, shackled in mind and body, straining against the yoke, yearning. This is their history.

SOURCE

Charles Nichols, *Many Thousand Gone: The Ex-Slaves' Account Of Their Bondage And Freedom* (Leiden, Netherlands: E. J. Brill, 1963), pp. 1–2.

Part One: Chattels

Chapter One: "O, Wasn't That A Wide River..."

Captain Collingswood's vessel set sail for Barbados with a fair wind and two hundred and sixty Negroes aboard. It was a large cargo for his ship, but no doubt many would die of consumption, "flux," scurvy or smallpox, and a trader had to show a profit in this hazardous business. Many of the blacks were treacherous and intractable, willing, if mutiny was impossible, to hurl themselves into the sea rather than submit. But a slaver was well equipped with screws, stocks and chains, and Collingwood's cargo was secure—stolid and mute.

As the Guinea coast fell away behind him, this eighteenth century slaver must have thought of the many risks he was taking. For if he escaped pestilence and mutiny there were always the unforeseen delays caused by bad weather and the fear that their stores of food and water might not last. Collingwood's passage was more fortunate than most.

One of the slaves on board was the boy, Venture, born in Dukandarra, Guinea, about the year 1729. His father, Saungm Furro, was prince of the tribe. A small party, including Venture and his mother, had set out from Dukandarra some days before, but they were soon captured by a tribe of about 6,000 men and made prisoners. It was this hostile tribe which sold the boy and his mother to slavetraders. "While we were going to the vessel," wrote Venture, "our master told us to appear to the best possible advantage for sale. I was bought on board by one Robertson Mumford, steward of said vessel, for four gallons of rum and a piece of calico, and called Venture, on account of his having purchased me with his own private venture."[7]

This son of a tribal prince soon found himself chained hand and foot to another slave and crowded into a space so small that he could only sit or, with difficulty, lie under the deck. Around him were the hapless victims—some stolid, others, moaning, all disgruntled. As the voyage lengthened the stench and filth became unbearable. The slaves sat in their own offal and vomit; the diseased quickly spread their contagion. Smallpox and "flux" ran riot. Daily the sailors threw their dead chattels into the sea. The more intractable blacks plotted mutiny, and a small group determined to stage a hunger strike. Everywhere there was the dull and empty look which bespoke their hopelessness and desperation.

What other privations Venture and his fellow passengers suffered we do not know except that there was great mortality by the smallpox.[8] Of the 260 slaves, fewer than 200 survived. Young Venture was not sold in Barbados but sailed with his owners to Rhode Island. Sold to other masters, he lived in Long Island and in Connecticut for more than sixty years. Evidently the boy grew to be a huge man, for he describes himself as weighing three hundred pounds and measuring five feet around the waist. His prodigious strength was legendary in Connecticut. The dictated account of his life was first printed in New London in 1798.

Nearly two decades after the kidnapping of Venture, Olaudah Equiano (later called Gustavus Vassa) was snatched from his African homeland. The youngest son of [the] leader of his tribe, he was born in 1745 in Essaka, Guinea in the kingdom of Benin. Abducted from his home by an unfriendly band, he was sold many times in Africa. Like the boy, Venture, he was about ten years old when he was bought by a European slave trader. After a long march to the coast Gustavus Vassa saw his first slave ship riding at anchor, gently rocking in the blue lagoon. Strange men with red faces and long hair directed the loading of cargo into the small boats. The boy had the most fantastic fears, for in his wonderment there was none to reassure him. Chained and driven like oxen the coffle was taken aboard. "I was immediately handled and tossed up to see if I were sound, by some of the crew," he wrote. "I was now persuaded that I had gotten into a world of bad spirits and that they were going to kill me.... When I looked around the ship, too, and saw a large furnace of copper boiling and a multitude of black people of every description chained together, every one of their countenances expressing dejection and sorrow, I no longer doubted my fate; and quite overpowered with horror and anguish, I fell motionless on the deck and fainted. When I recovered a little, I found some black people about me, who I believed were some of those who had brought me on board and had been receiving their pay.... I asked them if we were not to be eaten by those white men with horrible looks, red faces and long hair."[9] Gustavus Vassa was then put below the deck where the odors of perspiration and excrement were suffocating, and the cries of the manacled slaves filled him with horror. The boy refused to eat and longed for death. His captors attempted to force him to eat and flogged him when he refused. In desperation two slaves who were chained together threw themselves into the sea; a third, debilitated by scurvy, followed suit. For there were not enough guards among the crew to prevent this wretched human cargo from leaping overboard.

The whites were armed with whips and guns. The slightest pretext brought on the lash, and Vassa was amazed at the "savage manner" of the white men. "I had never seen among any people such instances of brutal cruelty." While on deck for his daily airing the slave boy witnessed the chastisement of a white sailor who was tied to the foremast and severely whipped. A few days later the man died, and "they tossed him over the side as they would have done a brute."

At length the ship arrived at Barbados, and while the crew greeted Bridgetown harbor with joyous shouts, Gustavus Vassa and the other slaves were confused and frightened; they still expected to be eaten. Some of the Negroes from the island who had become inured to their servitude came aboard to reassure the newly arrived cargo. With some difficulty the new arrivals were persuaded to disembark. Within two weeks Vassa was taken to Virginia where he was sold to a planter. Some time after this he was bought by Captain Pascal of the Royal Navy, given the name Gustavus Vassa, and taken to England. His exciting career continued, for he was engaged in several expeditions with the British navy, was a slave again in the West Indies and Georgia, eventually purchased his freedom and went to live in England. An enthusiastic abolitionist, he petitioned the British parliament in 1790 for the suppression of the slave trade. The first edition of Vassa's autobiography was published in 1789.

These two Africans, Venture Smith and Gustavus Vassa, produced the rarest historical documents, for millions of the men, women, and children who crossed the Atlantic during two or three centuries of the slave trade have left no word of their experiences. As Vassa's account shows, the trail of the slave trader often began far in the interior of the continent where hostile tribes enslaved or sold their prisoners of war. Some of these African peoples seemed to the Europeans more tractable and better suited to laborious toil on plantations in the new world than others. One planter insisted that the Ebbos, the Whidaws, the Pawpaws and the Aradas made the best slaves, while the Gaboons were physically weak and susceptible to debilitating diseases. The inhabitants of the Gold Coast were, he felt, hardy, robust and energetic, being a warlike people. "Yet bringing with them into slavery lofty ideas of independence, they are dangerous inmates of a West India plantation when implicit subjection must necessarily be exacted."[10] The Negroes of Senegal, however, handsome, tall and well-limbed, were "excellent for the care of cattle and horses and for domestic service," but adjusted poorly to field labor. "Many of them converse in the Arabic language, and some are sufficiently instructed even to write it." Similarly the Congos "captivate the eye by their appearance and the ear by their humour; though totally unfit for laborious occupations, they make good domestic servants and tradesmen." The Mandingoes our English planter found indolent and easily fatigued, "though less ferocious than the Minna and Gold Coast negroes." But it was the Ebbos and the Ebbo-bees (called Mocos) who constituted the greater part of the cargoes then carried from Africa to the British islands in the West Indies. They are "turbulent, stubborn and much addicted to suicide; yet they are hardy and susceptible of labour—the women in particular, who are superior to any other, and very little inferior to the men."[11]

Chapter Eight: "Pharoah's Army Got Drowned"

The career of William Grimes illustrates well the effect of caste status, deprivation and physical suffering on the personality. Born in 1784 in King George County, Virginia, William Grimes was the son of one of the wealthiest planters in Virginia. Old Grimes was a wild sort of man who murdered a neighboring planter, was tried, and was acquitted on the ground of insanity. He died early in William's life, and his half-white son became the property of another planter. In his early years, however, Grimes' masters were not unkind. But when he was old enough to work in the fields he was often whipped and cruelly driven by black and white overseers. One white overseer, says Grimes,

> Set us to making fence, and would compel us to run with the rails on our backs, whipping us all the time most unmercifully. This hard treatment continuing for some time I at length resolved to run away.[12]

Grimes went to another slave, George, confided to him his plans to run off and asked his help. But his fellow slave informed against him. The overseer came directly to Grimes' cabin and sent in George to question him while he listened without. George asked Grimes if he intended to run away, provided he would give him the jacket and some meal. Half asleep, Grimes answered that he did not know. George repeated the question several times and got the same answer. The overseer then shouted out, "Hey, you son of a bitch, you are going to run away are you, I'll give it to you! Bring him out here!" So they brought him out and horsed him upon the back of Planter George, and whipped him until he fell quivering in the dust. Bitter and resentful, Grimes did run away, but was seized by a neighboring slaveholder and brought back. Again he escaped to the woods and remained for three days. Then forced by hunger to return, he appealed to his master who gave orders that Grimes was not to be whipped without his owner's consent. But the overseer whipped him again, and the slave was afraid to complain. His next flogging came after Grimes had the "impertinence" to call a slave girl "miss." Meanwhile he was worked hard and had little to eat.

••••

William Grimes reveals himself throughout his autobiography as a high strung, nervous man, and he says repeatedly that he was "afraid," "fearful," "terrified." His surroundings affected him profoundly and whipping always filled him with horror. "I saw Bennett strip off James' shirt and whip his naked back part as if he had been cutting down a tree. I thought what was to be my fate." Of another slave he saw Grimes writes, "This poor man's back was cut up with the lash until I could compare it to nothing but a field lately ploughed." And again he says:

> I at this time was in such dread of the whipping post, where I daily saw so many human beings sacrificed to the lash of the tyrant that it struck me with horror. I prayed constantly to my God ... to protect and defend me in this adversity.[13]

Of one of his masters he writes: "He was cross to me, and I feared him like death." On one occasion Grimes was driving the coach for his mistress and lost his way, but so afraid was he of punishment for his error that he pretended to know the way and wandered about until he found the right road.

Unsuccessful in his attempts to run away, Grimes sought to mutilate himself, to break his own leg. He often pretended to be ill, went on hunger strikes and in one instance managed by this device to get a new master. Moreover, he drank heavily whenever he could get whiskey. His behavior also showed marked aggression. He fought with his master's other servant, Cato, and bit off the latter's nose. In another fight with a Negro driver Grimes beat the man, struck him with his head and bit him, "Hardly knowing what I was about, being so much terrified." At the same time the slave showed considerable indifference and carelessness about his work. His attitude incensed his master who beat him in the chest and face until he was "all in a gore of blood" and sent him to jail. The jail had no water for washing, nor were the slaves given any changes of clothing.

> The lice were so thick and large, that I was obliged to spread a blanket on the floor, and as they crawled up on it, take a junk or porter bottle ... and rolled it over the blanket repeatedly, and in the same way that I have seen people grind or powder mustard seed on a board.[14]

Shortly after this Grimes was released from prison and made his escape from slavery by stowing away on a ship bound for Boston. But even in the

North, years later, he was recognized by one of his master's friends, retaken, and "forced to purchase his freedom with the sacrifice of all he had earned." Nor was the North free of segregation and discrimination. It is not surprising that a man who suffered so much never really adjusted himself to the society around him even after he became a free man. He had persistent feelings of guilt, prayed, searched his soul and repented of his sins.

> My conscience used sometimes to upbraid me with having done wrong, after I had run away from my master and arrived in Connecticut; and while I was living in Southington, Connecticut... I went up on a high mountain and prayed to the Lord, to teach me my duty that I might know whether or not I ought to go back to my master....[15]

He finally decided that God had delivered him "out of the land of Egypt, and out of the house of bondage."

The same guilt over running away was experienced by Solomon Bayley, William Parker and others. Such guilt feelings are not only evidence of the effectiveness of the slaveholder's teaching, but also, and more significantly, they indicate how guilt follows closely upon fear and aggression. William Grimes, having escaped bondage, lived in a half-dozen cities in New England and engaged in a score of different occupations from janitoring at Yale College to keeping a barber shop in Providence. Moreover, he was constantly involved in law suits and was once tried for rape and acquitted. A restless and rather pathetic man, he did not find in the North the freedom that meant peace of mind.

Even though some of his behavior was pathological, Grimes was an ordinary man. He did not have the latent powers of a Frederick Douglass or the mind of a James W. C. Pennington. It is reasonable to suppose that thousands of fugitives were, perhaps, not unlike him in their suffering, in their fear, and in the difficulties they faced in freedom.

Similar case studies drawn from the narratives might be discussed, but it is not likely that they will throw more light on the particular problem under consideration. By the time they had achieved freedom the ex-slaves' personalities had set in definite molds. Elizabeth Keckley and Josiah Hensen, for example, continued to seek security by their close association with influential people, while Douglass, Bibb, William W. Brown carried on their protest within the wider framework of the abolitionist movement. William Wells Brown, Frederick Douglass, Henry Bibb, James Pennington and others achieved rare distinction [in] the country which had enslaved them. Other fugitives, like Josiah Henson and Austin Steward, were pioneers in the establishment of new communities in Canada. Their adjustment is an amazing instance of human adaptability. For the runaway slaves had to find jobs, homes, friends. They had to struggle to acquire an education. Moreover, they had to rid themselves of their feelings of inferiority and gain a sense of selfhood and independence. "There is one sin that slavery committed against me which I could never forgive," observed Pennington:

> It robbed me of my education; the injury is irreparable; I feel the embarrassment more seriously now than I ever did before. It cost me two year's hard labor, after I fled, to unshackle my mind; it was three years before I purged my language of slavery's idioms, it was four years before I had thrown off the crouching aspect of slavery; and now the evil that besets me is a great lack of that general information, the foundation of which is most effectually laid in that part of life which I served as a slave.[16]

Perhaps the greatest evil of slavery, as de Tocqueville pointed out, was that the men of the slavocracy "employed their despotism and their violence against the human mind."

In these chapters I have attempted to describe the Negro's reactions to enslavement. No investigation of this kind could ever claim completeness, but it has been shown that the narratives are instructive along certain general lines. First, they indicate that slave loyalty was directly related to rewards. Hayden and Henson offered their faithfulness to masters who gave them better incentives than their fellows received. Second, the narratives show that the great mass of slaves, who were field hands, led an enormously difficult life and reacted with considerable protest and aggression. Third, this literature presents no evidence to support the notion that there is anything peculiarly "African" or "inferior" in the behavior of the slaves, or that full blacks were more contented than mulattoes. Indeed the mulattoes, who were often house servants, showed greater faithfulness than the full blacks. Yet Henry Bibb, a mulatto, was just as determined to be free as was John Brown, a full black, for both experienced inhuman treatment. Fourth, it is evident, too, that many slaves, whether relatively well treated or not, had sufficient manhood to strike for freedom and deliberately planned rebellion to achieve that end. And finally, the foregoing discussion supports the findings of recent psychologists and sociologists who have shown that, by and large, the "haves" adjust and the "have-nots" do not. A sense of belonging, the opportunity to participate in the life of a community and to share in its rewards produces a stable, cooperative individual, loyal to the society that protects him. But physical punishment, lower caste status, the denial of every chance for improvement create a personality that is fearful, aggressive, guilty and disintegrated. It is impossible to estimate what the institution of slavery cost the Negro and American society generally, but the narrators have here indicated, in part, what bondage cost each of them.

Source

Charles Nichols, *Many Thousand Gone: The Ex-Slaves' Account Of Their Bondage And Freedom* (Leiden, Netherlands: E. J. Brill, 1963), chapter 1: pp. 5–13, chapter 8: pp. 119–120, 122–125.

Endnotes

1 Some consideration is given to the slaves' point of view in John Hope Franklin's *From Slavery to Freedom* (1947) and in Kenneth Stampp's *The Peculiar Institution* (1956); Cf. also B.A. Botkin, *Lay my Burden Down* (1945). (This and all following notes are from original.)

2 *Life and Labor in the Old South*, p. 219.

3 Lunsford Lane also wrote his own autobiography, *The Narrative of Lunsford Lane* (Boston, 1842).

4 *Emancipator*, Sept. 20, 1838.

5 *Incidents in the Life of a Slave Girl*, p. 7.

6 *Journey in the Seaboard Slave States*, I., pp. 198–199.

7 *Narrative of the Life and Adventures of Venture*, p. 12.

8 *Ibid.*, p. 13.

9 *The Interesting Narrative of Olaudah Equiano or Gustavus Vassa, the African*, Written by Himself, London, 1789, pp. 31–32.

10 Ulrich Phillips, *Documentary History of American Industrial Society*, vol. II, pp. 127–129.

11 *Ibid.*, p. 129.

12 *Life of William Grimes*, p. 10.

13 *Ibid.*, p. 36.

14 *Ibid.*, p. 48.

15 *Ibid.*, p. 28.

16 *Fugitive Blacksmith*, p. 56.

XI

George E. Sawyer
(1925–2002)

edited by Paul Kriese

GEORGE SAWYER was born in Kokomo, Indiana, on April 27, 1925, and died in West Lafayette, Indiana, on July 31, 2002. Sawyer was a long time member of Clear Creek Meeting in Richmond, Indiana. He held various positions in the American Friends Service Committee and was the first Director of Urban and Black Studies at Earlham College. Sawyer passionately advocated for civil rights for African Americans. It was in this situation where Sawyer came into disagreement with his European American Quaker cohorts. His son commented that white Quakers just did not understand the reality of the black community in Indiana and the United States. His father's vocal activities on race relations provoked strong opposition from people as central to Quakerism as Tom Jones, president of Earlham College. Sawyer participated in a vigorous debate with Jones and Fred Woods, the editor of *Quaker Life*, a major organ for Friends United Meeting, headquartered in Richmond, Indiana, following publication of his article ("The Stranger among You," included below) illustrating racial problems between white and black Quakers.

Sawyer argued that when African American Quakers raised their voice in opposition to discrimination, European American Quakers sought to have these African American cohorts tone down their argument and wait for better times. Sawyer expressed disappointment that European American Quakers were not on the barricades with them, expecting good people of faith, including Christian Quakers, to be outraged with human rights violations in the African American community. Sawyer suggested that Quaker consensus and Quaker silence were used at Earlham College to avoid rather than to confront racial tensions between white and black Quakers. Sawyer responded to justifications for why white Quakers could not be involved in the fight for human rights with the assertion that as long as blacks suffer from discrimination and Quakers do not step forward and fight for rights of their African American coreligionists, then Quakers are not being true to what they say they profess: human rights for all of God's creatures.

A Lawyer Finds His Way

On Saturday afternoon, in the year 1945, on the Island of Okinawa, in the South Pacific, I was confronted with what I thought was one of the most dastardly acts that could be perpetrated on a group of men. We were a Negro Marine Ammunition Company. We had seen and participated in the highest degree of human insanity—War. We had been spared, however, by the loving hand of God.

In celebration our company had joined with the White companies of our battalion and built an outdoor movie. This particular Saturday was our grand opening. This particular Saturday our Battalion Commander finished his tour and was replaced by a Colonel from Georgia. That Saturday evening when we went to our movie we found it segregated. The new Colonel had ordered signs erected showing where "White" and "Colored" should sit. It was at this moment that the idea of being a lawyer came into being.

I say the idea of being a lawyer because it was just an idea. There were many barriers which seemed to me insurmountable. Number one, I was a Negro—a Negro of average intelligence, but plagued with a terrible speech impediment. At times I stuttered so badly that I could not speak. Number two, I had no funds. Our family numbered eight boys and four girls and we were desperately, economically, poor. And so the idea lay dormant while I spent two more frustrating years in the United States Marine Corps and three years as a molder at the International Harvester Foundry in Richmond, Indiana. These three years were sufferingly frustrating. For the idea became a burning desire, but my human heart and mind had not the courage to grasp the challenge. My speech impediment grew worse and my lack of courage grew stronger. There was no longer the problem of finances, because I could avail myself of the G.I. Bill. My problem was that I knew not God. I, who had been raised by a minister father and mother—I who had practically lived in the sanctuary of the church from the cradle until I entered the Marine Corps—had not experienced, in my heart, the love of God and the guidance of the Holy Spirit. This was the source of my frustration. In retrospect, however, at the time of which I speak, I would have forcefully denied the statement that I knew not the love of God or the guidance of the Holy Spirit.

Through the prayers of my mother and sisters, however, I was guided to the ivy covered buildings of Earlham College and here entered into a grand and noble experience with God and the Holy Spirit. Out of this experience came the courage and determination to overcome my speech impediment, my fear of failure because of my race, and to become an able lawyer. After four years at Earlham College and three years at Howard University Law School in Washington, DC, the idea that began on a Saturday afternoon, on a Island in the Pacific Ocean, became a reality. Thirteen years after the germination of that idea, I became a lawyer.

The practice of law is a rewarding experience. There are so many varied cases and assignments that there is never a dull moment. There are happy moments, sad moments, and moments when you wonder what would have been the destiny of the human being who has committed larceny or robbery or rape or murder if God had been in his life. I was talking to a client one day and, as she left my office, I told her that I would pray for her. She stopped abruptly, turned to me, and said, "Do you pray?" And for a half an hour we talked about the power of prayer. I am convinced that whether you be a lawyer, doctor, dentist, merchant, laborer, man, woman, boy or girl, it is necessary and proper that we give thanks to God for daily blessings of life and that He is able to solve the seemingly insurmountable problems that we sometimes face in our everyday life.

The most exciting aspect of my life today, however, is not the actual practice of law, it is man's struggle for freedom. The struggle has been called "The Negro Revolution," but to me this is not a Negro Revolution, it is the revolution by White and Black men in America and throughout the world. We are all victims of prejudice. This is, and it is an inescapable fact, Godlessness.

We cannot profess to believe in God and pretend to live the Christian life if we ignore the "love thy neighbor" edict of the Holy Scripture. We cannot love God and hate man. We cannot admit the fatherhood of God and deny the brotherhood of man. So we are engaged in this "revolution," which began in 1619 and has been slowly gaining momentum. Today the cry for freedom rings so clear that it can be heard throughout the world. Man must be free. Our freedom will certainly be assured when man opens his heart to the Spirit of God, allows it to be purged of prejudice and hate and filled with the dignifying love of his fellow man. There is no other way. Man can by laws make man equal and equality will no doubt come in our time. But God will make us free.

The Young Friends of North America must know that my prayers are constantly with them for continued, and greater, success in their chosen areas of concentration. My prayers are especially with you in the controversial areas of Peace and Race.

Source

Thomas E. and Esther B. Jones Collection, FMS 21, Friends Collection and Archives, Lilly Library, Earlham College, Richmond, Indiana. Originally published in *Friends*, vol. 4, no. 10, published weekly by Friends Publications Board, 101 Quaker Hill Drive, Richmond, Indiana, Merle Brauer Publisher.

National Conference of Friends on Race Relations

Friends from various Yearly Meetings located in various geographic areas of the United States gathered in Washington, DC, at Trinity College from July 27 to July 31, 1970, and, under the auspices of the National Conference of Friends on Race Relations, struggled with the problem of white racism in our society and particularly in the Religious Society of Friends. The participants were called upon to look at and discover themselves, make an in depth determination as to whether there was white racism within, and, if there was, face the awesome responsibility of self-admission and the purging of self. The final and even more awesome responsibility was the commitment of themselves to the task of erasing white racism, which breeds black repression, from the face of our nation.

Repression was vividly brought to the attention of those attending the conference when a young participant arrived about 1:30 a.m. Tuesday, July 28, 1970. He was unable to get in contact with anyone to register him at this hour and, in accordance with the strict security measures at Trinity College, was asked by the security guards to leave campus. The young man was allowed to sleep in his sleeping bag on the grass but was kept under strict surveillance. One Friend was so indignant that she tore up her identification card at the morning meeting for worship. It suggested that perhaps the group had experienced a somewhat microscopic impression of the continual repression perpetuated against the black man in this country.

It seemed as though the above noted incident was the proverbial "straw that broke the camel's back." The leaders began the gathering with exercises of repression. The participants were told what to do, when to do it, and how long to do it. At times we were forced to move on to another exercise. There were cries "but we haven't finished," but these cries were unheeded. Participants began to become frustrated and angry and at Tuesday's morning session, less than twenty-four hours from the initial session, the revolt came.

The revolt came as a relentless outpouring of anger against the leaders. The leaders were eight in number, Caucasian in race and all trained in psychology or psychiatry and group therapy. One participant characterized the leaders as "the gang from Philadelphia." It was, at times, problematical as to whether the leaders would be able to carry out their assignment, but with a great deal of expertise, constant work, dedication, and the leading of the Spirit, they were able to complete it.

Participants, through the vehicle of youths from Upward Bound at Trinity College, were forced to face up to the relevancy of their nonviolent testimony. The session started with the usual white interrogation of the blacks. But then the black youths began to ask questions of the participants.

When the chips are down, when violent white racists come to take the lives of blacks, will Quakers bear arms in defense of their black brothers? If not, are Quakers willing to present their bodies? The dialogue became so heated that a participant called for silence. The black youths, however, would not comply. This raised the questions as to whether Quakers sometimes use the vehicle of "Quaker silence" to escape the confrontation of analyzing themselves and their Quaker beliefs.

One is reminded of the Negro spiritual "Wade in the Water, God's Gonna Trouble the Waters." The Spirit of God truly polluted the hearts and minds of the participants, and although we were at times frustrated and angry, on the final day we were overcome with God's love and filled with the total realization that white racism must be rejected.

Out of this great experience came a determination that there should be created a permanent, fully staffed Friends Committee for Human Justice. A Steering Committee was appointed to carry out this felt will of the gathering. The Steering Committee, under the direction of the gathering, met in business session, and, knowing the urgency of the problem, decided that the top priorities are as follows:

1. Notifying Yearly Meetings of the decision of the gathering and asking that each Yearly Meeting appoint a representative to the Board of the Friends Committee for Human Justice
2. The raising of funds
3. The hiring of an executive secretary or facilitator and staff secretary
4. The acquiring of a site for headquarters

Our choices for headquarters are: Plainfield, Ind., St. Louis, Mo., or Louisville, Ky.

We must be mindful of the urgency of this matter and must take immediate steps to appoint the above mentioned Yearly Meeting representative. We hope also that Friends will know the need for money and include the Friends Committee for Human Justice in your budget. Checks may be sent to the Friends World Committee for the Friends Committee for Human Justice. God grant us the fulfillment of our goal.

SOURCE

Quaker Life, Series 11, no. 9, pp. 26–27.

The Stranger Among You

It is lawyerlike, I suppose, to seek out and define the subject matter with which one is to deal. The definition of a stranger is interesting. Webster initially describes him as "strange." Now to be strange, one must be "not native to or naturally belonging in a place, foreign, alien, or external origin, not before known, heard or seen." Webster further describes the stranger as "a foreigner, a resident alien," a person or thing that is unknown or with whom one is unacquainted and finally "one who does not belong to or is kept from the activities of a group." The latter part of this definition contains the ingredients which maintain the mountain from which I must utter words which to some of you may seem unnecessarily cruel and improper.

It must be accepted as true, I think, that "the group" is White America. The "one who does not belong to or is kept from the activities of the group" is Black America. How can one be other than a stranger if he is shut out of the mainstream and enclosed in a stifling, stagnated, festering swamp?

History cannot help but reveal that the Black stranger that walks among you, the Black stranger that has managed to survive the swamp, has reason to strike out in violence against the group and to stand in the group's public places demanding reparations for the hideous atrocities perpetrated against him. For it can be no less than true that White America with its limited democracy, limited to Whites only, has with its tool of unChristian Christianity, created the conditions under which she now stands in awesome fear of the Black stranger.

Redundancy may run rampant, but America must be ever reminded that slavery, one of the most evil manifestations of the human mind, was foisted upon the ancestors of this Black stranger 350 years ago. Black human beings were kidnapped from their homes, loaded into slave ships, manacled and chained to the beams of ships, brought to the shores of America, and sold into slavery.

There was, during slavery, a separation of human beings, White and Black. There were not then, however, two separate societies. Slavery was legal and the slave was considered no more than a cow or a pig or a piece of chattel totally owned by the master.

In the *Dred Scott Case* (1847) the Supreme Court of the United States enunciated this doctrine. Thirty years after the war to save the Union the Supreme Court of the United States, speaking in the case of *Plessy vs. Ferguson* (1896) and speaking to the White-Black problems said, "As long as facilities are equal it is constitutional for them to be separate." With one opinion the Supreme Court have given White America the legal tool with which to keep the Black stranger in the festering swamp.

George E. Sawyer

In 1968, the President's National Advisory Commission on Civil Disorders said, "This is our basic conclusion: Our nation is moving toward two societies, one black, one white—separate and unequal." This opinion came as no shock to the Black stranger. The Supreme Court's 1954 decision notwithstanding, our nation was not then, and is not now, moving toward a Black and White society. It is impossible for an object to move toward when it has never moved away.

In the early years of the twentieth century, W.E.B. DuBois, in his book *Dusk of Dawn*, said

> It is difficult to let others see the full psychological meaning of caste segregation. It is as though one, looking out from a dark cave in a side of an impending mountain, sees the world passing and speaks to it; speaks courteously and persuasively showing them how these entombed souls are hindered in their natural movement, expression, and development; and how their loosening from prison would be a matter not simply of courtesy, sympathy and help to them, but aid to all the world. It gradually penetrates the minds of prisoners that the people passing do not hear, that some thick sheet of invisible but horribly tangible plate glass is between them and the world. They get excited; they talk louder; they gesticulate. Some of the passing world stops in curiosity; these gesticulations seem so pointless; they laugh and pass on.
>
> Then the people within may become hysterical. They may even, here and there, break through in blood and disfigurement and find themselves faced by a horrified, implacable and quite overwhelming mob of people frightened for their own very existence.

You must know that W.E.B. DuBois, who died in exile branded a communist because he dared speak out for racial justice in White America, was a Black prophet whose prophesy we have come to realize today. You must know that the Black stranger is breaking out of Dr. DuBois' impending mountain and that which I choose to describe as the stifling, stagnated, festering swamp.

You must know that the Black America that you once knew—the Black America that White America Christianized to the ethic of suffering—has come of age. You must know that the Black stranger with whom you must deal is no longer willing to end his suffering by "stealing away to Jesus" with the firm faith that there is a "long white robe" in that heavenly home with streets paved with gold.

You must know that the Black stranger has been with you long enough to embrace your might-maketh-right ethic and that there should be no hesitancy to commit violence. You must comprehend that of which Dr. DuBois spoke: "There was a man who walked among us. A man who spoke of love as the savior of America."

On January 14, 1963, at the National Conference on Religion and Race, Dr. Martin Luther King said, "America has brought the nation and the world to an awe-inspiring threshold of the future.... We have dwarfed distance and placed time in chains. But when we turn to the question of progress in the area of race relations, we face one of the most shameful chapters of the American scene. In spite of the jet-like pace of our scientific and technological development, we still creep at a horse-and-buggy speed in human relations. We must face the melancholy fact that one hundred years after the Emancipation Proclamation, the Negro is still dominated politically, exploited economically, and humiliated socially."

On August 28, 1963, at the foot of the Lincoln Memorial, my friend Martin had a dream:

> I have a dream that one day this nation will rise up and live out the true meaning of its creed: We hold these truths to be self-evident: that all men are created equal.... I have a dream that one day on the red hills of Georgia the sons of former slaves and slaveowners will be able to sit down at the table of brotherhood.

In 1966, writing for the *New York Times*, Martin Luther King, speaking of Black Power, that cataclysmic phrase that excitedly stimulates the fear syndrome of White America said:

> Black Power is no mere slogan. It is a movement dedicated to the exercise of American democracy in its highest tradition; it is a drive to mobilize black communities in this country in the monumental effort to remove the basic causes of alienation, frustration, despair, low-esteem, and hopelessness. Black Power is not Black supremacy, it does not mean the exclusion of White America from the Negro revolution, it does not advocate violence, and it will not start riots.

Yet on April 4, 1968 Martin, having been allowed the privilege of going to the mountaintop and seeing the promised land where racism and poverty did not exist, was struck down by a bullet from a rifle fired by White America.

Shock waves may rumble through the White conscience of this assemblage, and some of you may rise up in righteous indignation, but I challenge you to deny that your own forefinger gave aid, assistance and comfort to the assassin as he lined his sight and pulled the trigger that started the missile that forever silenced the voice of the Black prophet of love.

I cannot help but be reminded of a call that I received some years ago from the president of the Richmond, Indiana, Human Relations Council. She was also a chairman of the Social Concerns Committee of her Meeting. I was advised that the house next door to her was up for sale and the owner was willing to sell it to a Negro. I advised her that my wife and I would be happy to look at the house.

The next evening she called and asked us not to come. Her neighbor on the other side of the empty house did not approve and would break all relations with her if she encouraged me to buy the house. This was a blatant condonation of racism. She tearfully chose, however, to submerge her religiosity in the stagnant tank of racism in order to keep the friendship of a racist.

I hear anxious voices crying out to me: "But, George, we have been to the ghetto and visited the residents thereof. We clothed them when they were naked, we fed when they hungered, we visited them when they were in jail, as a matter of fact we went to jail with them." To which I answer how difficult it is for White America to understand.

Ten million Whites could spend a lifetime working in the ghetto day and night. Twenty million racists are working day and night to keep the Black stranger in subjugation while 150 million Whites remain frightened and silent.

You must unseal the lips of these silent millions. You must foment action in the White, silent, frightened ghetto. You must say to the White racist, I have seen the Black stranger, I have visited him, I have eaten with him.

Admittedly there is a difference in his color, but he is one of God's children. He is capable of loving and has the capacity to receive love. Racist, when you get to know him, then all the myths that you have believed will be destroyed and you will see him as he really is.

You must say to the silent, frightened millions: "Be not afraid of your racist brother. He is wrong." When you do, when you go out into the hinterlands of White racist America struggling to convince people that there is no sanity to the ideology of White supremacy, that there is no way that one human being can be superior to another because of the color of his skin and that America may well perish if she continues on this perilous path, then, and only then, will the Black stranger gain hope.

Let me share with you a little of that which it means to be a Black man in White America. I was born in a ghetto in Kokomo, Ind., moved to a ghetto in Anderson, Ind., at the age of six months, and moved to a ghetto in Richmond, Ind., at the age of nine years. My father was born in Nashville, Tenn., and was forced out of school to help support the family when he was in the fourth grade. My father could not get a decent job because he was Black. My mother was born in Ashland, Tenn., and was forced out of school for the same reason in the sixth grade.

I shall not forget my first day of school. I had been on the playground five minutes and a White child called me a Nigger. I whipped him. Racism starts early. In the second grade a little White girl took me to her home for lunch because we had not the money to buy lunch meat.

We lived in a rat-infested house. My brothers and I had an imperative evening chore. After dinner, and after the kitchen was cleaned, my mother would sprinkle bread crumbs on the kitchen floor. When the rats began to enjoy their dinner, my brothers and I would run into the kitchen, turn on the lights, stuff rugs into the rat-holes and beat the rats to death with sticks. This was imperative because we had younger brothers and sisters, and the fewer the rats, the fewer the rat bites.

A rat cannot form the necessary criminal intent to commit murder. But the White racist can. Calculatedly, White Society has relegated the Black stranger to the rat-infested ghetto. Intent can be proven by the outrage of the act—by the weapon used. White Society is guilty of the murder of hundreds of thousands of rat-mutilated murdered Black children.

White Society is guilty, but there is no forum that will hear the Black stranger's complaint. There is no grand jury that will indict and there is no judge or jury that will convict. A Kansas City barber, testifying before the National Advisory Commission on Civil Disorders, said: "We have marched, we have cried, we have prayed. We have voted, we have petitioned, we have gone out to Vietnam as doves and come back as hawks. We have done every possible thing to make this white man recognize us as human beings and he refuses. . . . You can understand why Jews who were burned by the Nazis hate Germans, but you can't understand why Black people, who have been systematically murdered by the government and its agents—by private citizens, by the police department—you can't understand why they hate white people."

One thing that White America must understand is that within the ranks of the Black stranger there is a revolution. There are those who cling to the Martin Luther King doctrine that "love force" is the only way, that the Black-White problem is a moral one and the only solution is love. "If there be blood in the streets of Birmingham" said Dr. King, "let it be our blood."

Dr. Price M. Cobb, co-author of *Black Rage*, said, however, "Nobody but a fool would accept this philosophy." Speaking to a group at Earlham College, Dr. Cobb indicated that Dr. King's death was unfortunate but the Black revolutionary had been the beneficiary. The love ethic espoused by Dr. King is the impossible idealism. For the White man has not the inclination or the capacity to love the Black stranger.

Today the Kingsian, Wilkinsian, and Youngsian clamor for non-violence and moderation is being obliterated by the cry that the only ethic that White America understands is the ethic of violence. Rev. Albert Clege, in his book, *The Black Messiah*, speaking to the Black church and speaking of the past said:

> The church was performing a valuable and real function.... You could go to church and shout and feel that God was just even though the world in which you lived was unjust.... White people were the oppressors. They were sinners, they were guilty.... Implicit in every ignorant preacher's sermon was the faith that God must eventually shake white people over hell fire and that after death black people were going to heaven.... But today the church must reinterpret its message in terms of the needs of a Black Revolution. We no longer feel helpless as black people. We do not feel that we must sit and wait for God to intervene and settle our problems for us. We waited for four hundred years and he didn't do much of anything, so the next four hundred years we're going to be fighting for ourselves.... As black preachers we must tell our people that God is fighting with us as we fight. When we march, when we take to the streets in open conflict, we must understand that in the stamping feet and the thunder of violence we can hear the voice of God.

Rev. Clege is saying to the Black stranger that he has been duped by the White man: that the Apostle Paul reconstructed Christianity to suit the White man's needs; that Jesus really was a Black Revolutionary leading the Black nation of Israel against the White Roman oppressors. He sees in the "Honkey," "Whitey," "hate the Whitey," attitude the beginning of a Black nation that will, in time, be capable of rising up and overthrowing the White oppressor.

I recently witnessed the thunder of violence in the streets of Indianapolis. I saw massive bricks landing in thunderous rapidity upon the fire trucks as the "Big 10" supermarket burned to the ground. I witnessed human beings, both Black and White, afraid for their very own existence. But I did not hear the voice of God. I did not feel the presence of God.

There was a sort of empty, sick, somewhat indescribable feeling. I suppose, as I deal with the luxury of hindsight, the feeling was what I will feel when death invades the sanctuary of the Sawyer household. I know that it is inevitable, but there is no way to be mentally or emotionally prepared.

The riot struck with the fury of a tornado, subsided briefly and then struck again: a Black man with a broken nose; a bloody White police officer with bowed and aching head; a Black man wounded because he had taken the bullet aimed at a friend, who lay unconscious on the floor, because the White policeman "always did want to kill a Nigger"; a Black man hospitalized from the "raid" on the Black Panther headquarters; a White police officer almost trampled to death by the steady stamping of eighty feet.

In the midst of this violent eruption, this breaking out of the cave in the "impending mountain," this violent escape from the stifling, stagnated swamp I did not have the vision of having been carried to the mountaintop. I was in the depth of an iniquitous chasm, and I saw the possibility of the violent annihilation of the Black stranger. The odds are 180 million against 20 million. And if the White racist juggernaut begins to roll against the Black stranger, he may well be wiped from your midst.

It seems to me that America is embroiled in what could be described as a deadly game of checkers. They can be named non-violence, moderation, and violence. The Black checker, violence, is near the kings' row. The White can block the violent checker, but he must be willing to give up his checkers of White Supremacy, White Racism, and White Power.

It seems to me, it's White America's move. God grant that it is made swiftly, decisively, and correctly.

Source

Quaker Life, October 1969, pp. 289–291.

XII

Vera Green
(1928-1982)
edited by Paul Kriese

Vera Green, an anthropologist, was a member of 57th Street Meeting in Chicago, Illinois. One of Green's major contributions to Quakers and race relations was her anthropological study titled "Blacks and Quakers: A Preliminary Report." Her small but still revealing sample of the fourteen respondents she interviewed in person showed that there was much diversity within the African American community. Her study illustrated many myths and half-truths that European American Friends had of African Americans in the United States. She found respondents viewed favorably Friends practice, casual dress, lack of ceremony, and understanding toward humanity. What was seen as less positive included values for patience, which was seen as a "cop out," and for nonviolence, which was seen as too close to submissiveness by the people in her study.

──────●──────

Blacks and Quakerism: A Preliminary Report (1973)

Sample:

The report is based on material collected from interviews (half in person, half by long distance phone) with 14 informants:

11 Black, includes 6 Friends (5 convinced, 1 birthright)
3 White, includes 3 Friends (2 birthright, 1 unknown).

The Black informants were primarily from the East and Mid-West; Three university professors, one high school teacher, three social workers, one university administrator, one business administrator, one housewife (married to a university professor), and one professional musician.

Blacks interviewed (except two) had contact with Quaker educational institutions as students and/or through teaching. Blacks with prior knowledge of Quakers were selected. Non-Friend informants (except one) were not attached to other Churches.

Informants were asked (a) what they felt was the general Black reaction to the Society of Friends, (b) what factors would motivate Blacks to attach themselves to the Society, and (c) what factors would hinder their attachment to the Society.

Findings:

Interestingly, the sharpest criticism of Friends came from those most closely connected with Friends activities. Informants tended to categorize both Friends and Blacks broadly. This really camouflages reality. When most of the informants were discussing Blacks, they were thinking about those of stable working class and lower middle class backgrounds. At least two informants felt there were differences between the approach of convinced and birthright Friends to problem solving, in terms of patience, spiritual insight as a learned phenomenon, etc., and that there were similar differences between programmed and unprogrammed Meetings.

The remarks of the informants, the writer included, are summarized under the question headings as follows:

1. *What kinds of Blacks are attracted to Friends Meetings?* When considering "the Blacks" en masse, it becomes important to see that Blacks are U.S. "products" as are the Whites and, except in issues directly related to race and color questions, their interests were until recently roughly parallel, depending on "class," geographical area, education, etc. This means that, as one would find a number of Whites turning to the Quaker and Unitarian faiths for status motives, so were some of the Blacks. Quakerism afforded some individuals an opportunity to follow a certain "intellectual," highly acceptable and different form of worship in an interracial setting. Consequently it attracted dilettantes as well as those who came in search of warmth and spiritual growth.

    Most informants indicated that Blacks and Whites attracted to Friends Meetings are those who are educated. Many stated that "No one knows about Quakers." A Philadelphia resident stated ". . . you don't even know where the Meetings are . . . like other churches, you have to go FIND them." Many of the non-Philadelphia informants knew about Friends historically. One Haverford graduate went to College expecting to find Friends dour and all dressed in black—not "doing" anything (drinking, smoking, dancing). ". . . but it wasn't like that at all." He later met other groups who were abstaining from these activities, and noted the variation which existed.

With the relative lack of knowledge of Friends as a living, breathing body, it is primarily through Friends schools, work camps, and to a lesser extent conferences that U.S. Blacks become close enough to Friends to actually entertain ideas of establishing lasting contacts. This would be especially true outside the Philadelphia area.

In view of the racially divided structural organization of this country, it is often only at the college level that Blacks (those not reared in small Northern towns or neighborhoods) had the opportunity for intermingling in social and institutional activities on anything approaching an equal level. As a result, it was primarily the educated Blacks who (1) having already the prerequisite skills in maneuvering within a White context, could feel more comfortable operating within the Friends setting, or (2) could overlook the fact that close participation in Friends activities means primarily participation in an "all white setting."

2. *What are the aspects of the Society of Friends which are most appealing?* Some informants felt Quakers were very liberal. Others thought they were perfect examples of the establishment ("most of them are University people") and very "class bound." An example of liberalism was "they can marry themselves . . . just like the hippies, Blacks and that. They don't want all that rigmarole." Another felt that Friends had comparatively more "understanding towards humanity" and the quiet, informal atmosphere was appreciated in contrast to the highly ceremonial worship services. He also appreciated the general "Quaker aesthetic values, simple pleasures, the contact with the environment." These same traits were described by another informant, noting that some Blacks working closely with Friends have never been able to appreciate their "austerity."

Certain informants appreciated the patience of Friends, though it is a trait which some Blacks criticize, being now equated with "copping out" from the Black, radical, and liberal points of view. There was a general feeling that Friends as a sect were respected in the Black community for honesty, etc.

3. *Which types of messages appeal to Blacks?* It was noted that Friends generally tried to teach brotherhood, and to practice this more than some other groups, especially in the past. The peace testimony was felt rather difficult to accept, for Blacks are highly "patriotic" (as though to be a C.O. is not). Socio-economic reasons have caused higher numbers of Blacks to join the armed forces.

One informant said Friends "intellectually think white . . . nonviolence is white, it is not a concept of third-world peoples." (He had forgotten its successful use by India.) One commented, "Most Blacks aren't passive—and rightly so. There was a time when they were. Now they're in a stage when they're not. They might even jump the gun (react violently when there is no immediate reason to do so). They have the whites really scared now, they don't know how to act." Thus some informants saw it in relation to particular experiences of Blacks, rather than as "not Black," and as something which, given changes in the outer environment, might become more important to the Negroid population.

It is fairly common to hear that Blacks avoid the Society of Friends because of the lack of emotionalism in its services, but this generalizes too far, I think. For one thing, a deeply moving silent Meeting can be very "emotional" in a less overt manner. Also, this statement assumes that ALL Blacks were traditionally in the Sanctified, Baptist, or Methodist churches. The historical records indicate that large numbers were also attached to other denominations, Catholic and Episcopal. With the wish to control their own services, meet with their own people, etc., some of these changed to Baptists and Methodists, just as is occurring today. A denomination with doctrines similar to Quakerism, and services like some programmed Meetings can be successful with Blacks, as shown by the growth of the Unity School of Christianity in Chicago, where Negroes started a center within a Black neighborhood.

One informant stated that Quakerism in the U.S. is *of*, *by*, and *for* members of the White community, in the same way that the Friends Meetings in Jamaica have their roots in the local population of Jamaica. The "Negro Church," as E. Franklin Frazier refers to the Baptist and Methodist churches, where after the Civil War ". . . nearly half the Negroes have remained, on the whole, to the present day."[1]

It was, in the opinion of one informant, ". . . the only thing that was really ours." In a country where rigid socio-structural separation existed in varying forms, both North and South, community feeling is immensely important. Although Friends have often worked among Blacks, few Meetings were established among them. (One informant reported a "Black Society" had been established in Philadelphia at one time.)

Discussion:

Due to the present militant mood of U.S. Blacks, it would seem logical that even fewer would embrace Quakerism. Even "birthright" Catholics are leaving the fold, as Catholicism "ain't Black." These persons are trying to "seek their roots" based on often inadequate information about the situation of U.S. Blacks at the time of Emancipation. With Black unity and a search for "our roots" being fostered by practically all segments of the Black population, and young militants hypercritical of "integrating," it can be easily understood why so few attach themselves to Friends.

Perhaps some of the same feeling operates among Afro-West Indian Friends coming to this country. Several members of New York Yearly Meeting indicated some concern that some Jamaican Friends stopped coming to Meeting after they arrived. It was thought they might be more comfortable in that "sedate, cultural group." They may have been made to "feel comfortable" but preferred to be in a setting which they can structure themselves. They may want a more "home" atmosphere, including socializing commitments to other Friends.

For this reason, a programmed Meeting as a solution for retaining Jamaican Friends may be spurious. Such a Meeting might be successful, as it would be a familiar community they would control. This action must come from within, however, or it runs the risk of being considered an attempt at deliberate separatism on the part of White Friends, thereby solidifying the possible stereotypes of Friends as "elitist," priding themselves on seclusion, guarding their sacrosanct class realm and therefore "pure establishment." A pastoral group among Jamaican Friends is natural, a continuation of something with historic roots in a live community. The same attempt among U.S. Blacks would be rather out of character for Friends and rather false, as it would lack historical continuity.

Actually a similar problem appears to be experienced in a number of Meetings outside the areas where Friends have traditionally lived and worked, and where almost all the members are convinced Friends. In such cases, activity at Meeting sometimes resembles the local PTA or departmental faculty meetings, without the spiritual or religious catharsis as found in some more traditional Meetings. One Black Friend complained rather bitterly of the lack of compassion and Spiritual comfort coming out of one such Meeting, which was manned primarily by younger convinced Friends, and implied an interest in seeking another spiritual home.

One informant stated that he generally looked to older persons for stability. In this way some of us look to traditional Friends and their experience for guidance, especially in the spiritual side of Meeting. Others felt that traditional Friends were too patient and reserved. This means that Friends are not moving fast enough in terms of actual action in Black and third-world movements. This has tended to annoy older Blacks (over 40) in the past, and consequently one "can't imagine too many of the young being attracted to Quakerism. The super militants are angry."

A number of informants were able to see the plight of Friends, for they are often caught between the establishment and their attempts to follow their beliefs according to the tenets of the Quaker faith. In some instances even rival groups of Friends are not in accord—witness the events of William Penn College in Oskaloosa at the time of the presidency of Cecil Hinshaw.[2]

One informant stated that ". . . if Friends had been interested in actively seeking Black converts 15 years ago, there would have been greater success (among the educated) than currently, when Blacks are going through a phase where non-violence and quiet introspection have little place. It is what many Blacks need, but not what they want." This condition may adjust itself within the next 5–10 years. At that point Whites and White institutions may be judged not on acting and reacting, or playing the liberal role, but rather on the soundness of judgment in matters relating to issues affecting the disadvantaged peoples of the U.S. and the world.

Then, when identity problems are under great control, Blacks and others shall, no doubt, be freer to seek groups where there is clear evidence of total religious commitment. A Black Friend stated sadly that some avant-garde Eastern Meetings were concerned with freedom for homosexuals, freedom for women, but there is almost no attention to Black, Puerto Rican, or third-world problems. This person also commented on their constant talk about peace without ever getting around to examine the causal factors of war. The implication is that some Friends are also playing the liberal suburban establishment game and not living up to the basic Quaker tenets. The same individual stated that Blacks who participate in Friends Meetings rarely get opportunities in the wider circle (committees, etc.). After some questioning (for this was not necessarily true in my experience) the informant explained that committee membership is expensive. One must pay one's own way. I stated that there were sufficient Blacks able to do this also. The answer was that few are ready or have enough security . . they are nouveau riche and not as free with money. I personally feel that this is a "cultural" problem involving primarily differential use of funds. In Baptist and Methodist churches some individuals pay their own expenses to committee meetings, etc. So I do not feel this criticism is really valid.

Summary:

The majority of Black informants felt that most Blacks know little about Quakers or Quakerism. The majority gained their knowledge through Friends schools, work camps, action programs, etc. Most felt that Friends schools were relatively "liberal"—accepting a number of Blacks. However, one Haverford student reported that during his college days one Black was accepted yearly, and some years "they skipped" whereas at Bryn Mawr one or two Blacks were faithfully accepted each year. Only one felt that Friends schools were "the last to integrate" and cited refusal of admission of Ralph Bunche's[3] daughter to one, adding that when he became famous at the UN, he was invited to speak at the same institution and refused.

The majority felt that non-violence is really a basic Christian tenet that most denominations other than Friends usually ignore. However, due to social and historical conditions in this country, most Blacks, the younger generation in particular, cannot accept this aspect, or only with difficulty. It is understood that non-violence is "right" but White Americans generally do not know that, and they must be spoken to "in language which they understand . . ." in effect with violence! Some Blacks may also feel that Friends are naïve, and/or place differential stress on Blacks reacting with passivity, while less stress is placed on Whites' treatment of Blacks in the same vein. Further there appears to be confusion between the terms "peaceful," "passive," and "passive resistance." Many Blacks only hear the passive in the term passive resistance, and translate that as the old "yes-sir Boss" and bristle.

The other messages of the Society of Friends were felt to be vital. There are some Blacks, primarily the educated and perhaps even some from the stable poor, who by their own needs will find Quakerism the answer. Most of the informants pointed out that those attracted to Friends would be primarily the same types as the Whites who are attracted, i.e. as a result of exposure to work camps, schools, etc. As a result of the quest for identity, self-expression and improved conditions in the U.S. a number who would ordinarily be interested cannot affiliate at this time, due to the strong pressures for dichotomizing—ours vs. theirs. Few wish to run the risk of being called Toms, Oreoles, etc. by intensive "integrating," which is less fashionable in Black circles these days. Various forms of Islam are picking up converts who would otherwise be seeking other Christian denominations. Birthright Catholics are leaving the church in order to embrace ". . . our culture," starting to sing spirituals, and operating in a *Black controlled* organizational setting. A number of informants felt this was a phase of Negro adjustment, which will leave U.S. Blacks more secure as to their identity and the places they wish to occupy in U.S. society.

Conclusions:

It seems that clarification of the Peace testimony, so that the value of passive *resistance* is emphasized, would be important in approaching Blacks. But there again, violence is a part of this whole society, and Friends would be fighting influences of TV, radio, and the movies! Perhaps involving Blacks in wider Quaker activities, work camps, etc. is useful. Even if they elect to stay with their own denomination, the influence of continued contact can be beneficial. I personally do not see that many Blacks shall ever become attracted to Friends unless Meetings are strictly oriented to Blacks, i.e., Black Meetings, which in this country is an unnatural, contrived event. Locating within a Black community without proselytizing (which I am not necessarily in favor of) does not bring in more members. It can possibly make Blacks more sympathetic, and over generations bring in members.

I am not in favor of trying to involve large numbers of Culture of Poverty type Blacks in Quakerism as perhaps some might advocate. I think the battle is too great, and requires intense multifactoral, almost social work approaches which Friends are not by and large trained to do. Sometimes more antagonism is built up by well meaning naïve people "going forth to do good."

It seems that if contacts are to be made they should be lateral (across to those Blacks more likely to respond, and then those influences could filter down into inner city groups, Culture of Poverty, and poverty groups). The experience in culture change theory is that individuals accepting a change often receive it if there is sufficient value for them (status, material, and personal). And it is often quickly accepted if introduced by their own members with sufficient status, or they are able to see immediate tangible benefits to themselves from the change.

Source
The files of Kenneth Ives, dated March 22, 1973.

Endnotes

1   E. Franklin Frazier, *The Negro Church in America* (New York: Schocken, 1964), page 28: The important factor which is often overlooked is what were the other half of the population. For example, the Catholic Church was spiritual head for most French speaking and a few English speaking Blacks in Louisiana. Blacks of all status ranks are born Episcopalians in parts of Southeastern U.S.

2   Cecil Hinshaw was misplaced in Iowa. He brought many "modern" practices to this mainly conservative region of the country and Quakerism. Hinshaw tried to integrate William Penn College with no success. He was replaced after only several years as President. For a fuller description of this set of events see Bill R. Douglas, "Penn in Technicolor: Cecil Hinshaw's Radical Pacifist-Perfectionist Experiment At William Penn College, 1944–1949," *Quaker History*, vol. 96, no. 2 (Fall 2007), pp. 54–68.

3   Ralph Bunche endeavored to place his daughter at George School and was turned down. Later, when Bunche was awarded the Nobel Peace Prize (1950), he was invited to speak at George School. He refused this invitation because his daughter was refused admission to the school. For more information see James Zug, "The Color of Our Skins: Quakerism and Integration at Sidwell Friends School," *Quaker History*, vol. 98, no. 1 (Spring 2009), pp. 35–47. The article is mostly about similar racial issues at Sidwell Friends, but there are other examples of this situation of which Bunche's is one.

Bibliography

Jervis Anderson. *Bayard Rustin: Troubles I've Seen: A Biography*. New York: Harper Collins, 1997.

Stephen W. Angell. "Howard Thurman and Quakers." *Quaker Theology* 9:1 (Fall-Winter 2009): 28–54. Available at: http://www.quaker.org/quest/issue16-angell01.htm.

Margaret Hope Bacon. *But One Race: The Life of Robert Purvis*. Albany: State University of New York Press, 2007.

Margaret Hope Bacon. "'The Double Curse of Sex and Color': Robert Purvis and Human Rights." *The Pennsylvania Magazine of History and Biography* 121 (Jan–April 1997): 53–76.

Margaret Hope Bacon. "New Light on Sarah Mapps Douglass and her Reconciliation with Friends." *Quaker History* 90:1 (Spring 2001): 28–49.

Margaret Hope Bacon. *Sarah Mapps Douglass: Faithful Attender of Quaker Meeting: View from the Back Bench*. Foreword by Vanessa Julye. Philadelphia: Quaker Press of Friends General Conference, 2003.

Henry E. Baker. "Benjamin Banneker, the Negro Mathematician and Astronomer." *The Journal of Negro History* 3:2 (April 1918): 99–118.

Silvio A. Bedini. "Benjamin Banneker and the Survey of the District of Columbia, 1971." *Records of the Columbia Historical Society, Washington, D.C.*, 69/70, pp. 7–30.

Silvio A. Bedini. *The Life of Benjamin Banneker*. New York: Scribner, 1971.

William Boen. *Anecdotes and Memoirs of William Boen, a Colored Man, Who Lived and Died Near Mount Holly, New Jersey. To Which is Added, The Testimony of Friends of Mount Holly Monthly Meeting Concerning Him*. Philadelphia: J. Richards, 1834. Accessible at http://docsouth.unc.edu/neh/boen/menu.html.

Ira V. Brown. "Cradle of Feminism: The Philadelphia Female Anti-Slavery Society, 1833–1840." *The Pennsylvania Magazine of History and Biography* 102:2 (April 1978): 143–166.

Henry Cadbury. "Negro Membership in the Society of Friends." *Journal of Negro History* 21:2 (April 1936): 151–213.

James T. Campbell. *Middle Passages: African American Journeys to Africa, 1787–2005*. New York: Penguin, 2006.

Devon W. Carbado and Donald Weise, eds. *Time on Two Crosses: The Collected Writings of Bayard Rustin*. San Francisco, CA: Cleis Press, 2003.

Charles Cerami. *Benjamin Banneker: Surveyer, Astronomer, Publisher, Patriot*. New York: Wiley, 2002.

John D'Emilio, *Lost Prophet: The Life and Times of Bayard Rustin*. New York: Free Press, 2003.

Shirley Graham DuBois. *Your Most Humble Servant*. New York: Messner, 1949.

Elizabeth. *Memoir of Old Elizabeth, a Coloured Woman*. Philadelphia: Collins, 1863.

Elizabeth. *Elizabeth, a Colored Minister of the Gospel Born in Slavery*. Philadelphia: Tract Association of Friends, 1889.

James A. Fletcher and Carleton Mabee, eds. *A Quaker Speaks from the Black Experience: The Life and Selected Writings of Barrington Dunbar*. New York: New York Yearly Meeting of the Religious Society of Friends, 1979.

Walter Earl Fluker and Catherine Tumber. *A Strange Freedom: The Best of Howard Thurman on Religious Experience and the Public Life*. Boston: Beacon Press, 1998.

Walter Earl Fluker. *They Looked for a City: A Comparative Analysis of the Ideal of Community in the Thought of Howard Thurman and Martin Luther King, Jr.* Lanham, MD: University Press of America, 1989.

Sheldon Harris, ed. *Paul Cuffe: Black America and the African Return*. New York: Simon and Schuster, 1972.

Kenneth Ives. *Black Quakers: Brief Biographies*. Studies in Quakerism, 12. Chicago: Progresiv Publishr, 1991.

Alonzo Johnson. *Good News for the Disinherited: Howard Thurman on Jesus of Nazareth and Human Liberation*. Lanham, MD: University Press of America, 1997.

Cynthia Earl Kerman and Richard Eldridge. *The Lives of Jean Toomer: A Hunger for Wholeness*. Baton Rouge: Louisiana State University Press, 1987.

Gerda Lerner. *The Grimke Sisters from South Carolina*. Boston: Houghton Mifflin, 1967.

Carleton Mabee. *Black Freedom: The Nonviolent Abolitionists from 1830 through the Civil War*. New York: Macmillan, 1970.

Carleton Mabee and Susan Mabee Newhouse. *Sojourner Truth—Slave, Prophet, Legend*. New York: New York University Press, 1993.

James Earl Massey. "Bibliographic Essay: Howard Thurman and Rufus M. Jones, Two Mystics." *Journal of Negro History* 57:2 (April 1972): 190–195.

Bibliography

Donna McDaniel and Vanessa Julye. *Fit for Freedom, Not for Friendship: Quakers, African Americans, and the Myth of Racial Justice*. Philadelphia: Quaker Press of Friends General Conference, 2009.

Wilson Jeremiah Moses. *Classical Black Nationalism: From the American Revolution to Marcus Garvey*. New York: New York University Press, 1996.

Richard S. Newman and Patrick Rael. *Pamphlets of Protest: An Anthology of Early African-American Protest Literature, 1790–1860*. New York: Routledge, 2001.

Nell Irvin Painter. "Representing Truth: Sojourner Truth's Knowing and Becoming Known." In Judith Weisenfeld and Richard Newman, eds., *This Far by Faith: Readings in African-American Women's Religious Biography*. New York: Routledge, 1996.

Nell Irvin Painter. *Sojourner Truth: A Life, A Symbol*. New York: W.W. Norton and Co., 1996.

P. Lee Phillips. "The Negro, Benjamin Banneker: Astronomer and Mathematician: Plea for Universal Peace." *Records of the Columbia Historical Society, Washington, D.C.* 20 (1971): 114–120.

Alton B. Pollard, III. *Mysticism and Social Change: The Social Witness of Howard Thurman*. Martin Luther King, Jr. memorial studies in religion, culture, and social development, vol. 2. New York: Peter Lang, 1992.

Benjamin Quarles. *Black Abolitionists*. New York: Oxford University Press, 1969.

Leigh Eric Schmidt. *Restless Souls: The Making of American Spirituality from Emerson to Oprah*. New York: HarperSanFrancisco, 2005.

Luther E. Smith. *Howard Thurman: The Mystic as Prophet*, rev. ed. Richmond, IN: Friends United Press, 1991.

Erlene Stetson and Linda David. *Glorying in Tribulation: The Lifework of Sojourner Truth*. East Lansing: Michigan State University, 1994.

William Still. *The Underground Railroad*. New York: Arno Press, 1968. Originally published, 1872.

Lamont D. Thomas. *Rise to Be a People: A Biography of Paul Cuffe*. Urbana: University of Illinois Press, 1986.

Sojourner Truth. *Narrative of Sojourner Truth*. Olive Gilbert, ed. New York: Vintage Books, 1993.

Juliet E. K. Walker. "Racism, Slavery, and Free Enterprise: Black Entrepreneurship in the United States before the Civil War." *The Business History Review* 60:3 (Autumn 1986): 343–382.

Margaret Washington. *Sojourner Truth's America*. Urbana: University of Illinois Press, 2009.

Rosalind Cobb Wiggins. *Captain Paul Cuffe's Logs and Letters, 1808–1817: A Black Quaker's "Voice from within the Veil."* Washington: Howard University Press, 1996.

Rosalind Cobb Wiggins. "Paul and Stephen, Unlikely Friends." *Quaker History* 90:1 (Spring 2001): 8–27.

Shirley J. Yee. *Black Women Abolitionists: A Study in Activism, 1828–1860*. Knoxville: University of Tennessee Press, 1992.

Henry J. Young, ed. *God and Human Freedom: A Festschrift in Honor of Howard Thurman*. Richmond, IN: Friends United Press, 1983.

Acknowledgments

Harold D. Weaver, Jr.

It is impossible to recall all the names of the hundreds of people who have helped me in this endeavor (2003–2010), from the concept, to research, to realization to publication. I apologize to those not mentioned by name, but rest assured that I am grateful for all the help rendered by so many people, at a variety of locations in the United States and abroad. I offer my thanks

- First and foremost to Anne Steere Nash for being at my side, carrying out many tasks from beginning to end.

- To the W.E.B. Du Bois Institute for African and African American Research at Harvard University for space in winding down this anthology, and for stimulating ideas in our field: Skip Gates, Vera Grant, Abby Wolf, Delphine Kwankan, and Tom Wolejko. I am especially grateful to the late Dick Newman for his suggestions in ways to address the various voids in research in so many areas of African American Studies, including my own family history. Retired Harvard Professor Martin Kilson, 2010 Du Bois Lecture honoree, offered a broad range of suggestions. Bill Wilson offered insight about the importance of Rustin's "From Protest to Politics."

- To Blue Mountain Center for Writers, Artists, and Activists: my gratitude for the encouragement, support, great cuisine, and hospitality of the nurturing administrators (Ben Strader and Harriet Barlow), staff, and fellow writers, artists, and activists in the Fall beauty of the Adirondacks.

- To Friends General Conference (FGC): Bruce Birchard, the Committee for Ministry on Racism and its former clerk Jean-Marie Barth, Vanessa Julye (who shared some of her collected materials for photocopying), Barbara Hirshkowitz, Barbara

Mays, Alyson Scott, and others for stimulating and encouraging the ideas from concept to reality. Chel Avery has done a remarkable job pulling it all together.

- To Pendle Hill: especially its former executive director, Steve Baumgartner, from the beginning a strong backer of the anthology, for providing a communal environment that during my time as Friend in Residence in Spring 2004, led to interaction with, advice from, and encouragement from such Quaker scholars as John Punshon and Marge Abbott. John Meyer invited me to offer two weekend courses for discussing some of this anthology's material: (1) "Lift Every Voice and Sing": Paul Robeson and Bayard Rustin (2007) and (2) Black Fire: Black Quakers on Spirituality and Human Rights (2009). Steve Angell joined me as co-facilitator in the latter course. I am grateful for feedback from and dialogue with students, including committed activists for racial justice inside and outside the Society of Friends, Marion Fuson and Carolyn Keyes. My appreciation also goes to Niyonu Spann, Walter Sullivan, Lauri Perman, Judith Hudson, O, and Dorothy Day for their logistical support.

- To Casa de los Amigos, Mexico City: Nick Wright first provided me with a copy of the AFSC pamphlet *Speak Truth to Power* while noting the absence of the name of a key co-author, Bayard Rustin. For the past several years, la Casa, with Nick as the director, has provided a warm, nurturing hospitality for my writings for this anthology while I spent weeks each year at this Quaker center for peace, social action, and hospitality.

- To the American Friends Service Committee (AFSC): the archives' staff was helpful in providing memos, letters, field reports, and itineraries related to its longtime employee Bill Sutherland. I am appreciative that the Board of this Nobel Peace Prize winning organization in September 2010 restored the name of Bayard Rustin to his rightful co-authorship of the influential pamphlet, *Speak Truth to Power*.

- To IAGO, Oaxaca, Mexico: artist-philanthropist Francisco Toledo and his staff have provided a home away from home at

Acknowledgments

these graphic arts and photography institutes for much of my writing on a beautiful patio during Oaxaca's warm, sunny winter months.

- To the Haverford College Quaker Collection: Emma Lapsansky-Werner (since retired) and her competent, devoted staff. They were especially helpful in locating bibliographical and biographical materials by and about Ira Reid.

- To the Swarthmore College Quaker and Peace Collections: Chris Densmore, Wendy Chmielewski, and colleagues for help in finding materials on Jean Toomer, Bayard Rustin, and others.

- To New England Yearly Meeting: Jonathan Vogel-Bourne, Shelby Grantham, Donna McDaniel, James Varner, Dwight and Maureen Lopes, Lisa Graustein, and other members of the Ministry and Council Working Party on Racism.

- To Wellesley Monthly Meeting: the entire community for supporting my ministry, The BlackQuaker Project; the Ministry and Counsel's Ministry for Racial Equality and Justice (MORE): Roland Stern, Cynthia Ganung, Lyn Danforth, Bonnie Norton, Patsy Shotwell, Beth Collea, Anne Nash, Chris King; members of my care/support committee: Cynthia Ganung, Bonnie Norton, Ann Cook Frantz, Dody Waring, Rud Ham; and to my recently activated The BlackQuaker Project Fund Committee, whose function is to oversee fund raising and funds disbursement in support of the Project's ministry: Nancy Haines, Ann Cook Frantz, and Rud Ham.

- To fellow scholars gathered at the Quaker Institute for the Future during our collective study-worship-writing-sharing sessions at the College of the Atlantic, Bar Harbor, Maine, in summer 2005: Gray Cox, Leonard Joy, and other Quaker scholars who made insightful suggestions, both for this publication and for other creative, nonprint approaches to reaching a wider public. This includes a dramatic re-enactment of one of Rustin's letters, which has become the springboard for a play about Rustin that The BlackQuaker Project is currently writing.

- To all other organizations and individuals who took the time to provide creative, scholarly, and technical services to the editors of this anthology.

Paul Kriese

I want to acknowledge my father who first taught me about God's grace and God's justice. There are also nameless people who have taught me about forgiveness and F(f)riendship when one might think that they would think differently. I want also to thank Anne Thomason, Assistant Archivist at Earlham College, who found material on George Sawyer which has been critical to the focus and thesis of my part of this book. I also wish to acknowledge the hard and consistent work of Rena Holcomb who did many of the jobs so necessary for a successful book but which are not often enough recognized when the project is complete.

Steve W. Angell

I would like to thank John Meyer, Walter Sullivan, and Lauri Perman at Pendle Hill for making it possible for Hal and me to offer a workshop on the writings of African American Quakers and to try out some of this material in a live presentation and discussion format. Thanks also to the eleven wonderful, gracious, and engaging Friends who attended this workshop.

I am grateful also to Dorothy Day at the Pendle Hill bookstore for tracking down some of those hard-to-find books for me—at the right price, too!

The editorial assistance provided by the QuakerPress of FGC, especially Barbara Mays and Chel Avery, has been invaluable. This project would not have gotten as far as it has without the hard work of these dear Friends.

As always, I'm grateful to my colleagues and students at Earlham School of Religion, Bethany Theological Seminary, and Earlham College; they have often been great listeners and wise counselors on this and others of my scholarly projects.

I am also grateful for the encouragement of students and colleagues for my work in African American religious history, while I was teaching at Florida A & M University. I fondly remember the many terrific years that I spent with them in Tallahassee.

I am grateful to my father, Stephen L. Angell, who made the point of telling me, while he was recuperating from an operation in his hospital bed, how happy he was that I was embarking on this project, four years ago when I was invited to join the team of editors. And thanks also to my dear spouse, Sandra, who perhaps does not know just how much she helped this project along, but who did help in many ways.

About the Editors

Harold D. Weaver, Jr.

Hal Weaver, Fellow at the W.E.B. Du Bois Institute for African and African American Research at Harvard University, was the founding Chairperson of the Department of Africana Studies at Rutgers University. He has taught African American, American, and African Studies at the University of Paris VIII-Vincennes/St. Denis (France), Smith College, Commenius University (Bratislava, Slovakia), National Jiao-Tung University (China/Taiwan), Beijing USA College (China), Laval University (Quebec City), Long Island University, and Southern University of New Orleans, where he served as dean of the School of Education.

Hal's research and publications on actor-activist-scholar Paul Robeson, African filmmaker Ousmane Sembene, and Russian-African cultural relations were pioneering efforts aimed at restoring the truth to mainstream media and correcting scholarly misinformation and disinformation. His doctorate from the University of Massachusetts at Amherst is in cross-cultural and international communication and education. He wrote his dissertation on *Soviet Training and Research Programs for Africa*. Through The BlackQuaker Project, The ChinaFilm Project, and The BlackFilm Project, Hal, in retirement, is currently using film, moving images, and the arts around the world to facilitate international understanding and racial justice.

Hal is active locally, regionally, nationally, and internationally in the Religious Society of Friends (Quakers). He is a member of Wellesley Friends Meeting of New England Yearly Meeting, a member of the boards of directors of the American Friends Service Committee and Pendle Hill, and has served as a delegate to international meetings of the Friends World Committee for Consultation.

Paul Kriese

Paul Kriese is professor of political science at Indiana University East. He specializes in African and African American studies, gender studies, and multicultural politics. He serves on the executive committee of the Global Studies Association and is the 2005 recipient of the First Excellence in Education Award from the Indiana Chapter of the National Association for the Advancement of Colored People. He received a Ph.D. in political science from Purdue University in 1977.

Stephen W. Angell

Stephen Angell is Leatherock Professor of Quaker Studies at Earlham College, Richmond, Indiana. He has a doctorate from Vanderbilt University. He is co-editor with Paul Buckley of *The Quaker Bible Reader* (Earlham Press, 2006). His book reviews have appeared in scholarly journals, including: "The African America History of Florida" (*The Mississippi Quarterly*, 2005), "Religion and the Rise of Jim Crow in New Orleans" (*Journal of Southern History*, 2006), "The Black Church in the Post Civil Rights Era" (*Church History*, 2006). Stephen is an active member of Oxford Friends Meeting, Ohio Valley Yearly Meeting.

'Courageous and Visionary' Book Shreds a Myth, Challenges Quakers on Issues of Racial Justice

Fit for Freedom, Not for Friendship
Quakers, African Americans, and the Myth of Racial Justice

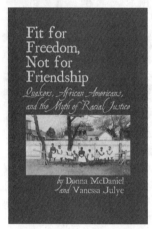

by Donna McDaniel and Vanessa Julye
www.fitforfreedom.org

"Quakers were always against slavery, and most Quakers were active in the Underground Railroad." Not so. Fit for Freedom, Not for Friendship documents the spiritual and practical impact of more than three centuries of racial discrimination within the Religious Society of Friends. This detailed history also acknowledges those who worked—and who still work—for racial equity and confront the current racial issues within the Religious Society of Friends. Addressing racism, the authors believe, will be the first step in ending it. Includes photos, glossary, Quaker bibliography, index, and extensive notes.

Quaker Press of FGC, 576 pages, hardcover $45.00, paperback $28.00

Praise for Fit for *Freedom, Not for Friendship*:

"The legendary status of Quakers in the struggle for Black freedom undergoes serious scrutiny and critique in this courageous and visionary book. This timely examination is a challenge to us all in the age of Obama."
— Cornel West, Princeton University

"Donna McDaniel and Vanessa Julye's prodigious research has given us a provocative overview of the complex—sometimes inspiring, sometimes disheartening—experience of American Friends and race."
— Thomas Hamm, Earlham College

To Order:

1216 Arch Street, 2B, Philadelphia, PA 19107
bookstore 800.966.4556 | www.QuakerBooks.org